IMAGES
of America

GRINNELL

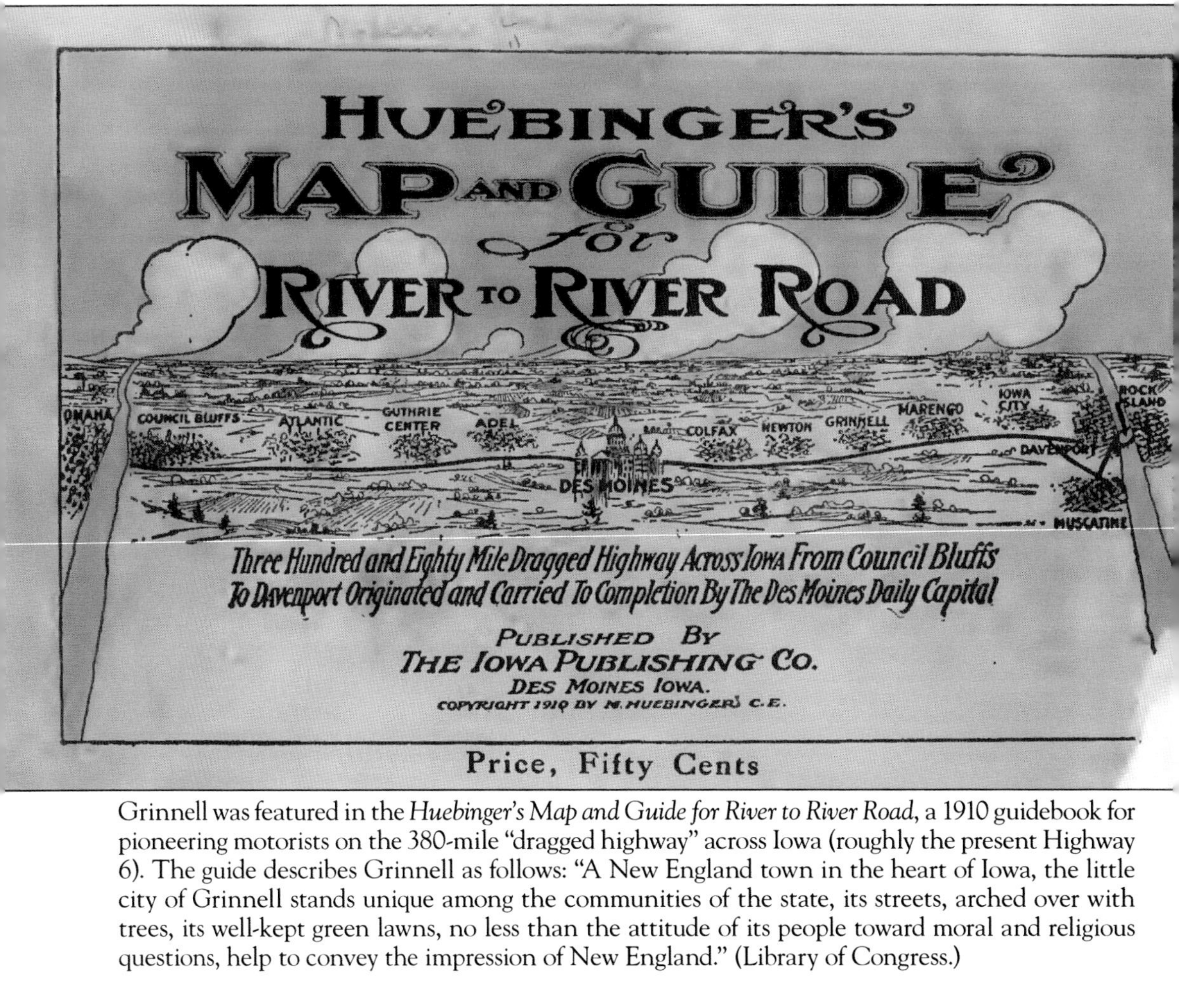

Grinnell was featured in the *Huebinger's Map and Guide for River to River Road*, a 1910 guidebook for pioneering motorists on the 380-mile "dragged highway" across Iowa (roughly the present Highway 6). The guide describes Grinnell as follows: "A New England town in the heart of Iowa, the little city of Grinnell stands unique among the communities of the state, its streets, arched over with trees, its well-kept green lawns, no less than the attitude of its people toward moral and religious questions, help to convey the impression of New England." (Library of Congress.)

On the Cover: Automobile enthusiasts in Grinnell in the early 1900s showed off their vehicles and advertised their town on daylong road trips that wound through the nearby countryside. To protect themselves from the dust and mud of the dirt roads, many drivers wore long dusters, goggles, and caps. (Grinnell Historical Museum.)

IMAGES
of America

GRINNELL

Lynn Cavanagh and Mary Schuchmann

ARCADIA
PUBLISHING

ISBN 978-1-4671-1419-6

Published by Arcadia Publishing
Charleston, South Carolina

Printed in the United States of America

Library of Congress Control Number: 2014958863

For all general information, please contact Arcadia Publishing:
Telephone 843-853-2070
Fax 843-853-0044
E-mail sales@arcadiapublishing.com
For customer service and orders:
Toll-Free 1-888-313-2665

Visit us on the Internet at www.arcadiapublishing.com

To Dorrie Lalonde, volunteer archivist at the Drake Community Library. There is little Dorrie doesn't know about Grinnell history, and what she doesn't know, she will find out.

Contents

Acknowledgments		6
Introduction		7
1.	Building a Town	9
2.	Establishing a College	25
3.	Making a Living	53
4.	Teaching and Preaching	67
5.	Living in Community	79
6.	Meeting the Challenges	93
7.	Walking around Town	101
8.	Celebrating the Good Times	115

ACKNOWLEDGMENTS

We are grateful to the individuals and organizations who gave freely of their time and knowledge to make our book possible. Marilyn Kennett, director of the Drake Community Library, planted the seed for this project, and local historian Bill Menner encouraged us to give it a try. The staff and volunteers at the Drake Community Library, the volunteers at the Grinnell Historical Museum, and the staff at the Grinnell College Archives provided invaluable assistance to us along the way.

We appreciate the willing and excellent help with research, technology, and general guidance we received from Karen Groves, Chris Jones, Dorrie Lalonde, Dorothy Louden, Cheryl Neubert, Monique Shore, and Wally Walker. We thank the many individuals and organizations who were willing to share their early Grinnell historical photographs, and even family histories, with us: Claude W. and Dolly Ahrens Foundation, Eddie Andersen family, Bruce Blankenfeld, Annette M. Cech, Jim Cunningham, Ruth Greenwald, Grinnell Fire Department, *Grinnell Herald-Register*, Grinnell Mutual Reinsurance Company, Karen Groves, Jerry Hagen, Joan Postels Heimsoth, Marjorie Hillmann, Dorothy Louden, Bill McNally, Mary Moffitt, Mickey Munley, Karen Packard, St. John's Lutheran Church, and Sue and Rick Ramsey.

The photographs used in the book are courtesy of Drake Community Library (DCL), Grinnell College Libraries Special Collections and Archives (GCA), and Grinnell Historical Museum (GHM), or the individuals or businesses mentioned in the courtesy line.

The authors' proceeds are being donated to the Drake Community Library in Grinnell in appreciation for the volunteers and staff who work together to enhance life in our community.

Finally, big thanks go to our husbands, Michael Cavanagh and Russ Schuchmann, who were patient with us when the "book project" took over our dining room tables, as well as our lives, for month after month.

INTRODUCTION

The influence of the first settler in any community is never lost. Character bears better fruit than acres. It is not the trees of the streets that have made the town famous but its men and women.

—Rev. David Otis Mears, son-in-law of J.B. Grinnell

A vision of a New England town on the Midwestern prairie led Josiah Bushnell Grinnell, a 33-year-old Congregational minister, to advertise in a New York newspaper in 1854 for "men of good character and high ideals and some means" to help him establish a new community. Acting on a valuable tip from the builder of the Rock Island Railroad, J.B. eyed a spot in east central Iowa where two rail lines would one day intersect. Further advertising attracted three men who shared J.B.'s Congregationalist ties—Homer Hamlin, Henry Hamilton, and Dr. Thomas Holyoke. The four traveled together by rail, wagon, and foot in March 1854 to a grove four miles south of. the promised rail juncture, near what is now the Jacob Krumm Nature Preserve.

After a lively debate over locating the settlement on the open prairie instead of near a river where timber would be readily available, J.B. got his way, and the town was established at a treeless spot where red flags marked the future rail intersection. Another debate centered on a name for the town. Hamilton wanted to name it Stella, but J.B. prevailed once again, and it was called Grinnell.

Decisions made, J.B. journeyed to Iowa City to file a claim for 5,000 acres that were divided among the four men. J.B. platted the town and directed the construction of a primitive shelter for new arrivals as well as a combination church and school. From his own holdings, he set aside land for a park, donated land for a cemetery, and sold lots to arriving settlers at cost.

As families from the East began to appear, J.B. took the leadership role for the new settlement. In keeping with his desire for a moral community, the deeds for sales of land in the early years stipulated that if liquor were sold on the premises, the title would revert back to J.B. The constitution of the church stipulated that "no intoxicating wine shall be used at the Lord's Supper, nor shall any intoxicating liquor be used by the members as an article of drink or traffic."

The abolition of slavery was also written into the church constitution: "No person shall be admitted to the church, or allowed to remain in it, who either practices or is not earnestly or actively opposed to buying or selling human beings, or holding them in slavery for gain."

J.B. was fervent in his desire "to make the church and school paramount and attractive institutions from the start." In addition to building a school for the town's children, he donated 20 acres to establish what he named Grinnell University. Hamilton also demonstrated his commitment to university education by donating a percentage of the profits from the sale of his land holdings to the future university.

Before any buildings were constructed or students enrolled, however, J.B. lured an existing college, Iowa College in Davenport, to merge with Grinnell University and move to Grinnell. The school, known as Iowa College until it was renamed Grinnell College in 1909, has shaped the town's character from the beginning to the present day.

Although J.B. picked a site for his town because of the promise of intersecting rail lines, it was not until 1863 that an extension of the east-west Rock Island Railroad, known then as the Mississippi & Missouri Railroad, actually reached Grinnell. The north-south extension of the Central Railroad of Iowa arrived in 1869. J.B. himself built a third rail line in 1875 to connect the town to the county seat of Montezuma, 22 miles to the south. The enterprise was called the Grinnell & Montezuma Railroad Company.

The young town had its share of setbacks. A cyclone in June 1882 killed 39 people and destroyed the entire college campus as well as 120 buildings in town. Rebuilding took place almost immediately, and commencement at the college went on as scheduled. In 1889, a fire destroyed the major part of the business district. Merchants immediately relocated to temporary shanty quarters in the park across the street while new buildings (brick and stone this time) went up to replace the burned-out wooden structures.

While agriculture dominated the town's early years and continues to have a major influence on the local economy, manufacturing has also played an important role. First, it was buggies and gloves and then automobiles, washing machines, and shoes. In more recent years, products have included playground equipment, farm machinery, sportswear, mufflers, signage, and windows and doors.

Grinnell's location has benefitted more from proximity to major roadways than to the railroad tracks. First, it was the River to River Road, the first road across the state (roughly the present Highway 6), built in 1910. Later, it was Interstate 80, the cross-country highway that passes three miles south of the city. The portion of Interstate 80 near Grinnell was completed in the early 1960s. Because of the increasing popularity of automobile travel, the last passenger train stopped in Grinnell in 1970. The train depot, abandoned for many years, was restored and turned into a restaurant in the late 1990s.

Grinnellians over the years have made their marks on the world. A young aviator, Billy Robinson, invented a rotary airplane engine, built his own plane, and set a record for continuous flight in 1914. His dream of manufacturing airplanes in Grinnell under the name Grinnell Aeroplane Company ended with his death in 1916 in an attempt to set an altitude record. During the Great Depression, Harry Hopkins was an advisor and confidant of Pres. Franklin D. Roosevelt, and Hallie Flanagan ran the Federal Theater Project. Robert Noyce helped revolutionize modern technology by coinventing the integrated circuit and cofounding Intel Corporation.

Today, Grinnell is known for its wealth of architectural styles from the late 1800s and early 1900s, including Gothic Revival, Italianate, Queen Anne, Richardsonian Romanesque, Neoclassical, Foursquare, Shingle, and Prairie.

The city is represented in the National Register of Historic Places with two historic districts and 15 individual buildings. The Merchants National Bank, designed by Louis Sullivan, is a National Historic Landmark.

One

Building a Town

In 1855 there was not a tree within three miles of Grinnell. We could see for miles, and all my longings for vast open spaces were satisfied.

—Joanna Harris Haines, who arrived in Grinnell at age 11

Although J.B. Grinnell left his pulpit in New York and headed west in 1854 in part because of voice problems that interfered with his preaching, he had no trouble inspiring a small band of followers to help build a town on the Iowa prairie.

With the help of three like-minded companions—Homer Hamlin, Henry Hamilton, and Dr. Thomas Holyoke—J.B. laid out the new community, set up a church and school, designated a park, and donated land for a cemetery and a university.

The first buildings included a temporary shelter called the Long Home, a general store operated by Anor Scott, and a combination church and school.

In accord with the founders' abolitionist fervor, the town became a stop on the Underground Railroad that transported runaway slaves north to Canada. In 1859, J.B. Grinnell opened his home and barn to activist John Brown and 16 slaves Brown had freed in Kansas. At a church service the following Sunday evening, Brown spoke passionately against slavery. The congregation responded with prayers and a collection of money and food to aid the travelers.

Despite a cyclone (1882) and a major fire (1889), the town developed and prospered. By the early 1900s, there were two newspapers, a library, hospital, theater, opera house, and separate high school building. The 1910 city directory listed 4 banks, 9 lawyers, 10 grocers, 13 physicians, and 17 painters and paperhangers. Public utilities included water, streetlights, and a steam heating system in the downtown. Paving of streets began in 1909. The population in 1910 was 5,036.

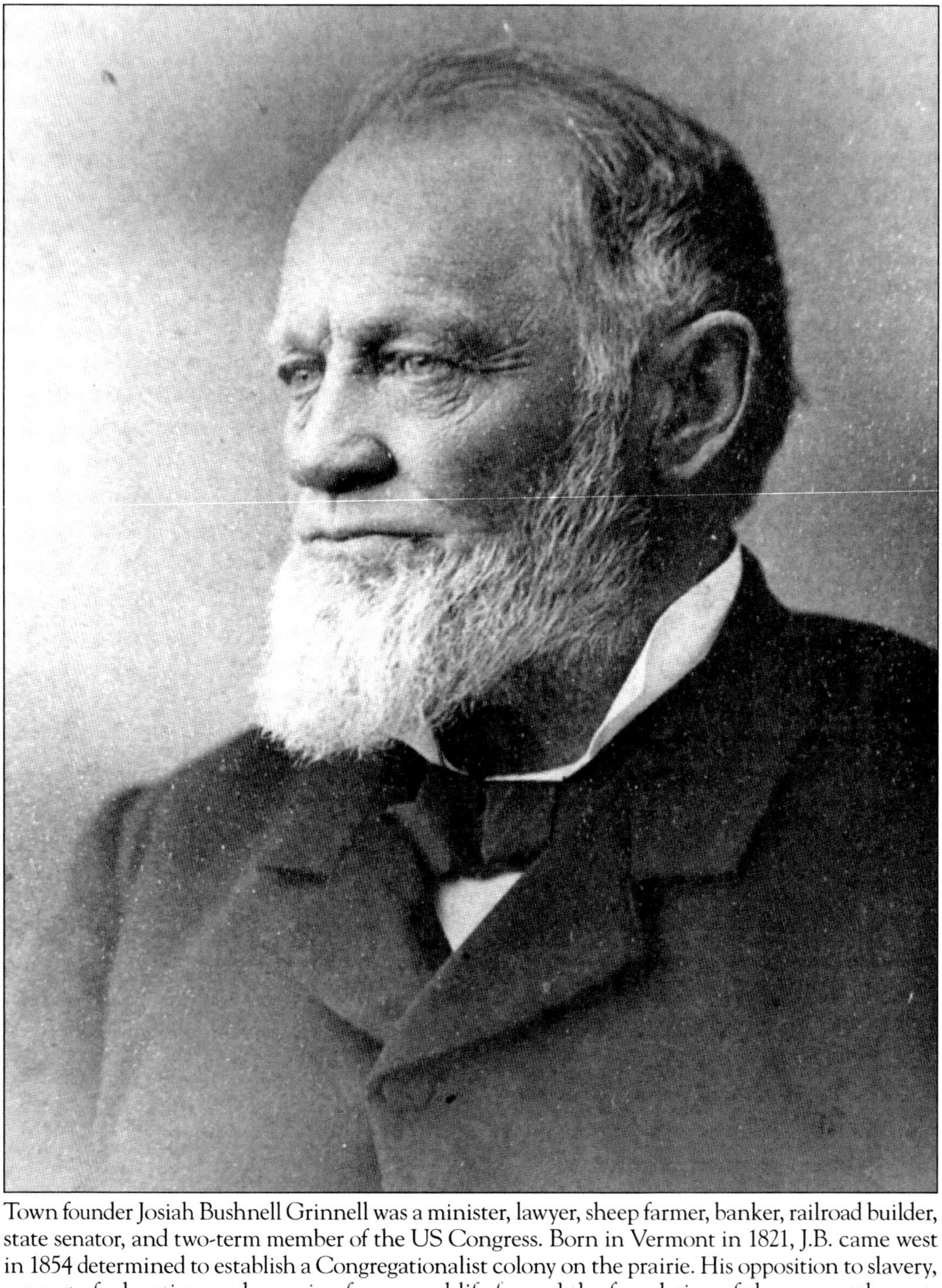

Town founder Josiah Bushnell Grinnell was a minister, lawyer, sheep farmer, banker, railroad builder, state senator, and two-term member of the US Congress. Born in Vermont in 1821, J.B. came west in 1854 determined to establish a Congregationalist colony on the prairie. His opposition to slavery, support of education, and yearning for a moral life formed the foundation of the new settlement. His fervor and determination spurred its rapid development. A cousin wrote the following of J.B.: "There was never any one else in the family like Cousin J.B. . . . He had a vision and a plan to carry out that vision. While others might hesitate, he was on his way—impetuous, inspired, ready to do for any good cause that came to his attention." (DCL.)

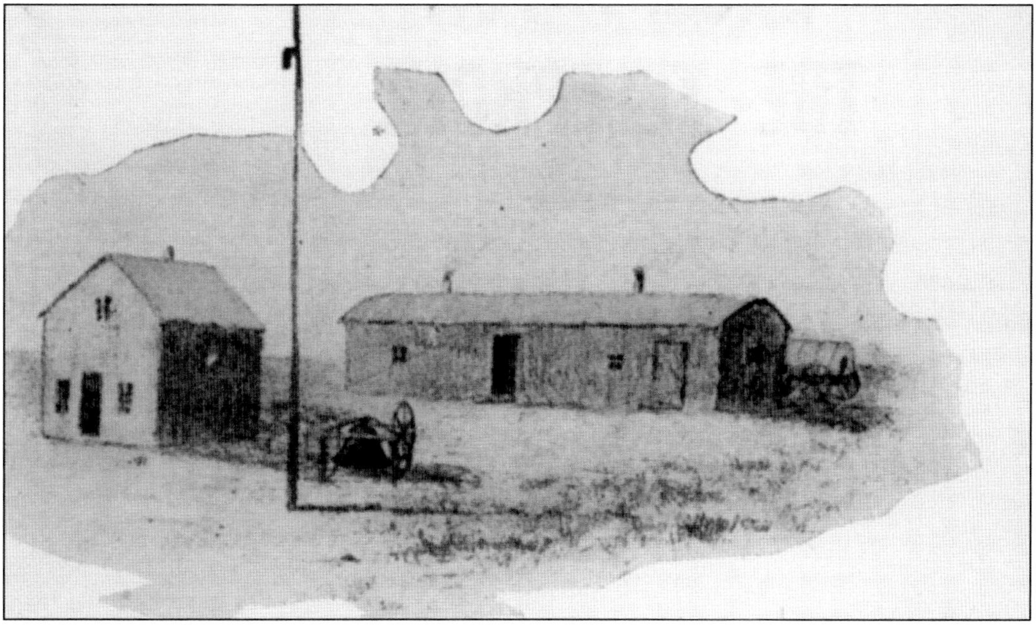

The first settlers lived in a 16-by-80-foot building (right) partitioned into small, makeshift rooms. It was called the Long Home. Outside, a lantern guided travelers, and a bell summoned newcomers to worship and public gatherings. Nearby was a general store (left) operated by Anor Scott. The buildings were located on what is now Broad Street south of Sixth Avenue. The site was marked in 1914 with a bronze tablet by the local Daughters of the American Revolution. (DCL.)

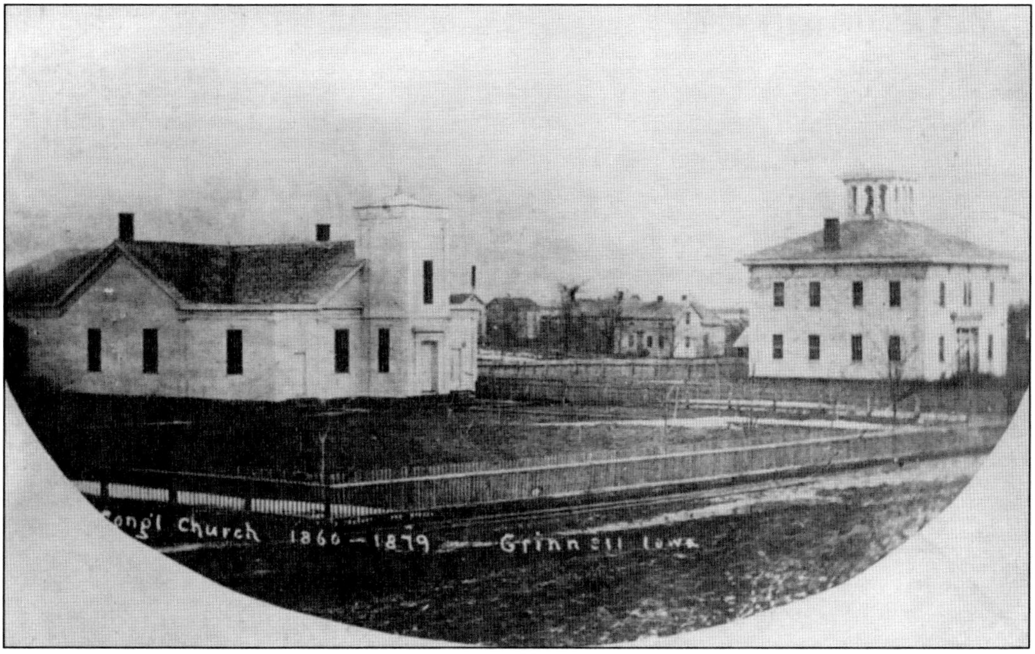

A two-story frame building (right) was constructed in 1856 to serve as school and church until a separate church (left) could be constructed in 1860. The school was destroyed by fire in 1871. At the time, it had 350 students. The buildings were located on Broad Street between Fourth and Fifth Avenues. (DCL.)

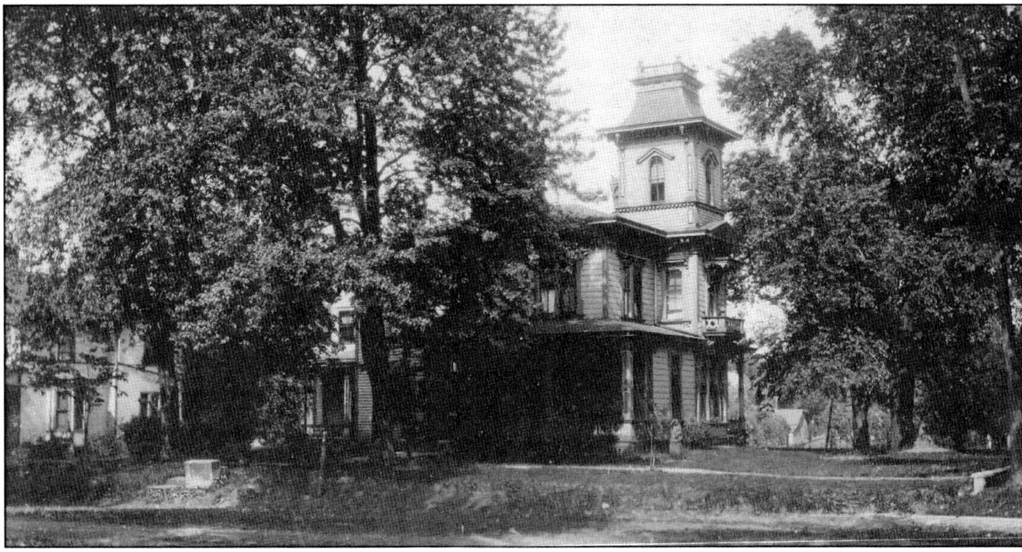

In the late 1850s, J.B. Grinnell built for himself and his wife, Julia Chapin Grinnell, an impressive Italianate home on Park Street. The couple entertained many notable visitors, including Henry Ward Beecher, Horace Greeley, and John Brown. One night during a blizzard, 44 people took shelter there. The sheep barn near the house was a well-known stop on the Underground Railroad, which aided runaway slaves on their flight to freedom. (GHM.)

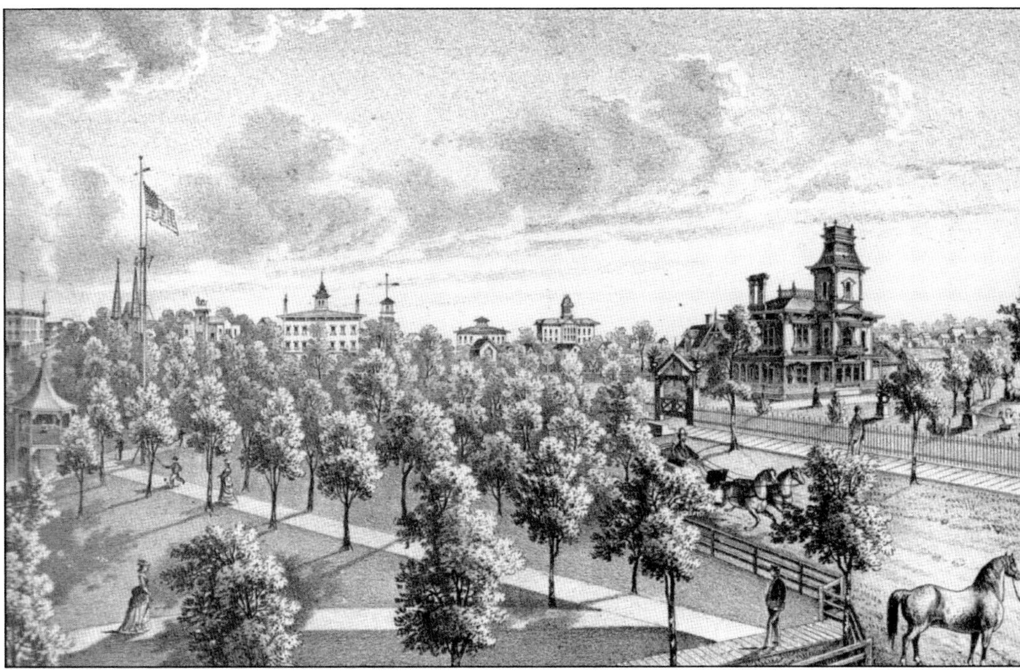

The importance of J.B. Grinnell and his grand home was highlighted in an engraving of early Grinnell contained in A.T. Andreas's *Illustrated Historical Atlas of the State of Iowa*, published in 1875. In the artist's stylized representation, J.B.'s home soars above its surroundings, with churches and college buildings portrayed as tiny in comparison. (DCL.)

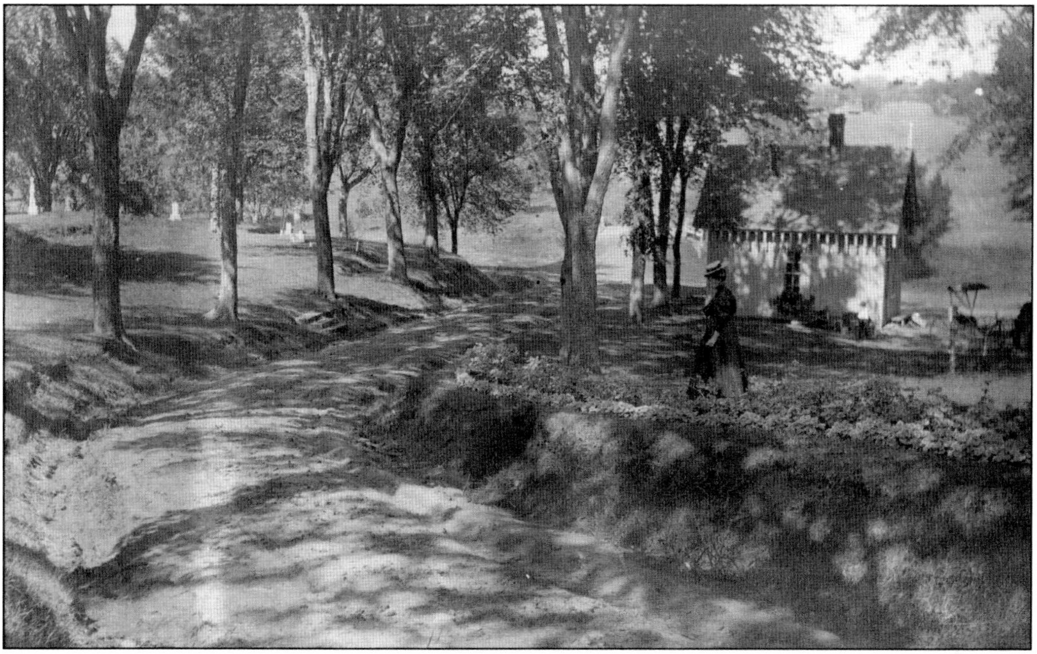

Hazelwood Cemetery was established in 1854, the same year the town was founded, with a donation of 13 acres from J.B. Grinnell. In keeping with J.B.'s lofty ideals, he specified that burial throughout the cemetery should be open to all, no matter their means, race, or social standing. J.B. Grinnell's grave is a designated site on the National Park Service's Underground Railroad Network to Freedom. (GHM.)

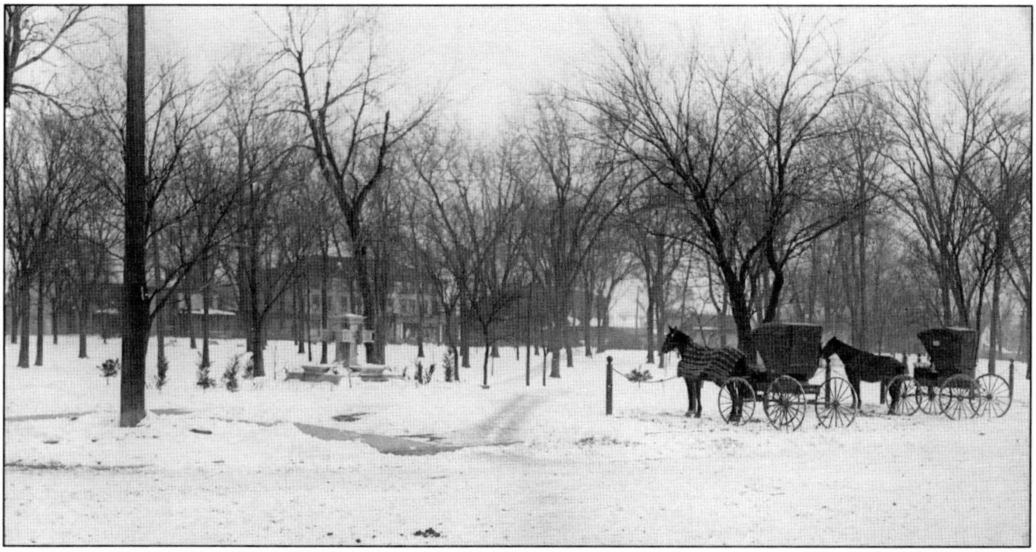

When J.B. Grinnell platted his part of the new community, he designated one block for a park, which became known as Central Park. Tree-planting took place almost immediately. By 1880, according to one account, "there was a forest of over 300 shade trees." The undated photograph, taken from the corner of Fourth Avenue and Broad Street, shows the Clark Memorial Fountain at left and the Monroe Hotel in the background. (Mickey Munley.)

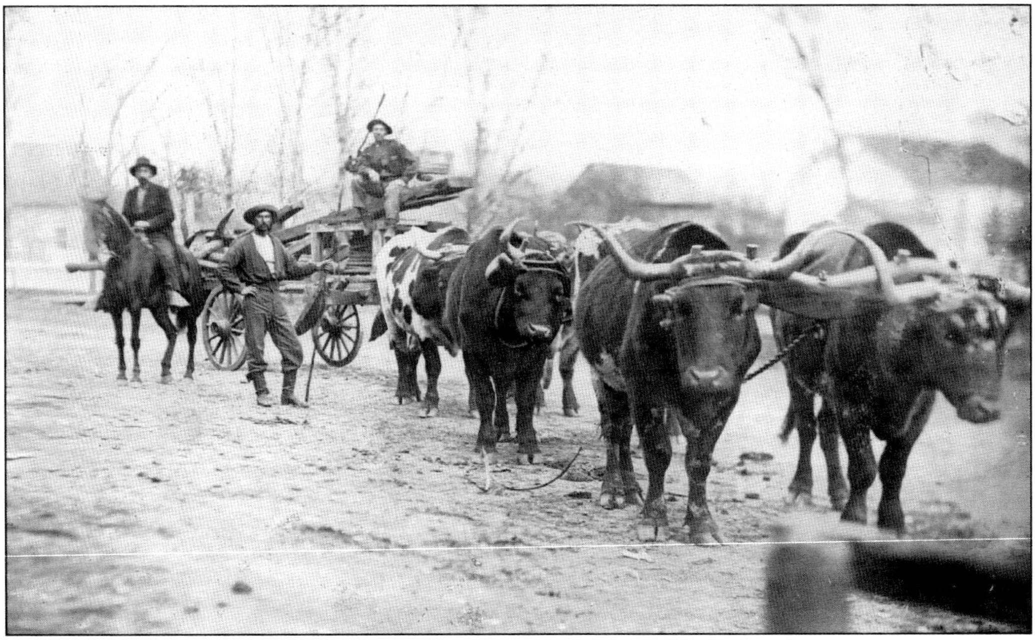

A team of oxen hauled wood to Grinnell in 1872 from Sugar Creek Township, located four miles west of town. The Sugar Creek area, which was crossed from northwest to southeast by the Skunk River, was an early source of timber for homes, stores, and sidewalks in Grinnell, which had been established on the treeless prairie. The photograph was taken on Broad Street. Note the hitching post in the foreground. (DCL.)

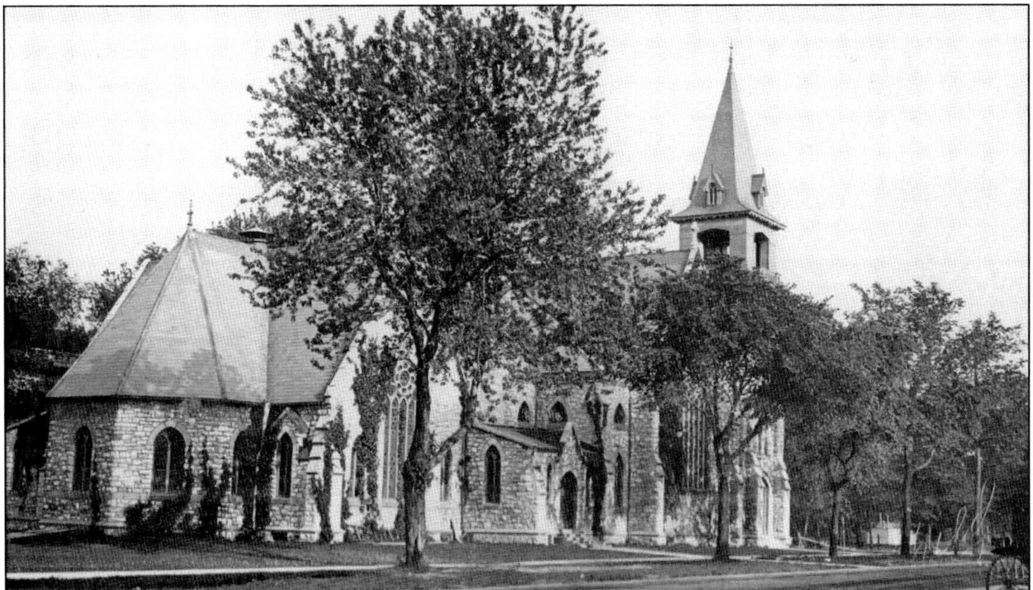

The Congregational church, built in 1878 and known as the Old Stone Church, was the dominant church and the center of community life in Grinnell for many years. Located at Fourth Avenue and Broad Street, it replaced an earlier frame building on the site. In the church's first years, J.B. Grinnell was among the preachers, and the church constitution limited membership to those who opposed slavery and practiced temperance. (GHM.)

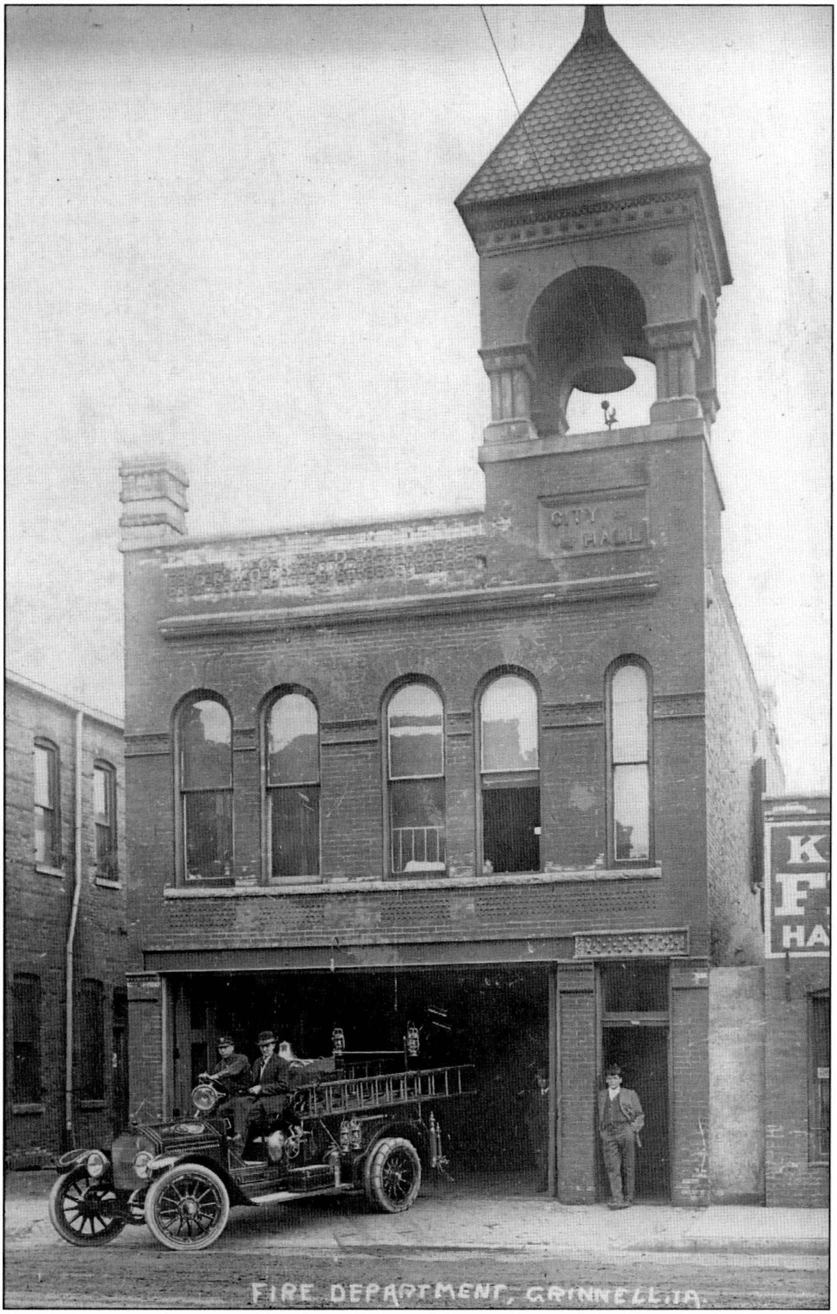

A fire station was built in 1889 on the south side of Commercial Street. The ground floor contained the city jail as well as the fire department. A firemen's hall was on the second floor. Fire apparatus in the building included an engine, hook and ladder, hose, and hose cart. Although the building was also intended to be the city hall, there was no room for the city offices, and so city business was conducted in rented space in the basement of the Citizens National Bank across the street. Historical records barely mention a police department. A 1911 history of Poweshiek County reads as follows: "As the city is a quiet and peaceful one, with no saloons, dives or other places to cause trouble, a small police force is all that is necessary." (DCL.)

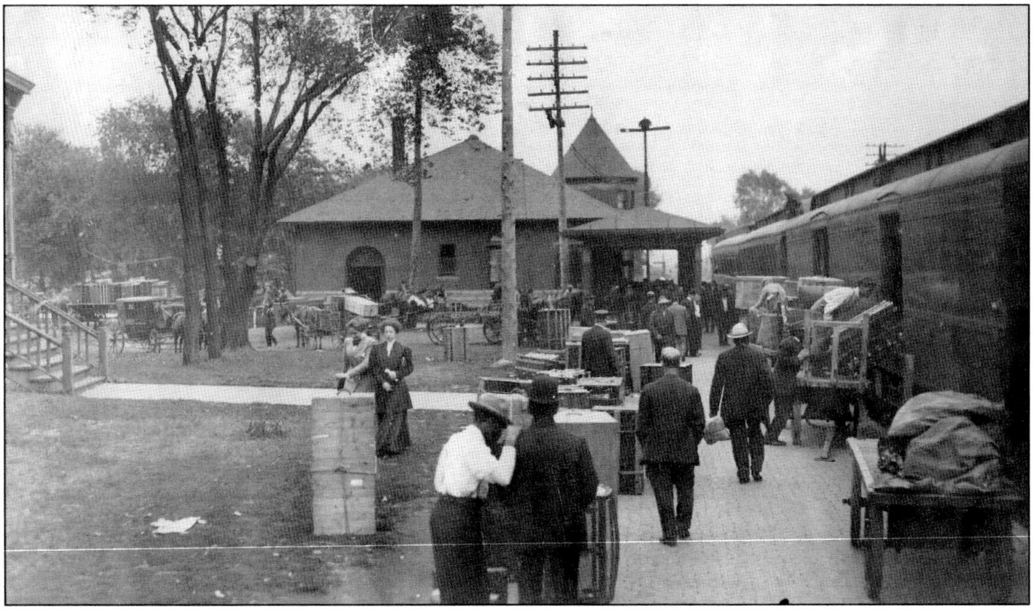

The convergence of two rail lines made Grinnell a bustling railroad center for many years. The Union Depot, built in 1893, had two waiting rooms, baggage room, lunch counter, and offices. At one time, 21 trains passed through Grinnell daily, and generations of college students arrived and departed from the platform. When passenger service ended in 1970, the depot was abandoned. It was restored in the 1990s and is a restaurant today. (Mickey Munley.)

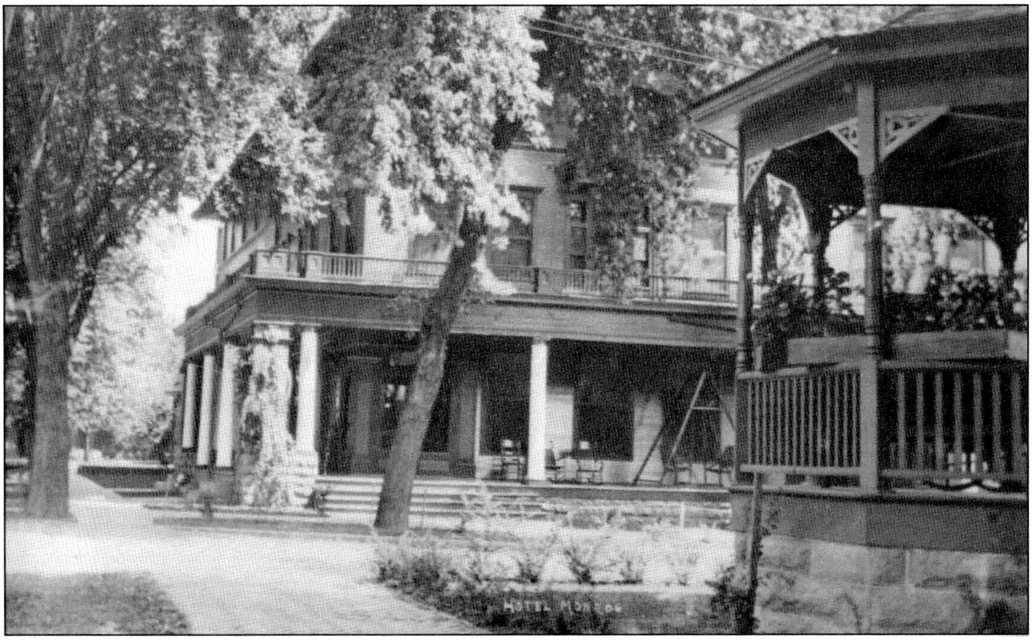

The Monroe Hotel was built in 1899 across from the Union Depot on what had been the front lawn of J.B. Grinnell's home. An impressive three-story building surrounded by a broad veranda, its elegant dining room attracted travelers and locals alike. The lobby floor, inlaid with silver dollars, was a tourist attraction. As passenger trains dwindled and business declined, the hotel fell into disrepair. It was razed in 1971. (DCL.)

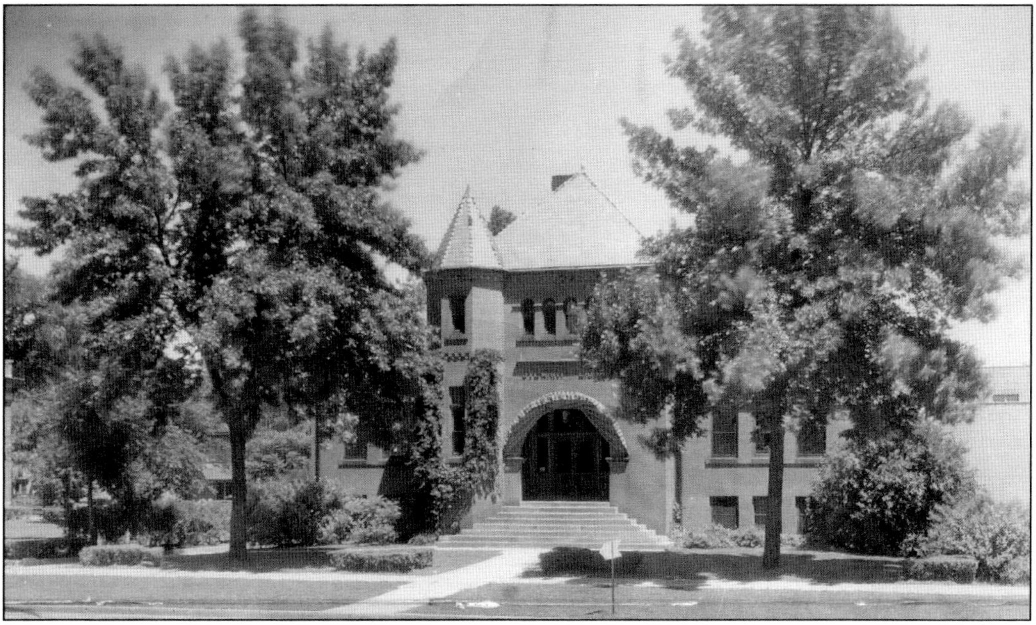

Stewart Library was opened in 1902, thanks to the generosity of Joel Stewart and his wife, Anna. Joel Stewart, a native of New York State who arrived in Grinnell in 1868, furnished the money ($15,000), arranged for the building contract, and supervised construction. Designed as a vernacular expression of the Romanesque Revival style, the building became the Grinnell Arts Center in 2009 after a new library was constructed. (DCL.)

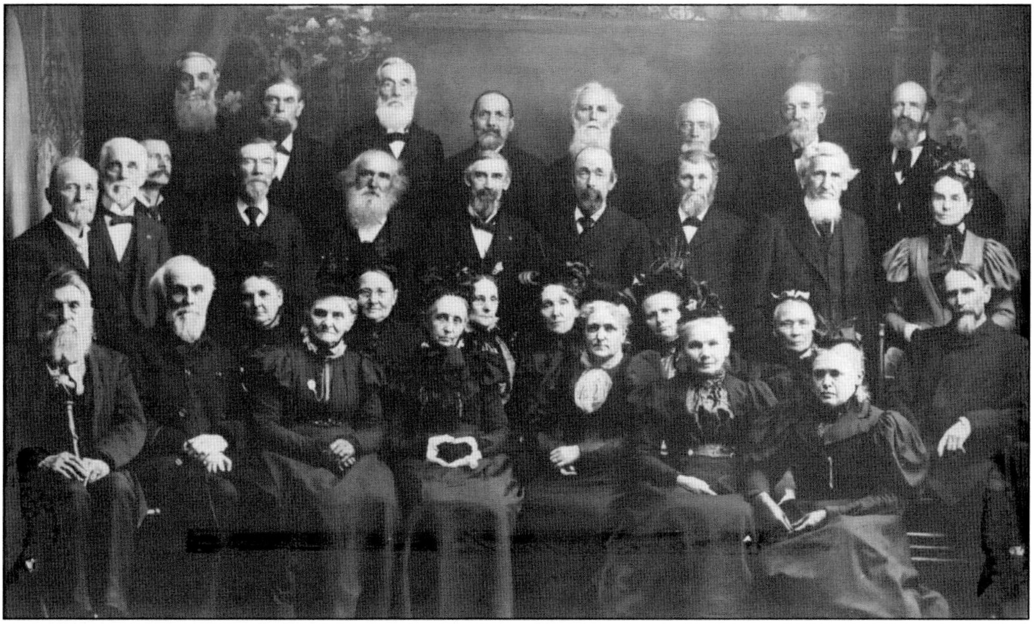

The Old Settlers Association was founded in 1894, the year of the town's 40th anniversary. Membership in the group was open to all who had arrived in Grinnell in the first five years. Its purpose was to "cherish the friendships and to perpetuate the memories of the early days." In this 1898 photograph, Julia Chapin Grinnell is seated fifth from left in the front row. J.B. Grinnell died in 1891. (GHM.)

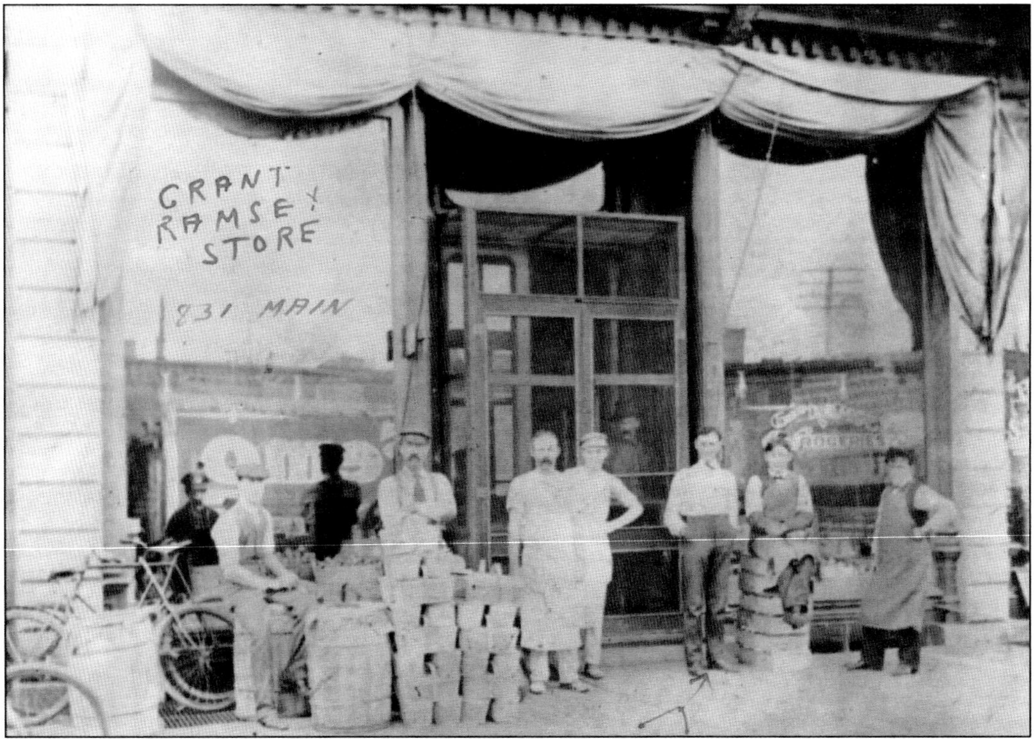

Grant Ramsey (third from right) started his career in the early 1900s as a grocer at 831 Main Street. An advertising brochure reported that he was "widely known as the busy grocer, butcher and baker of Grinnell." He sold the store in 1923 and opened Ramsey Realty, a business now in its fourth generation as Ramsey-Weeks. The photograph is dated 1902. (Ramsey family.)

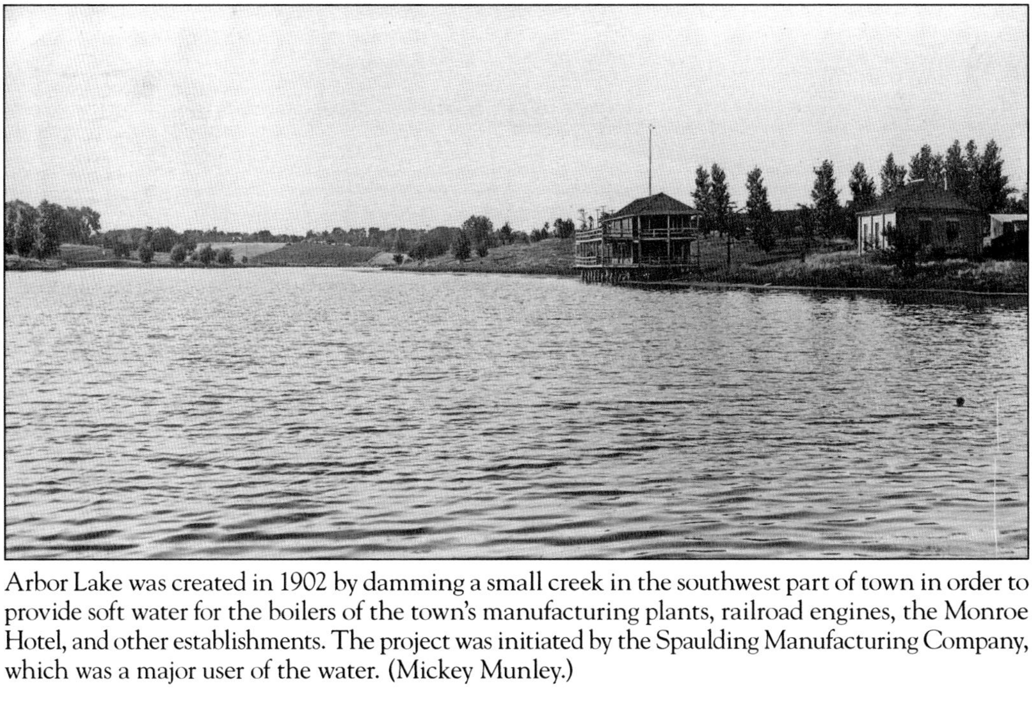

Arbor Lake was created in 1902 by damming a small creek in the southwest part of town in order to provide soft water for the boilers of the town's manufacturing plants, railroad engines, the Monroe Hotel, and other establishments. The project was initiated by the Spaulding Manufacturing Company, which was a major user of the water. (Mickey Munley.)

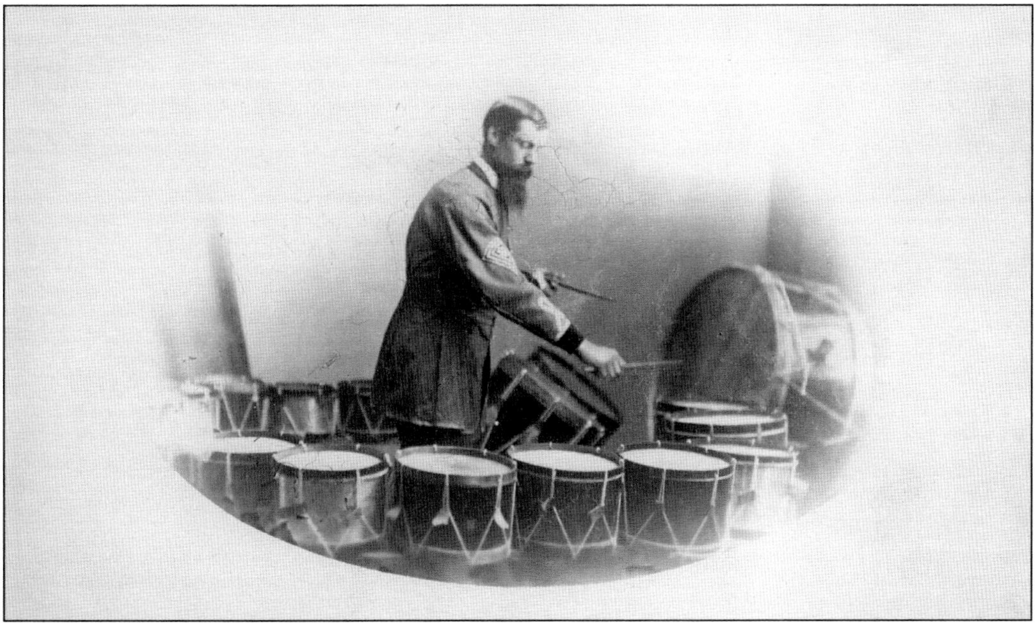

Physician Elbert Warren (E.W.) Clark was a noted percussionist with two local cornet bands. A 1916 newspaper article recalled the following: "One of his feats was to place 21 drums in a circle and play as he passed from drum to drum, never missing a beat." Clark was also mayor and served on the school board and in the state legislature. A fountain in Central Park was named in his honor. (DCL.)

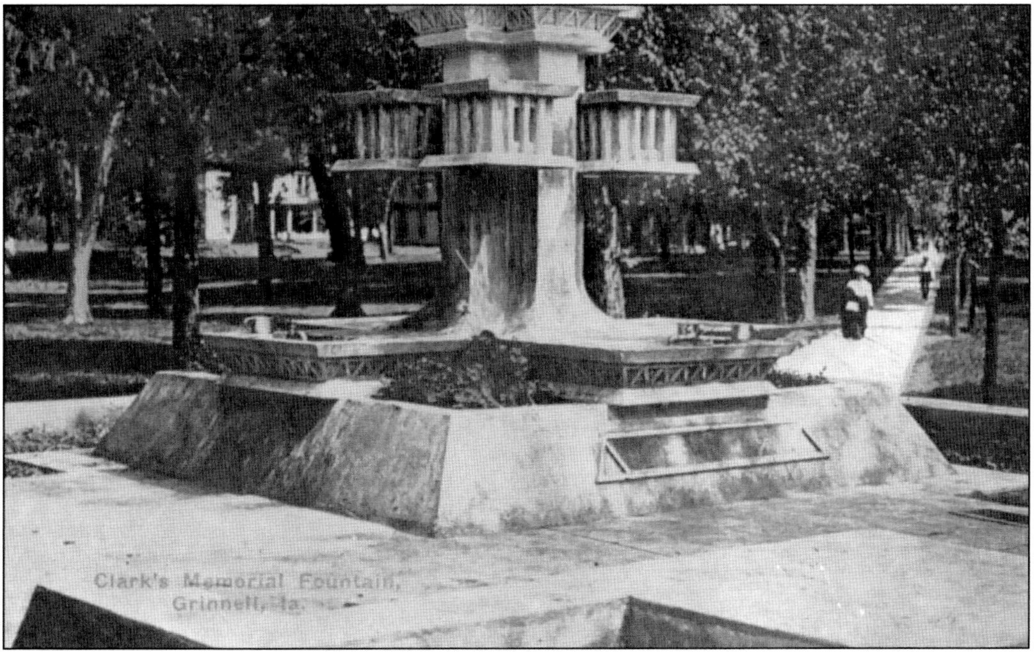

The centerpiece of Central Park for many years was the Clark Memorial Fountain, installed in 1911 and named for beloved physician Dr. E.W. Clark. The designer was Walter Burley Griffin, a noted Prairie School architect who also drew the plans for a home for Benjamin J. Ricker at 1510 Broad Street. The fountain was moved from the northwest corner to the center of the park in 1931 and then removed entirely in 1954. (DCL.)

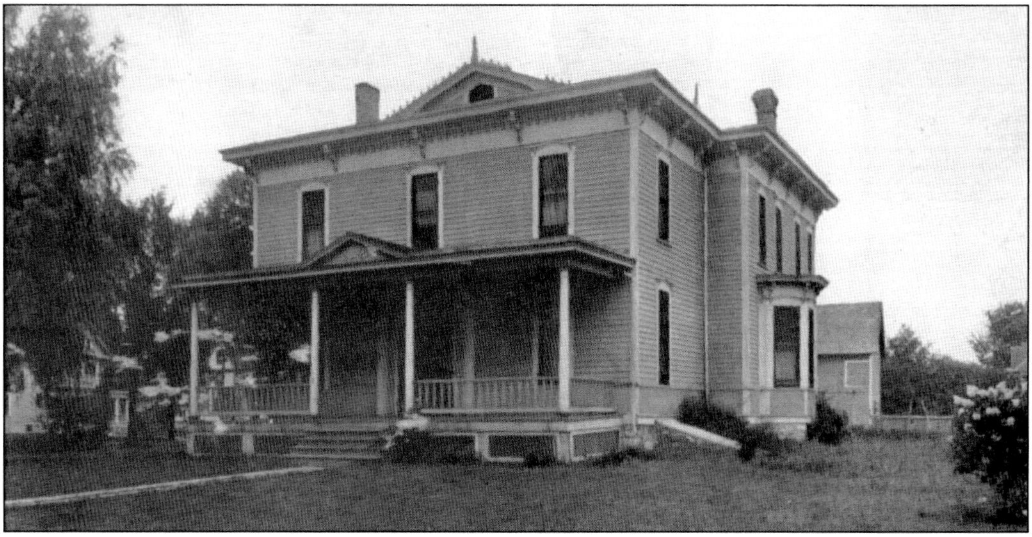

Thanks to a local fund drive, Grinnell's first municipal hospital opened in 1908 at 1030 Elm Street. Just as for a newborn baby, the community held a "shower" to assemble needed supplies. The building had six private rooms, an operating room, infant room, nurses' room, kitchen, reception area, dining room, and laundry facilities. It was replaced in 1919 by two new hospitals. The building is a private residence today. (DCL.)

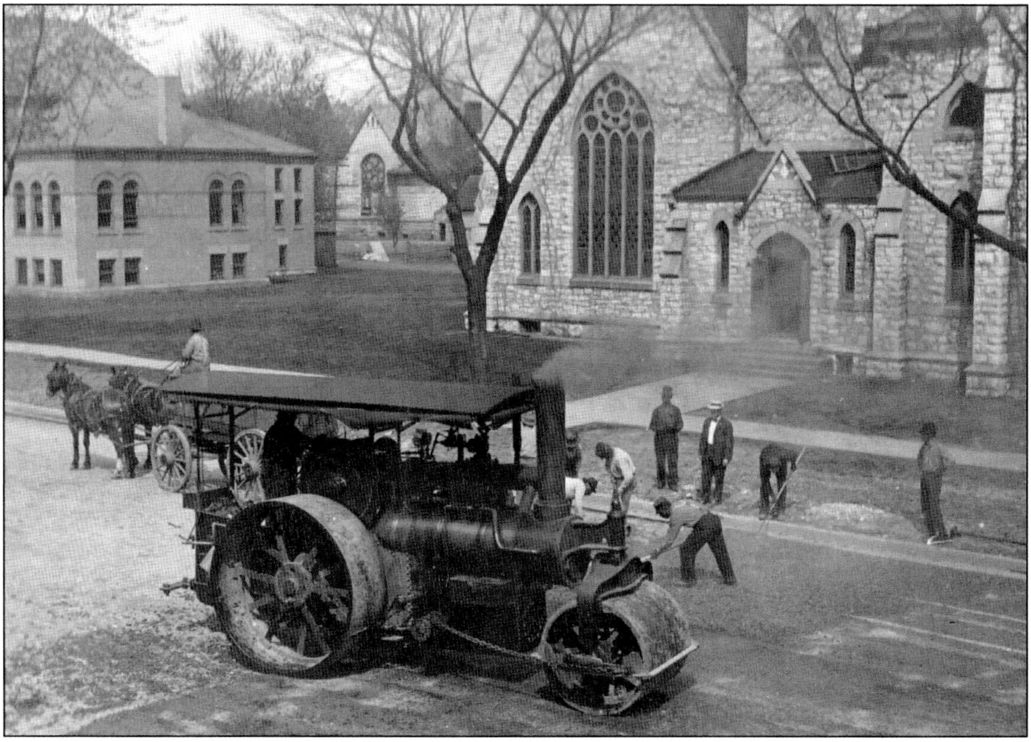

Dirt (often mud) roads were replaced with pavement in Grinnell starting in 1909 with work on eight blocks in the business district. By the end of 1910, a total of 5.5 miles of roadway had a hard surface—the largest single paving contract in the state at that time. By 1929, Grinnell had 14 miles of "the best paving on earth and everybody is glad for it," according to a newspaper account. (GHM.)

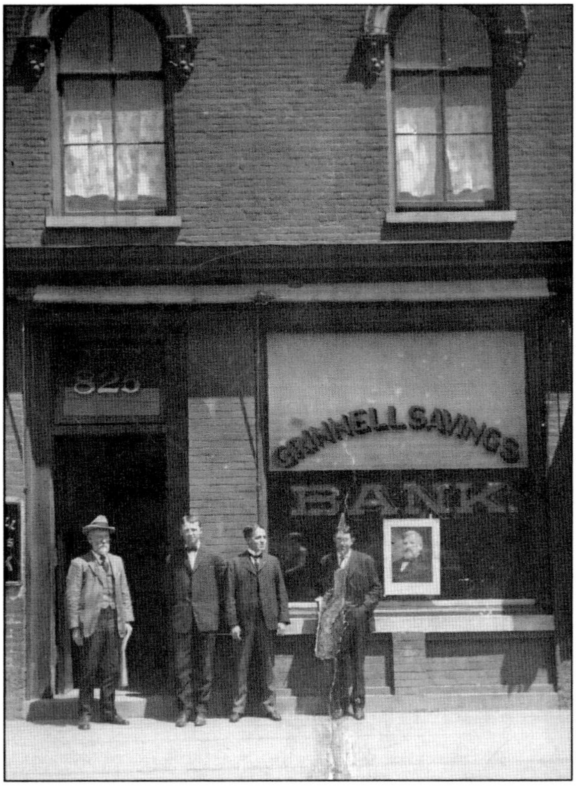

Grinnell Savings Bank opened in 1877 as the town's second bank (after the First National Bank). Its founders included J.B. Grinnell. Pictured in this 1908 photograph are, from left to right, unidentified, Carl Childs, Samuel Pooley, and George Walker. The bank moved in 1914 from the north side to the south side of Fourth Avenue, to the present site of Grinnell State Bank. (DCL.)

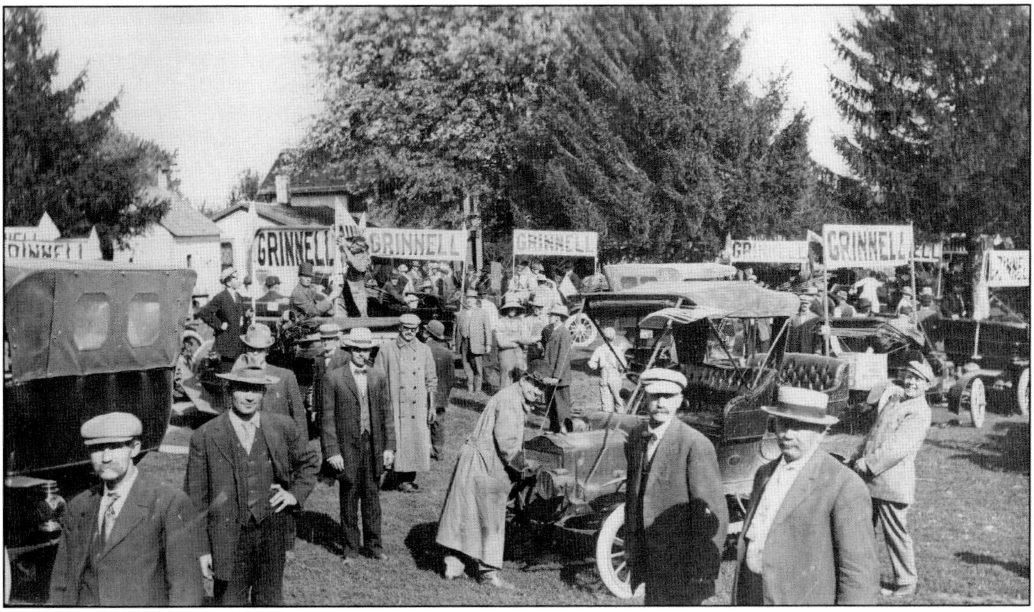

Horseless carriages were still a novelty when a group of local businessmen called the Grinnell Boosters began all-day excursions into the countryside to advertise Grinnell. One tour in September 1910 included 33 automobiles spaced at 100-foot intervals. In a summary of the trip, the *Grinnell Herald* reported the following: "We will pass over the list of punctures and blowouts and accidents, for they are incidents of automobile trips." (GHM.)

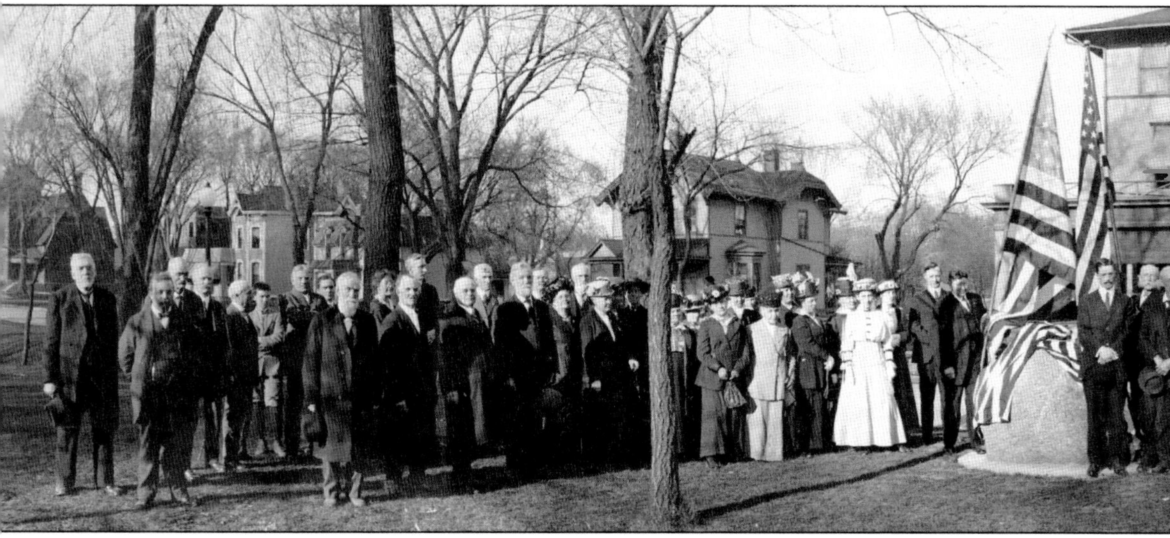

The Daughters of the American Revolution gathered in 1916 on the east side of Central Park to dedicate a bronze tablet marking the location of J.B. Grinnell's home across the street. Two years earlier, the rear of the house had been torn down and the front part moved to the 700 block of Broad

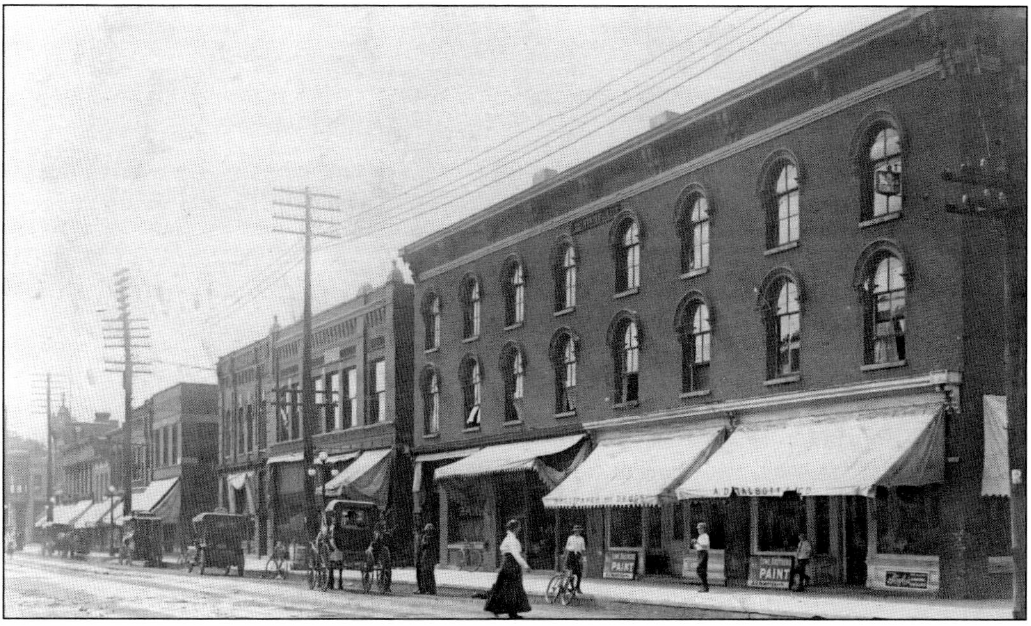

Fourth Avenue between Main and Broad Streets was Grinnell's retail hub in the early 1900s. Merchants occupied the space on the ground floors, while the offices of lawyers, doctors, and dentists were on the upper floors. The photograph was taken prior to 1914, when the Merchants National Bank was built on the corner of Fourth Avenue and Broad Street. (Mickey Munley.)

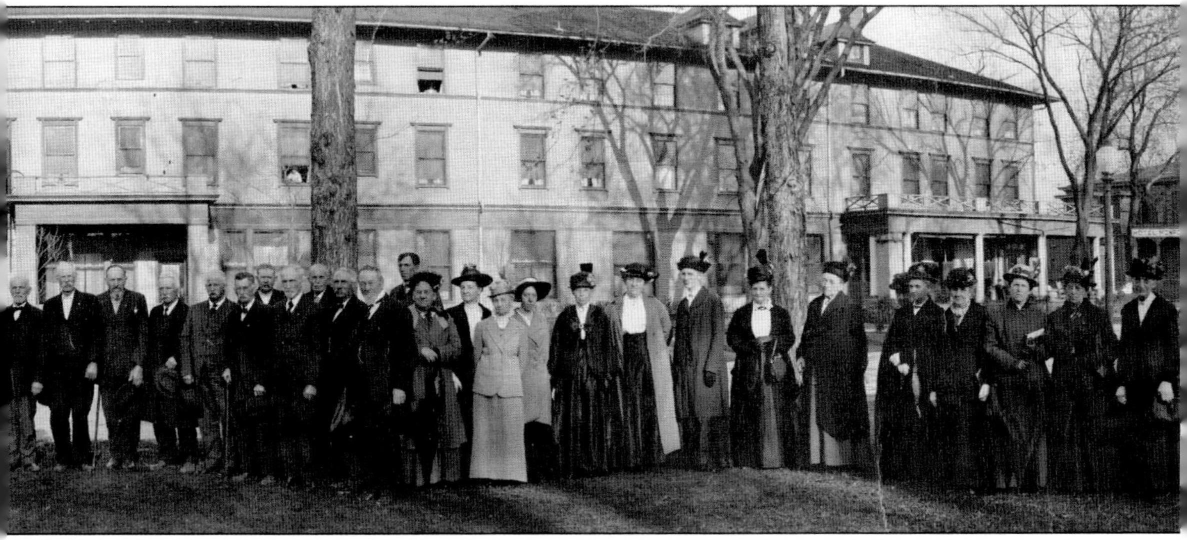

Street, where it was divided into apartments. It was razed in 1984. A stained-glass window saved from the house is on display at the Grinnell Historical Museum. In this panorama photograph, the Monroe Hotel can be seen in the background. (GHM.)

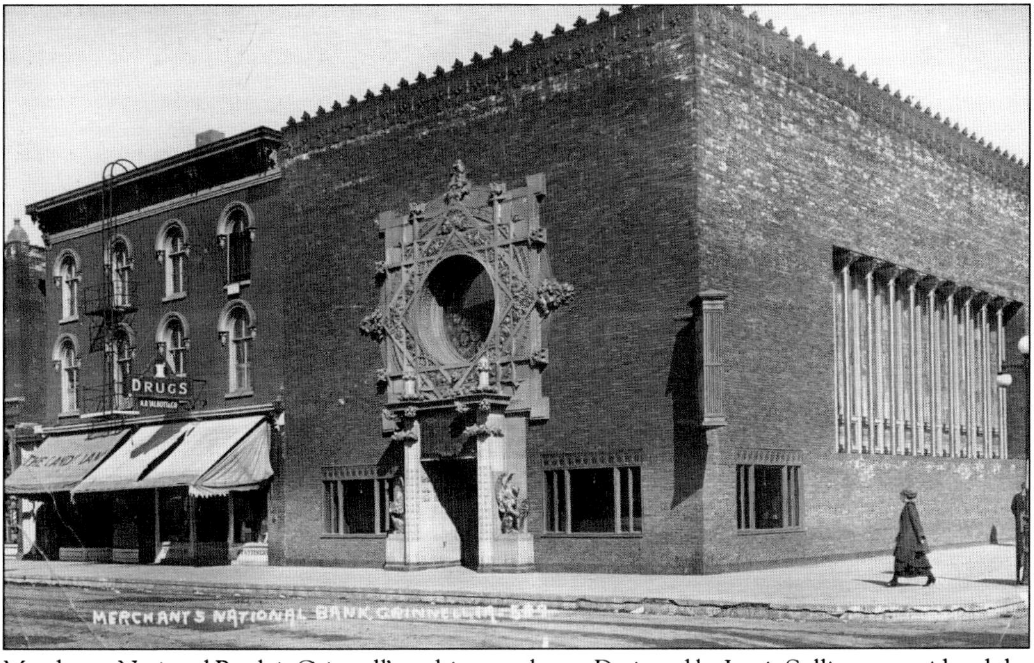

Merchants National Bank is Grinnell's architectural gem. Designed by Louis Sullivan, considered the father of modern American architecture, it was built in 1914 at a cost of $60,000. One of Sullivan's eight "Jewel Box" banks in the Midwest, it features stained glass, colored tile, marble counters and floor, and gold-plated terra-cotta ornamentation. The original urns had plumbing to water the ferns. The building was designated a National Historic Landmark in 1976. (GCA.)

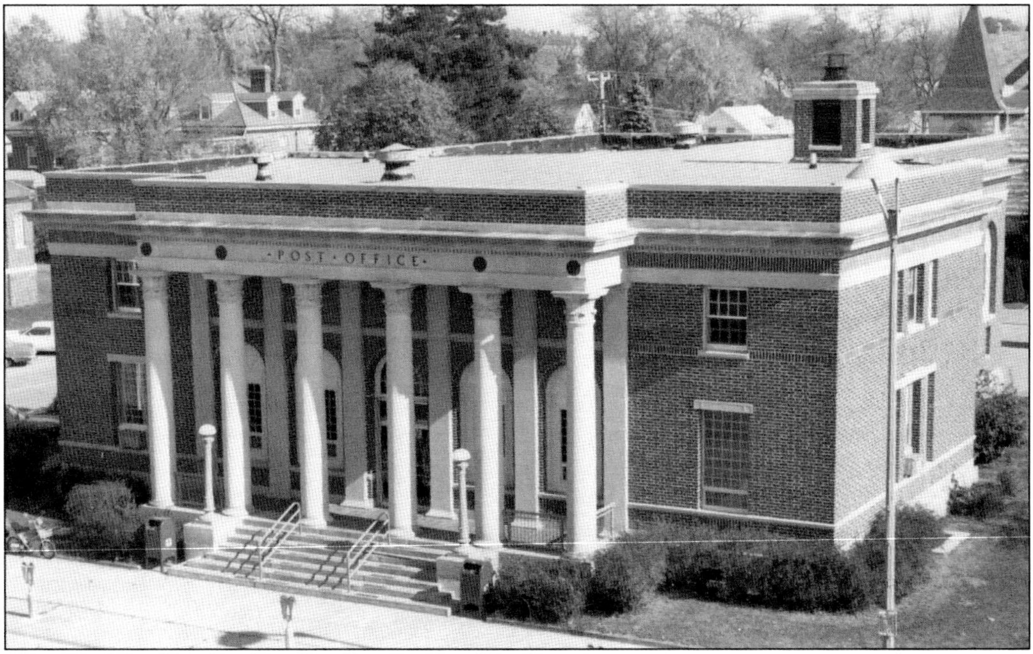

In 1916, business owners wanted a new post office on Broad Street enough to match a $15,000 government appropriation in order to buy a site at the southeast corner of Fifth Avenue and Broad Street. The building (above), designed in the Palladian Revival style, was constructed at a cost of $68,500. Newspaper articles on the opening day reported that the building contained "the best materials throughout," including toilets "finished in marble" and "a splendidly equipped shower which is the pride of Postmaster Nelson's heart." Delivery of mail in the Grinnell area started in the early 1900s, with seven rural routes. House-to-house delivery in town began a few years later. In the photograph below, postal workers posed in September 1917 on the steps of the new building. It is not known if the women in the back row were postal employees or family members of employees. (Both, DCL.)

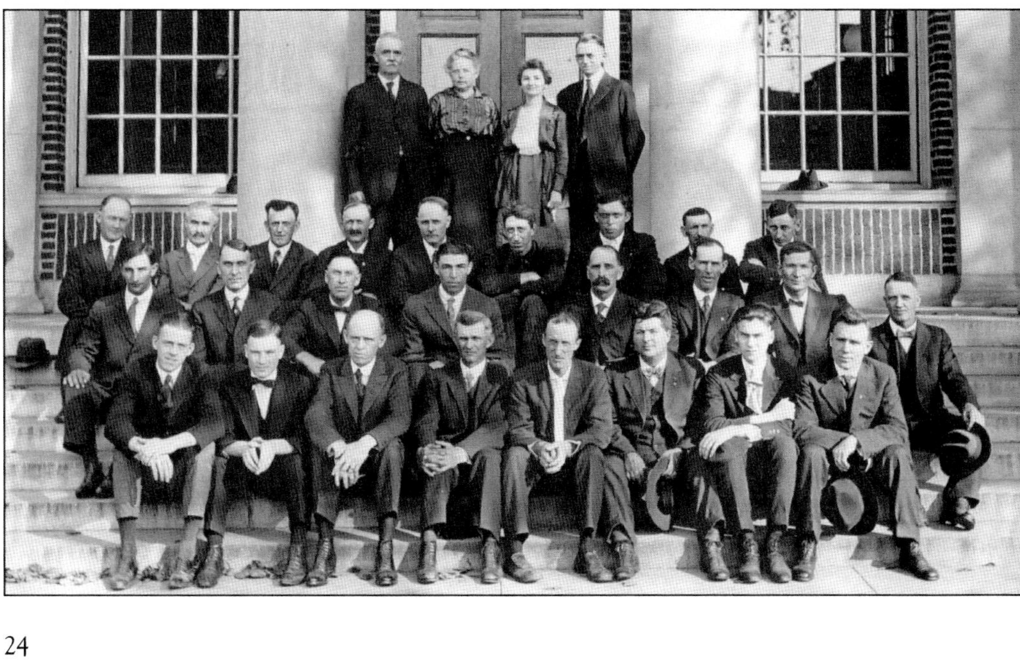

Two

Establishing a College

The ideal has been to give these young people the equipment and the will to help make this a better world.

—Howard R. Bowen, President, Grinnell College, 1955–1964

In 1848, an idealistic band of 11 young men, mostly Congregationalists from Andover Theological Seminary in Massachusetts, established Iowa College in Davenport, Iowa, a city on the Illinois-Iowa border. It was one of the first colleges west of the Mississippi River.

Ten years later, seeking a more hospitable location for their venture and attracted by J.B. Grinnell's offer of financial support, the college's trustees voted to move Iowa College to Grinnell and merge with Grinnell University. A wagon loaded with books, scientific equipment, the college charter, and $9,000 arrived in Grinnell the next year. The first classes were held in the new location in 1861.

From the beginning, the college and the town were drawn together in a common vision that embraced antislavery, temperance, and progressive ideals. The establishment of one of the country's first political science departments (1883) and a Department of Applied Christianity (1893) made the college a national center for the Social Gospel Movement—a belief that biblical teachings can and should be applied to solve social problems. By 1909, when Iowa College changed its name to Grinnell College, the school was widely known for its commitment to social justice—a reputation that continues to this day.

Over the years, the college has survived cyclones, fires, wars, economic uncertainties, and societal changes. During the challenging times, the college relied on the town's support and encouragement. In return, the college has provided a strong economic base and diverse cultural offerings.

Today, Grinnell College is one of the country's leading undergraduate liberal arts colleges. Its 1,672 full-time students (2014–2015 enrollment) come from all 50 states and 46 countries. Its endowment of $1.5 billion is one of the largest of any educational institution in the country.

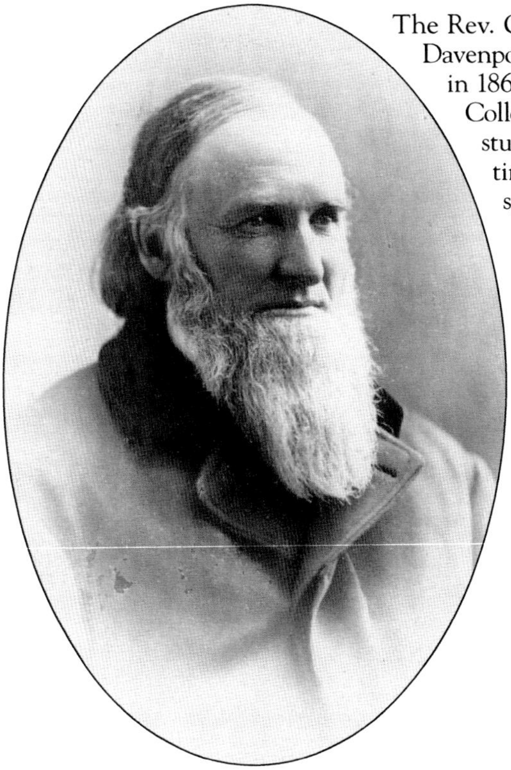

The Rev. George Magoun, a Congregational minister in Davenport and trustee of Iowa College, was inaugurated in 1865 as the first president of the newly merged Iowa College and Grinnell University. With most of the male students fighting in the Civil War, enrollment at that time depended largely on females. Magoun, an able speaker and a strong writer, sustained the college through this shaky beginning, which also included a fire in 1871 and a cyclone in 1882. (GHM.)

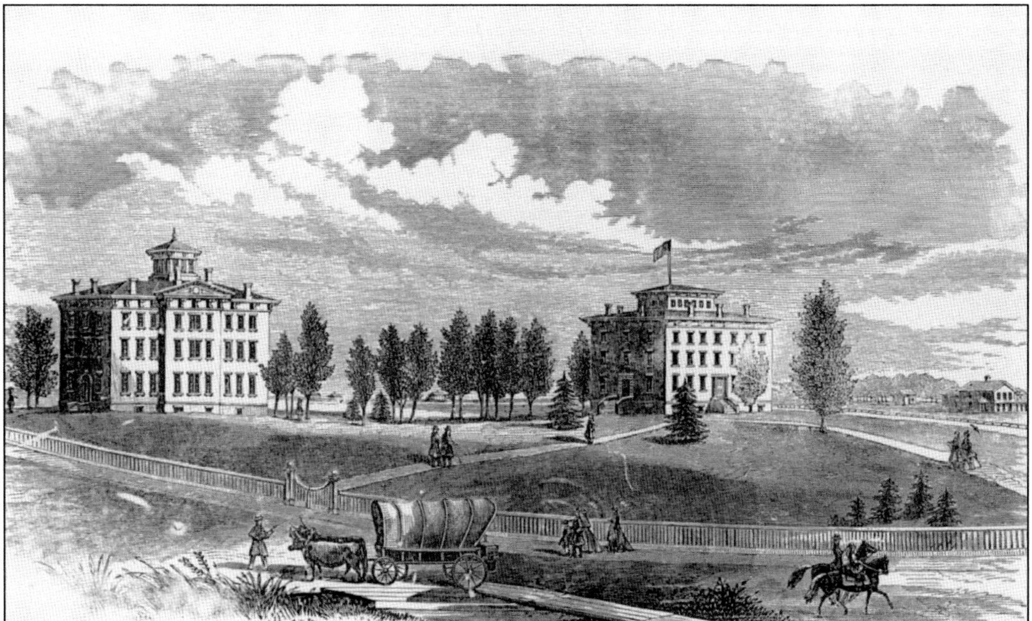

East College (right), the first building to go up at the newly established Iowa College in Grinnell, opened in 1861. It was heated by a stove in each room. West College (left) opened in 1867 and, although it contained no flush toilets, no pressure water supply, and no central heat, it did house 4,000 books in its library. (GCA.)

Joanna Harris Haines was the first woman to graduate from Iowa College in Grinnell. The year was 1865. Her father and four older brothers were serving in the Civil War during her college years. Years later, she recalled the following of those days: "Often the entire recitation period would be devoted not to the parsing of French verbs but to the latest news from Vicksburg and Gettysburg." (GCA.)

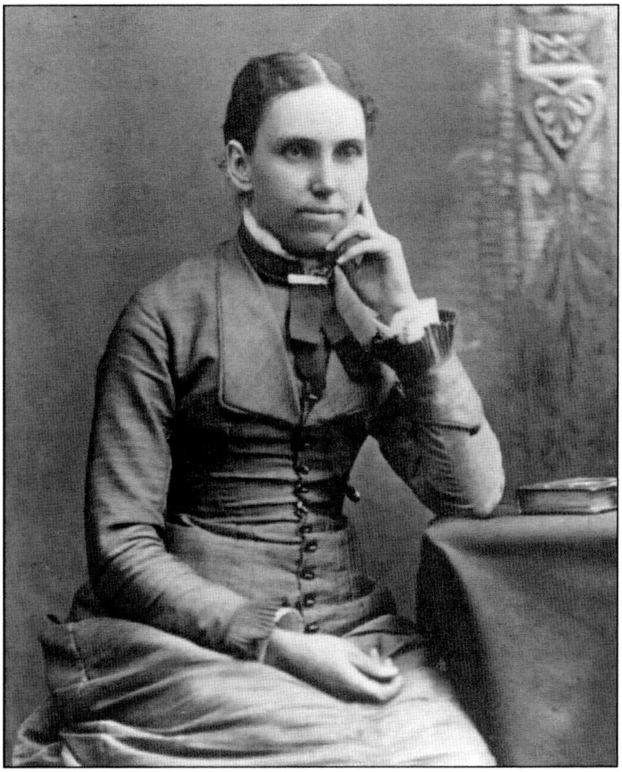

All the buildings and trees on the campus were destroyed in a devastating cyclone that struck Grinnell with fury on the evening of June 17, 1882. Thirty-nine people, including two students, were killed. Commencement went on as previously scheduled. The photograph shows what remained at the corner of Seventh Avenue and Broad Street. (DCL.)

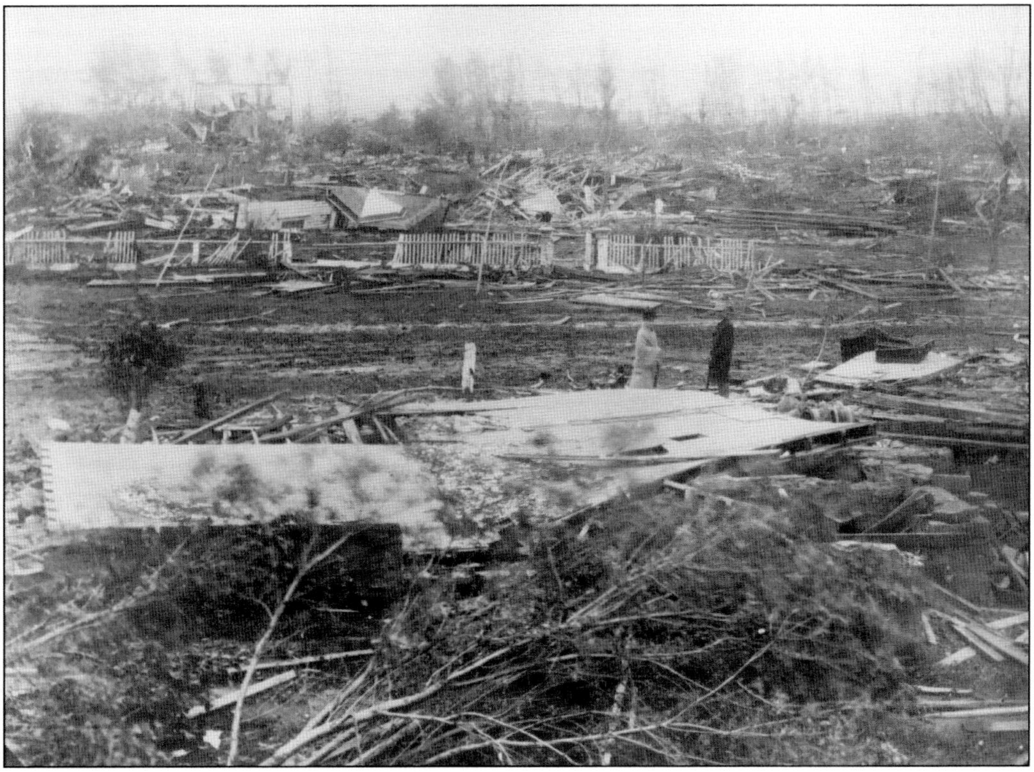

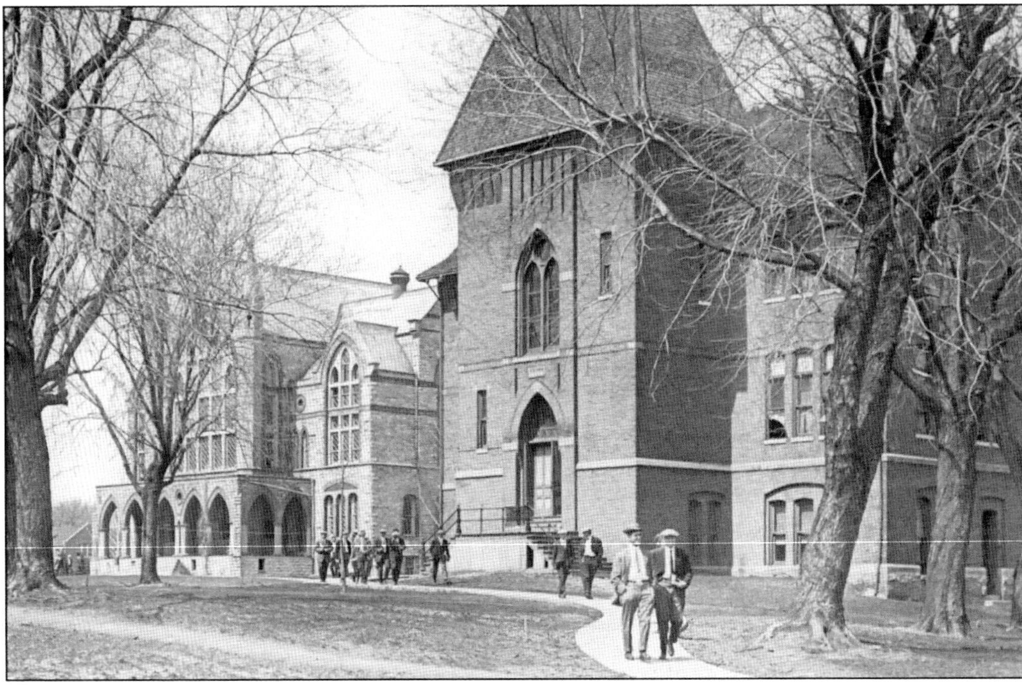

Alumni Hall (above right) was the first building constructed after the cyclone. Its cornerstone was laid just nine days after the disaster. Funds for both the walls and the roof of the building were furnished by the class of 1882, which became known as the "cyclone class." Blair Hall (above left), a late-19th-century Victorian Gothic building with vertical lines and cathedral-like arched windows, was finished during the next year. Blair Hall housed a science museum on its second floor. The image below shows women doing laboratory work in a biology class in Blair Hall aided by electric lights, which were added in 1898. Enrollment at the college at that time was 270 college students, 125 academy-college prep, 111 music students, and 19 graduate students. (Above, Mickey Munley; below, GCA.)

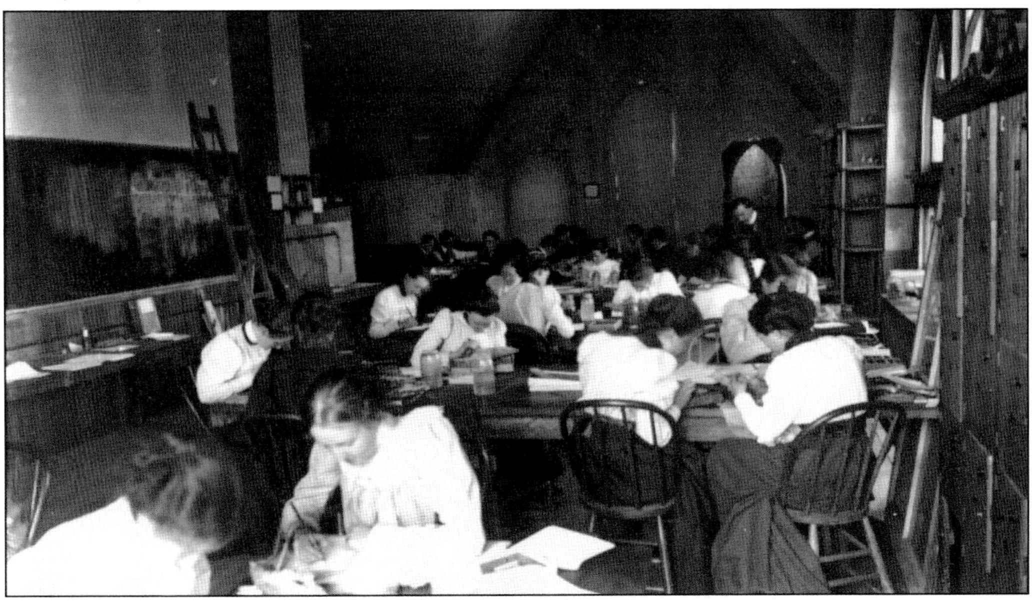

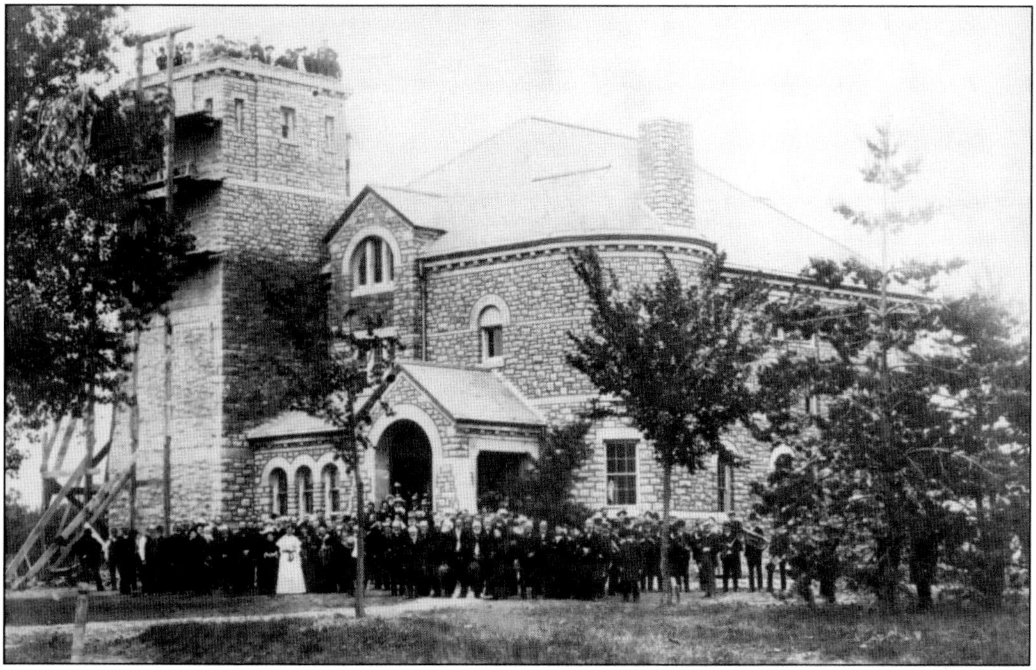

Immediately after the 1882 cyclone, J.B. Grinnell headed east to raise money to rebuild the college. He believed personal contact would generate more funds than a written appeal, and he was correct. Goodnow Hall (above) was built in 1885, the last of the four new structures constructed after the disaster. An example of Richardsonian Romanesque architecture, it currently houses the anthropology department and global development studies. It is the oldest building on campus. (GHM.)

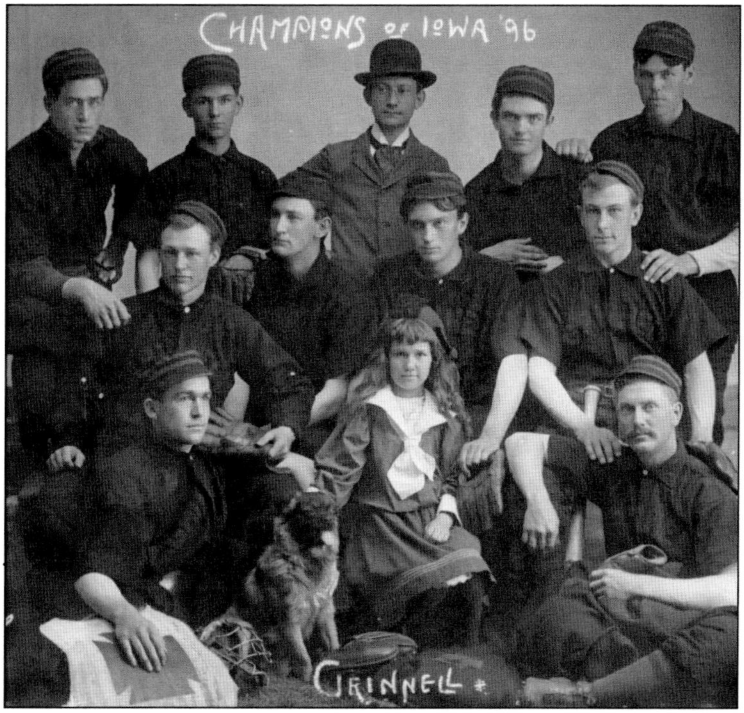

The first intercollegiate baseball game in Iowa was played in Grinnell in 1868, with Iowa College facing the University of Iowa. Iowa College won 24-0. After an Iowa College–University of Illinois baseball game in 1885, an Iowa College graduate wrote the following: "The spirit of athletics is in the air with winning teams in baseball, football, and track." The school colors were changed from pale pink to bold scarlet and black to reflect the enthusiasm. The photograph shows the 1896 championship baseball team. (GCA.)

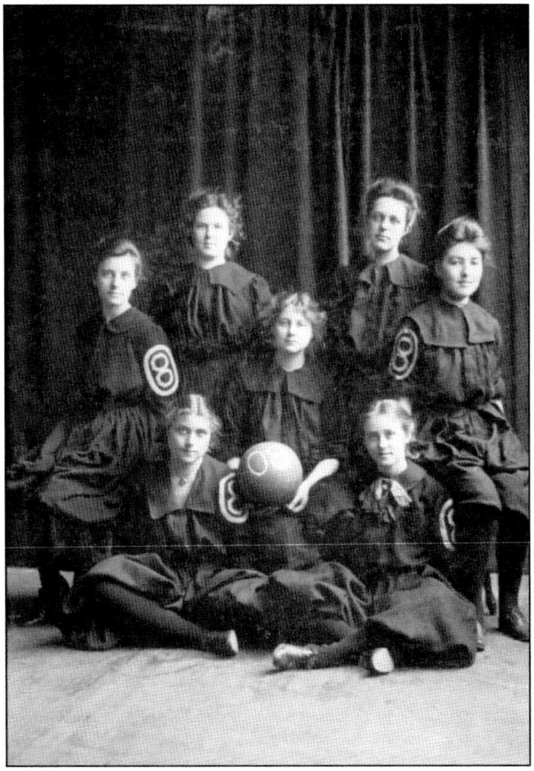

Although physical activities for female students were limited in the late 1800s, the first two women's basketball teams at the college were organized in 1896, two years before men's basketball was started. Ernest Atherton, class of 1895, won a contest to design an insignia for the athletic uniforms—the Maltese cross with the black letter G. It is still used today. (GCA.)

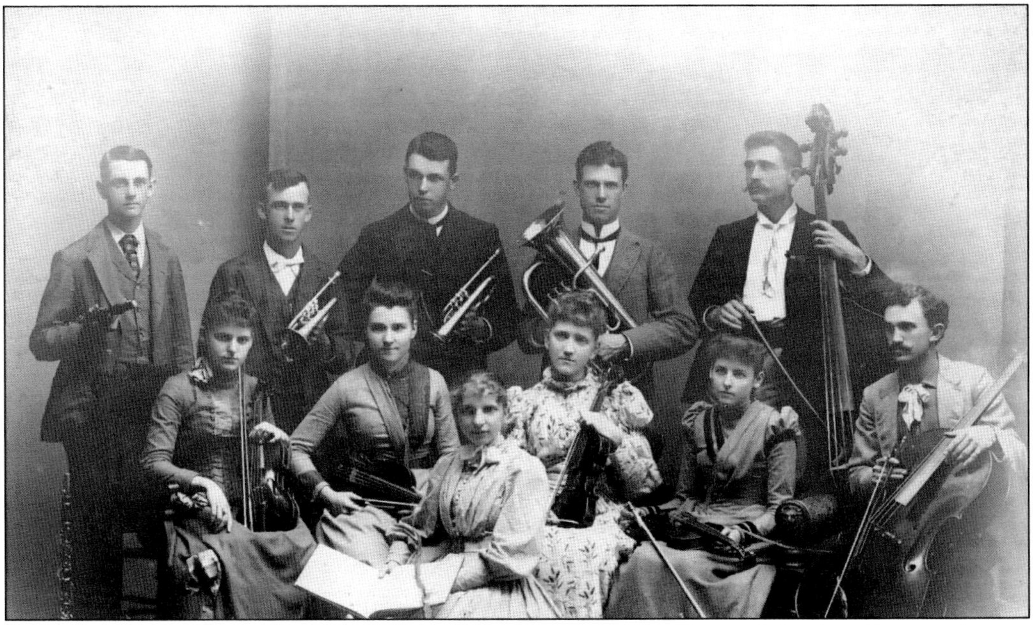

Prof. Rossetter Cole established the Amphion Orchestra in 1894, with both college and town musicians. Isabella Beaton (first row, center), a local girl who attended the college, went on to become a world-famous pianist. Cole also organized the college glee club, which toured the Midwest. James Norman Hall, class of 1910 and coauthor of *Mutiny on the Bounty*, recalled the following: "Belonging to the glee club was my heaven on earth at this time." (GCA.)

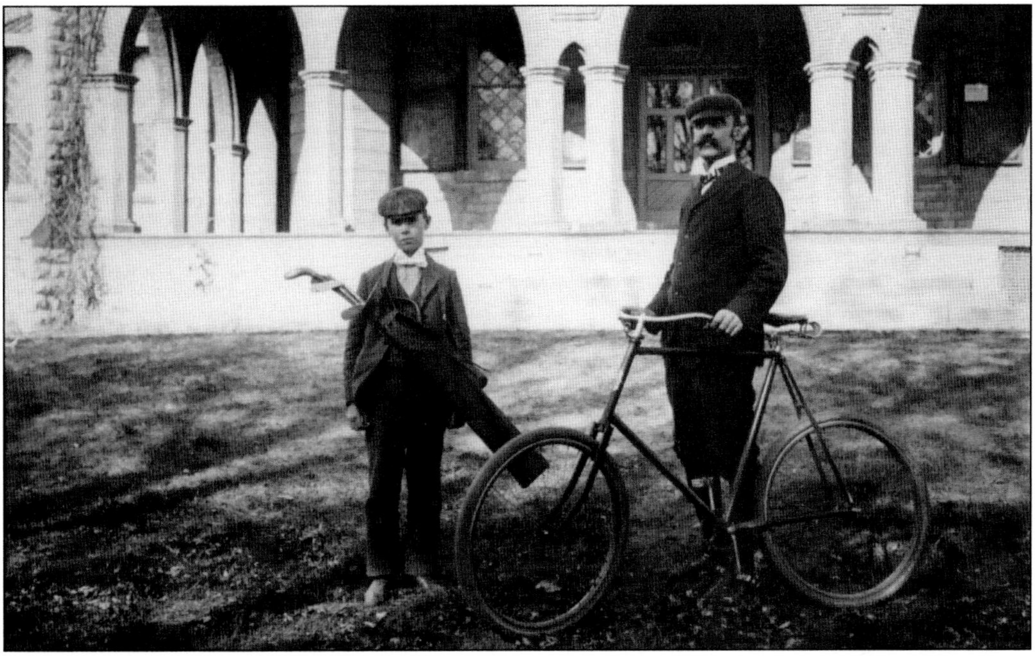

Prof. Walter Hendrixson and his son posed in front of Blair Hall, the most impressive of the four buildings constructed after the 1882 cyclone. Hendrixson taught in the chemistry department for 35 years, working to make it an effective center for scientific research and teaching. Hendrixson loved sports, especially the new game of golf, and was instrumental in starting the Grinnell Golf and Country Club in 1899. (GCA.)

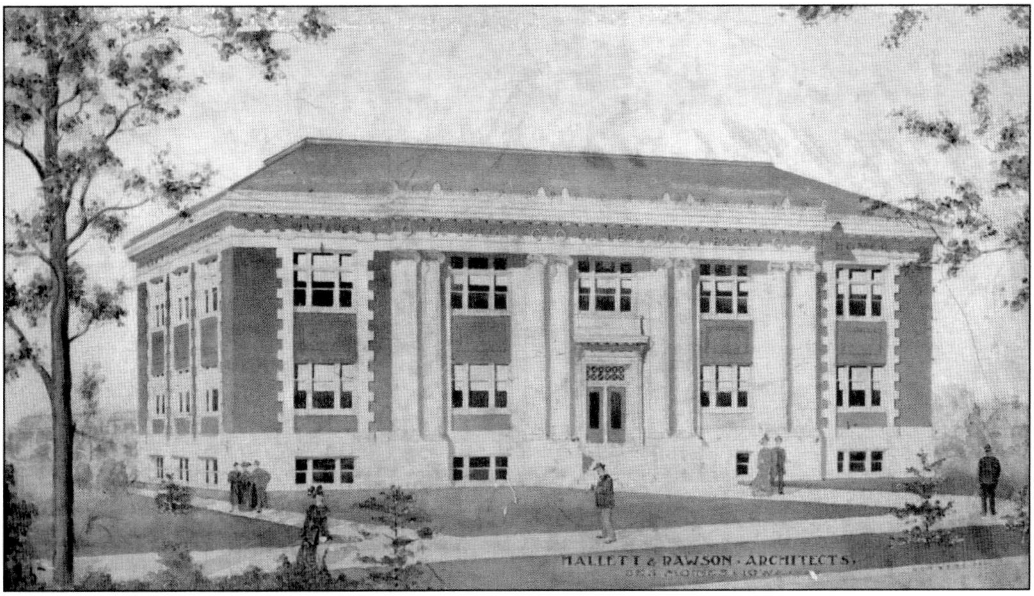

Carnegie Library, built in 1905, was financed in part by a grant of $50,000 from philanthropist Andrew Carnegie. It was one of the few college libraries Carnegie funded. Harry D. Rawson, class of 1895, designed the building in the modified Classical style. When Burling Library was opened in 1959, Carnegie was remodeled for use as classrooms, lecture halls, faculty offices, and the college bookstore. (GCA.)

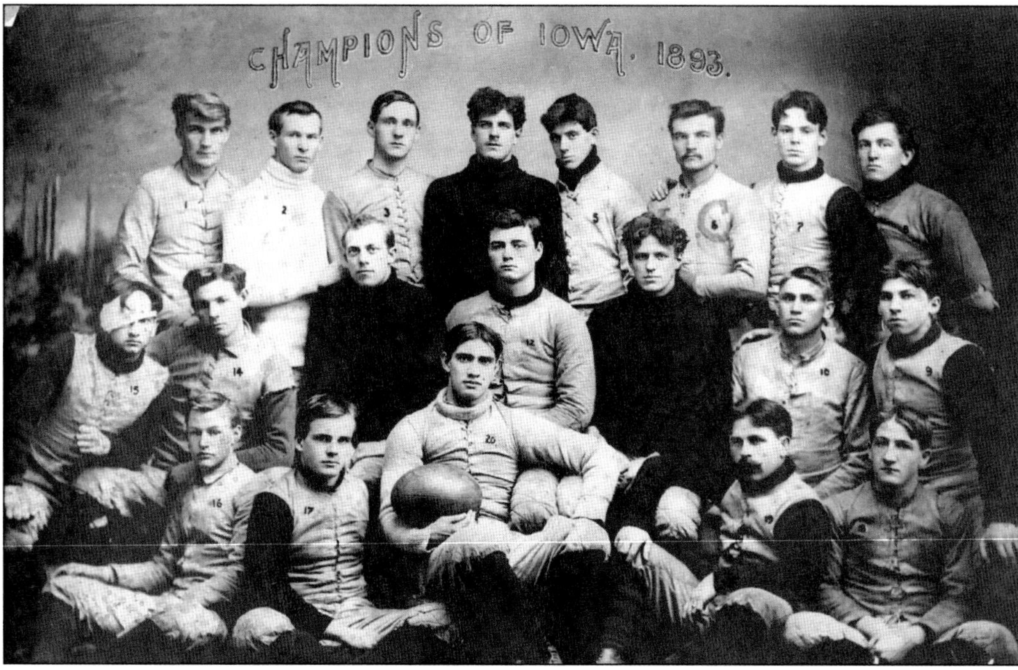

In 1889, Iowa College defeated the University of Iowa in football 24-0. The team went on to win five Iowa football championships by 1895, including wins over the University of Iowa, Iowa State College, the University of Nebraska, and the University of Minnesota. The north athletic field was dedicated by the class of 1895 to Herbert Ward, a student "of most exemplary character," who died two years after his graduation in 1890. The photograph is dated 1893. (GCA.)

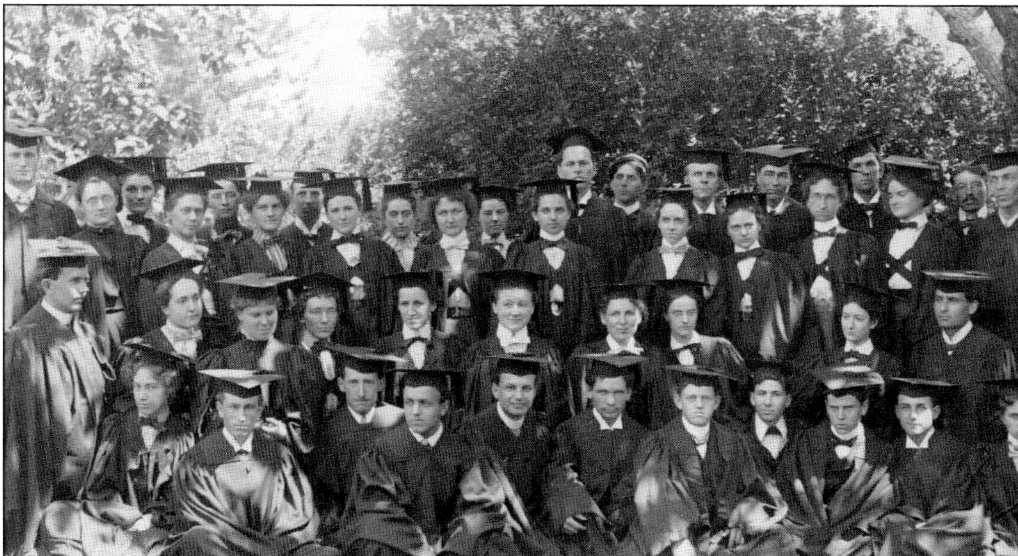

The class of 1898 was the first class to wear caps and gowns at graduation. The students also put on the first senior play, *As You Like It*. During the late 1890s, under the presidency of George Gates, the college promoted new courses in history, politics, literature, and modern languages as well as fostering a new emphasis on the arts. (GCA.)

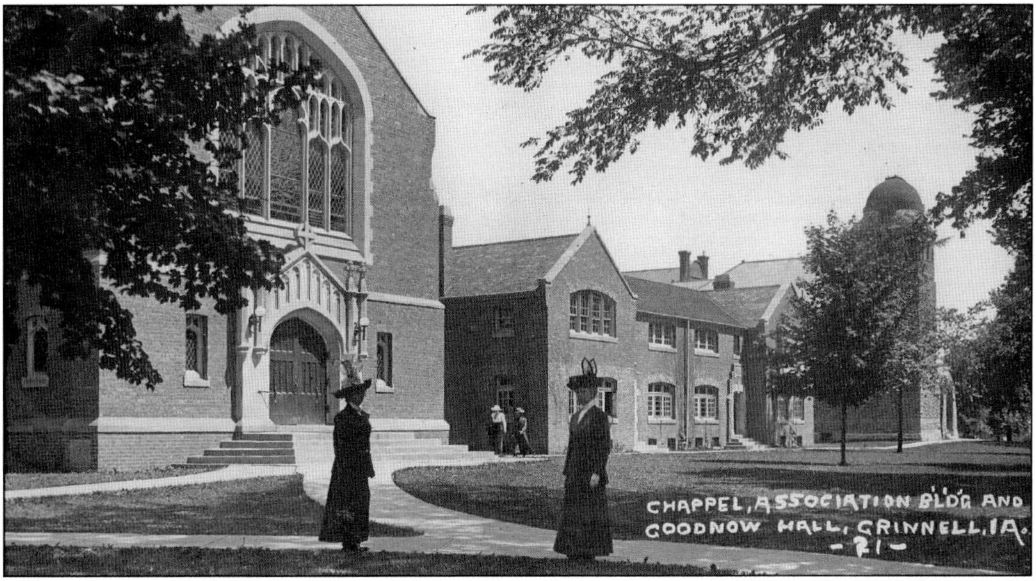

John Main, president of the college from 1906 to 1931, said the following of Herrick Chapel when it was built in 1907: "It is remarkably perfect in acoustical properties." The chapel, in a central location on campus, has been a popular venue for convocations, concerts, recitals, lectures, and weddings. Interfaith worship services, coordinated by the Center for Religion, Spirituality, and Social Justice, are held here. (GCA.)

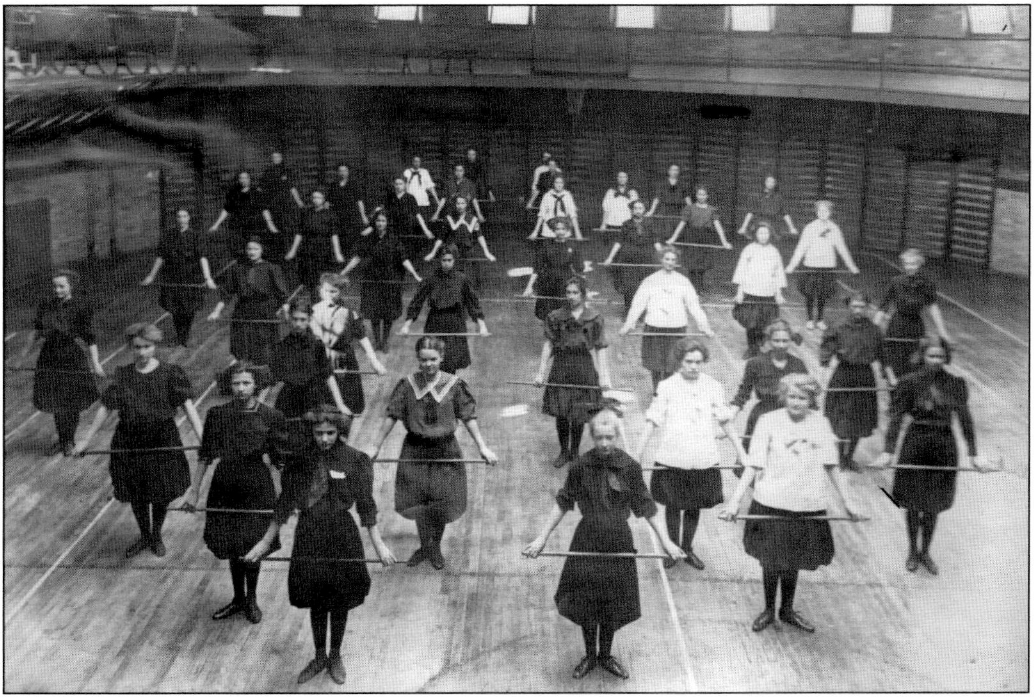

Rand Gymnasium, built in 1897, was a gift to the women of the college from Carrie Rand, instructor in social and physical culture. Lore has it that male students were aware of the times of the women's physical education classes and would choose those times to take their daily runs on the elevated track around the gym. (GCA.)

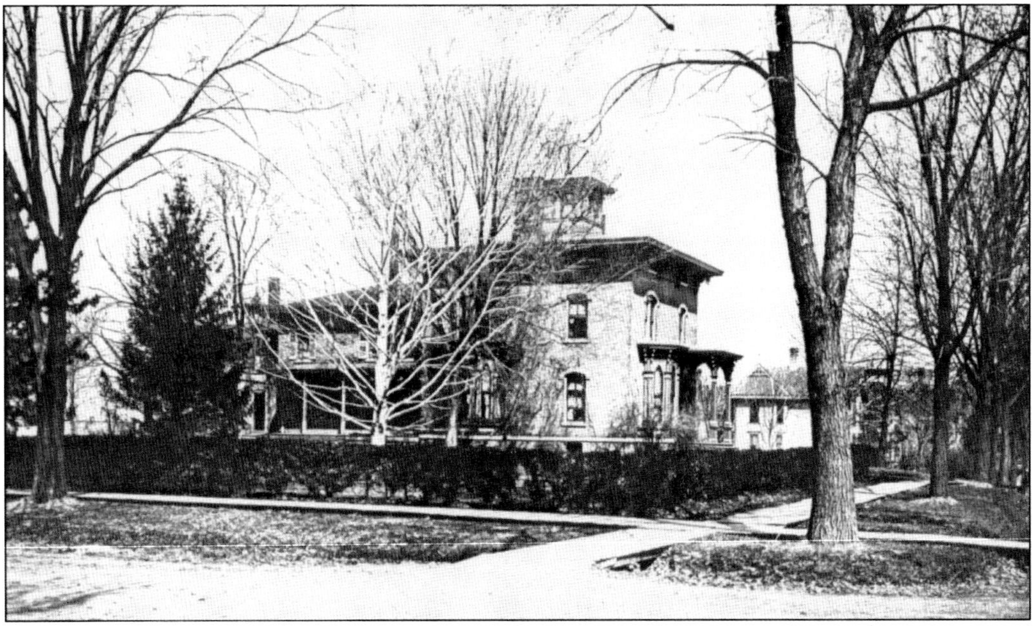

Henry G. Little, who came to Grinnell in 1867, built this brick house on the northwest corner of Fifth Avenue and Park Street. He sold it to the college in 1887, and it became the residence for college presidents for many years. It was replaced in 1917 by Grinnell House, which served college presidents and their families until 1961, when a new residence was built at 1600 Park Street. Today, Grinnell House is used as a college inn and an official faculty and administrative hospitality center. (GCA.)

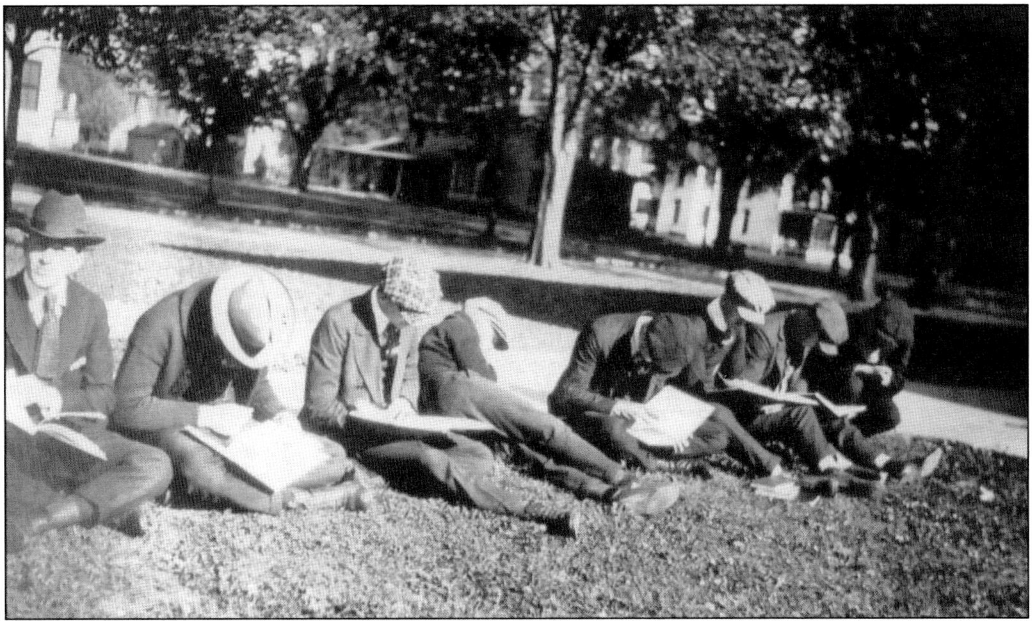

In the early 1900s, a group of serious-minded students used the Park Street curb to do some extra studying. Academics have always been a priority at the college. A Phi Beta Kappa chapter was established at the college in 1907. It was the 70th chapter in the nation and the second in Iowa. (DCL.)

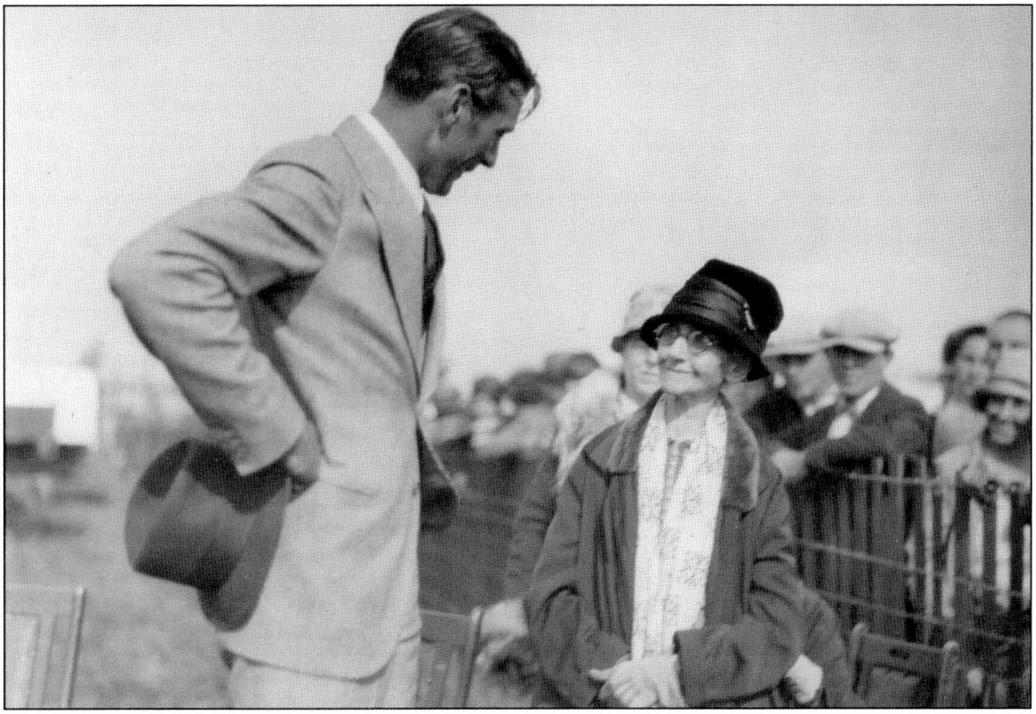

Actor Gary Cooper, who attended Grinnell from 1923 to 1925, greeted the college's first woman graduate, Joanna Harris Haines, class of 1865, when he visited the campus in 1929. Nicknamed the "Cowboy" by his fellow classmates, Frank James Cooper from Helena, Montana, attempted to join the drama club three times but failed. He did, however, go on to win two Academy Awards for his starring roles in *Sergeant York* (1941) and *High Noon* (1942). (GCA.)

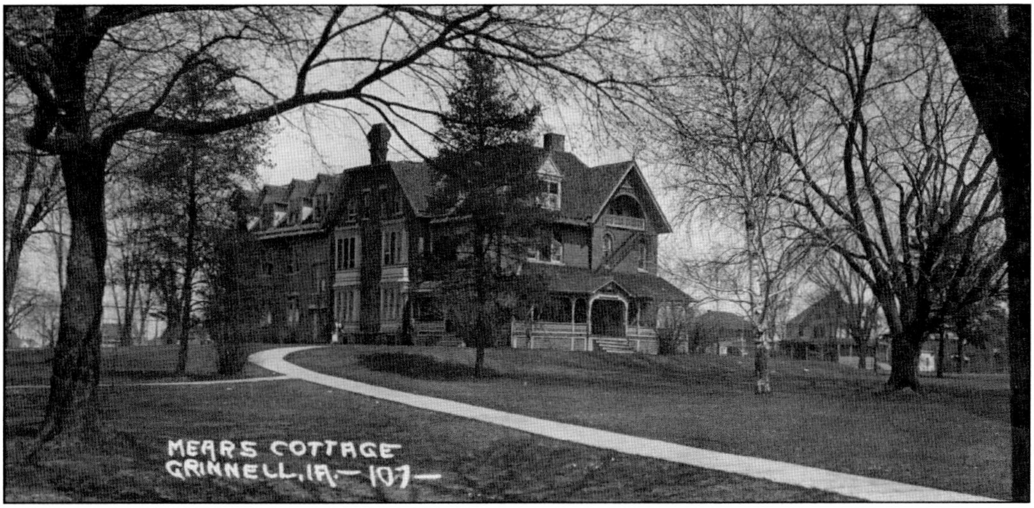

Before dormitories were constructed on campus, students lived in private homes near the college. The first residence hall was built for women in 1888. Called Mears Cottage, it was named for Mary Grinnell Mears, an 1888 graduate, daughter of J.B. Grinnell, and wife of David O. Mears. The three-story Victorian structure housed 28 women and provided "quiet ambiance for study and genteel social interaction." The building was enlarged in 1904, became coeducational in 1978, and was renovated in 1986. Mears Cottage now houses the offices of the English and history departments. (GCA.)

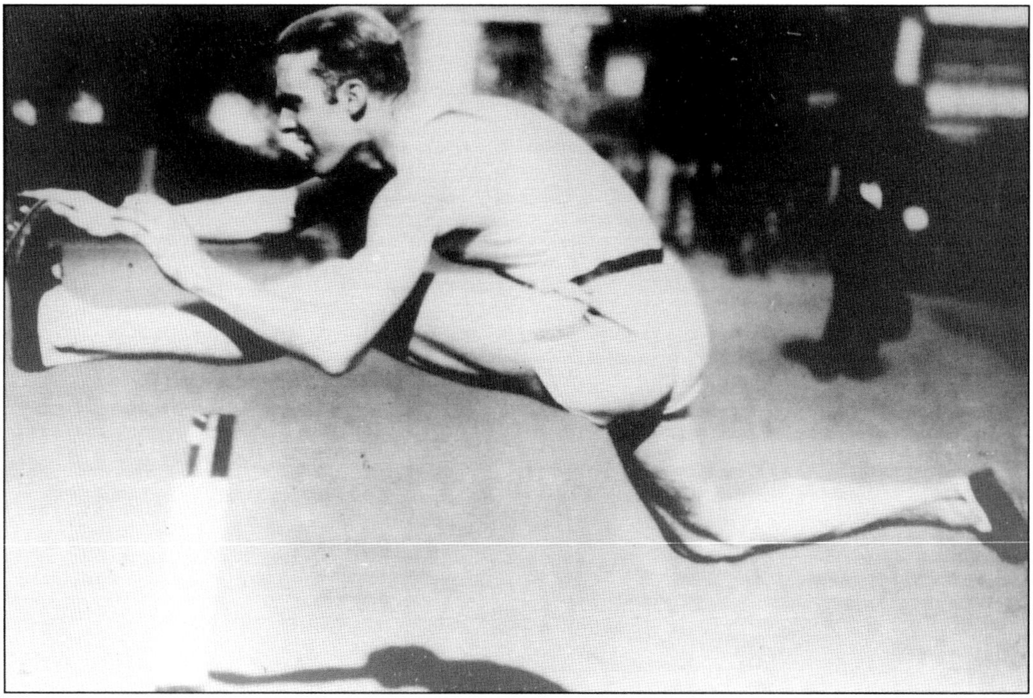

Morgan Taylor, class of 1926, won the gold medal in the 400-meter hurdles at the 1924 Olympics. Taylor went on to win a bronze medal in the same event in both the 1928 and 1932 Olympics. Taylor was involved in more than sports at Grinnell. He acted in the drama *The Goal*, sang tenor with the glee club, and held several student government offices. (GCA.)

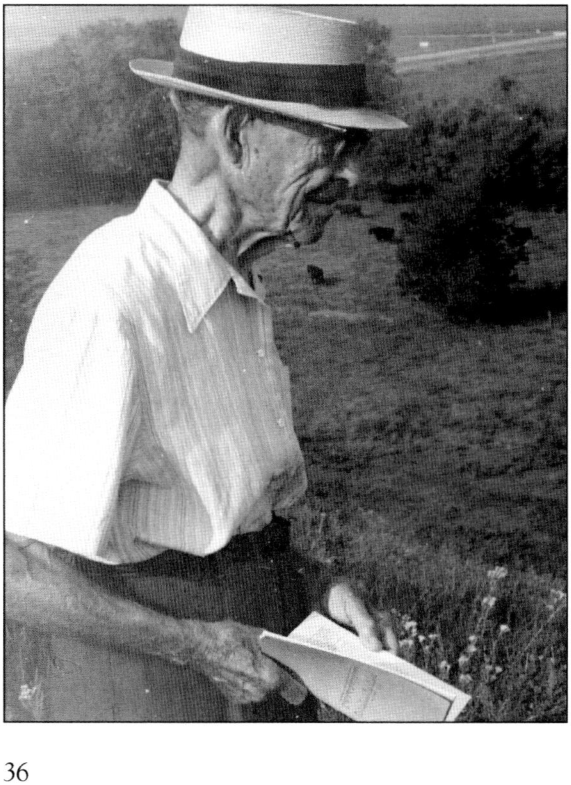

Henry Conard taught botany at the college for 39 years, retiring in 1944. He established an international reputation as a bryologist (expert on mosses). The Henry S. Conard Environmental Research Area (CERA), a 365-acre tract of land 11 miles southwest of Grinnell, was established in his honor in 1969 as a field lab for class use in the study of ecology as well as for student and faculty research. (GCA.)

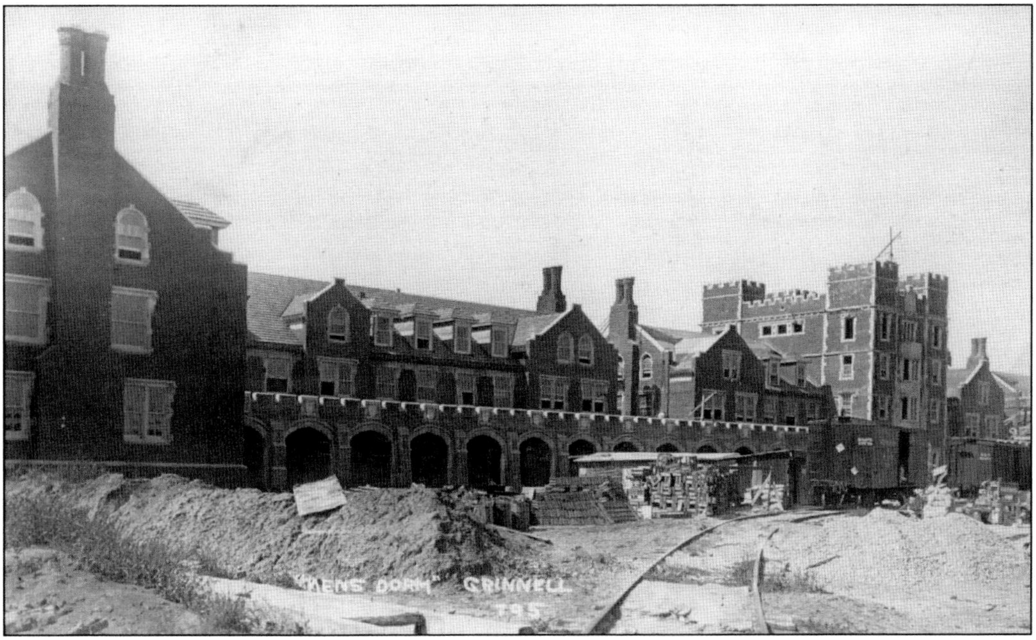

Under the leadership of Pres. John Main, Quad Hall for women, with six residence halls and a dining room, was built in 1915 on what is known as South Campus. Quad Hall for men (above) followed in 1917 on North Campus. The residence halls on each campus were built in the Oxford-Cambridge collegiate style and were connected by arched walkways or loggias. Both complexes had their own dorm rooms (below), reading rooms, game rooms, and dining halls. Enrollment in 1917 was 709. (Both, Mickey Munley.)

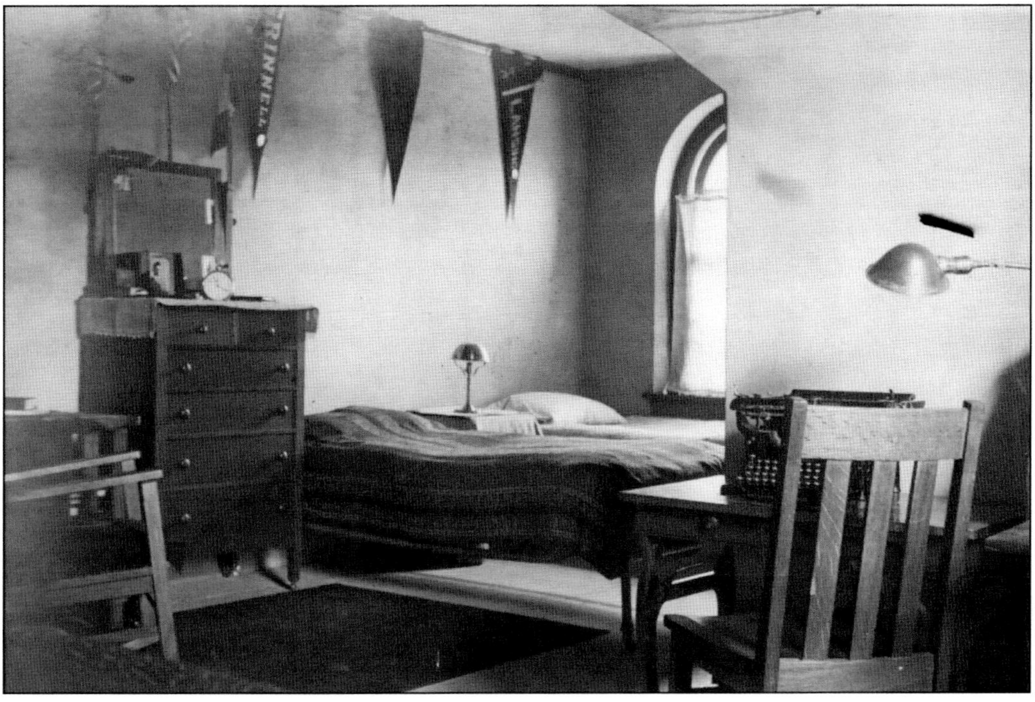

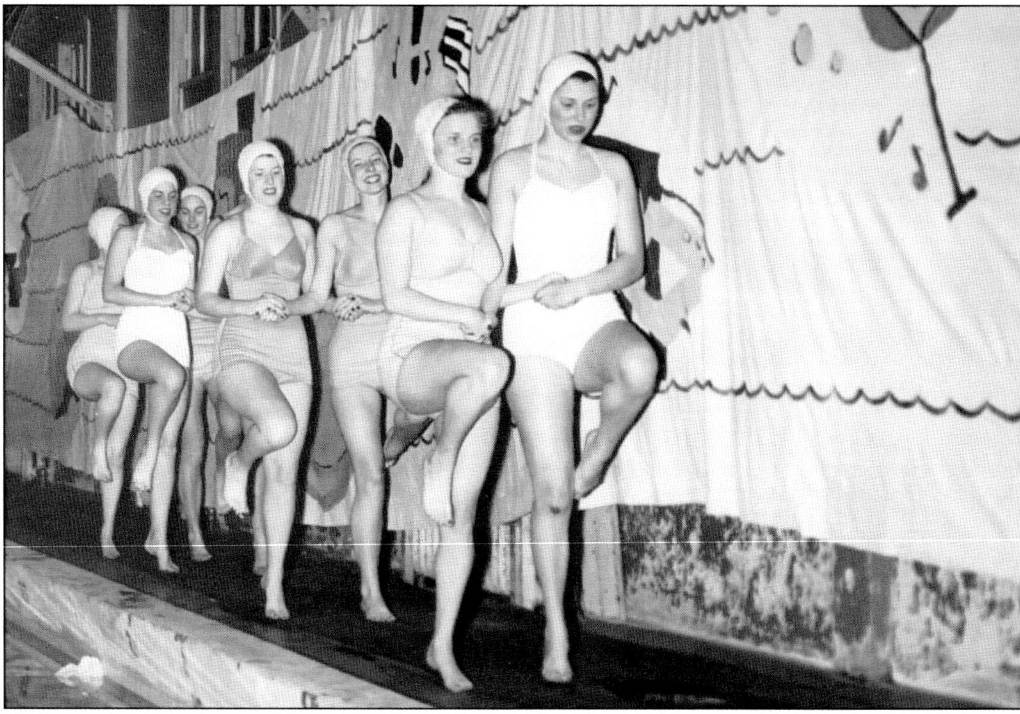

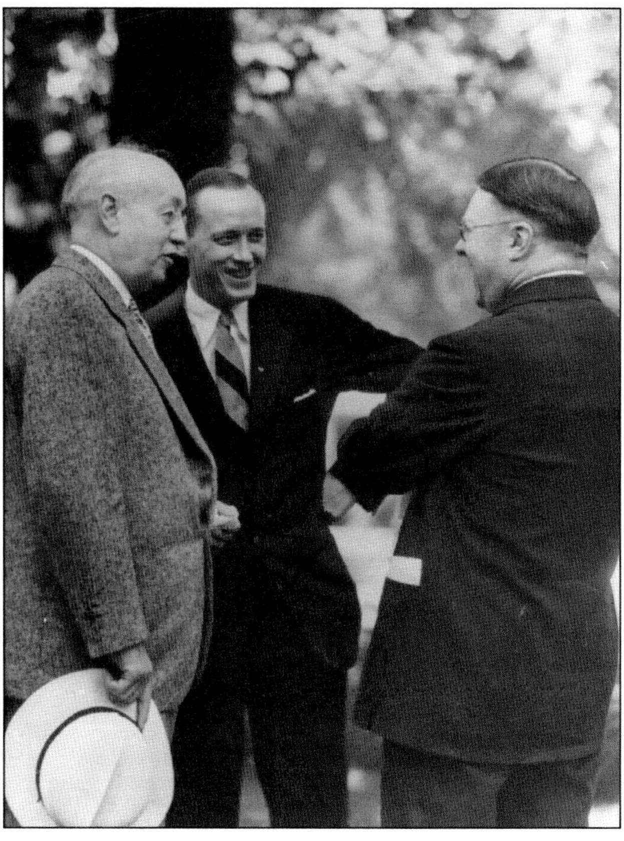

The natatorium, built in 1926 in a small frame building south of Eighth Avenue, was the setting for the White Caps, a women's synchronized swim team. The group, sponsored by the Department of Physical Education for Women, performed swimming routines to music. A 1934 program titled "Professor Bullfrog's School" listed a 14-piece orchestra as accompanying the swimmers. Note the lipstick and nail polish. (Karen Packard.)

In 1935, Chester Davis (left), class of 1911, and Harry Hopkins (center), class of 1912, returned to campus to accept honorary degrees from Pres. John Nollen. Davis directed the Agricultural Adjustment Administration and Hopkins, a local boy, directed the Works Progress Administration, both during the Franklin D. Roosevelt years. Hopkins was a confidant of both Roosevelt and Winston Churchill. (GCA.)

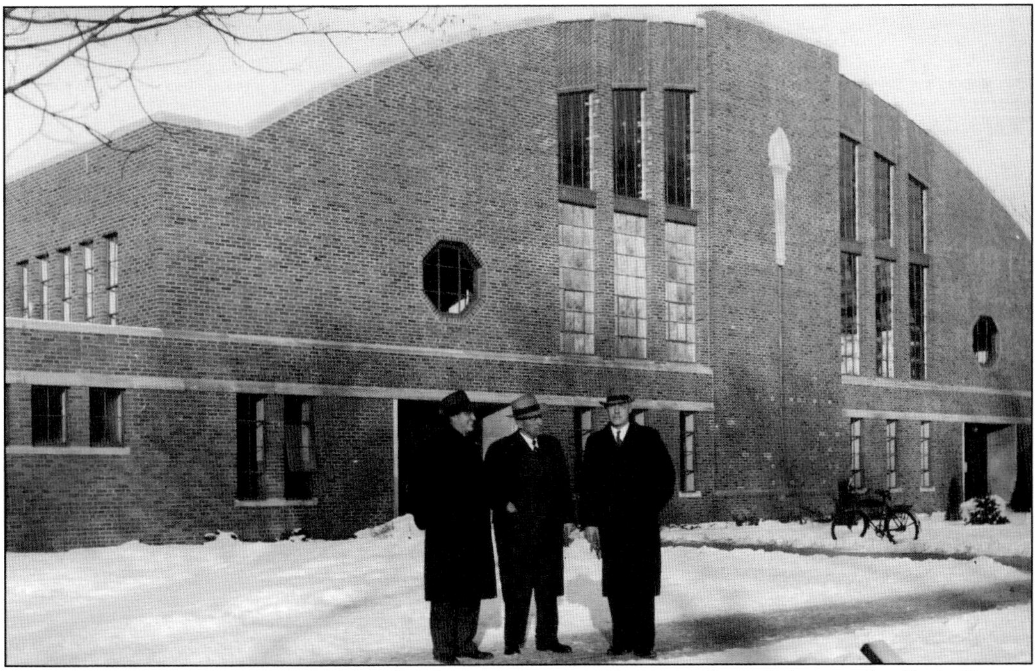

Viewing the newly constructed Darby Gymnasium in 1942 are, from left to right, Jack Heath, president of the board of trustees; John Frederick Darby, class of 1895, who excelled in several sports and provided a large portion of the building funds; and Pres. Samuel Stevens. A shortage of structural steel during World War II led to the use of a wooden lamella roof that added character to the popular gym. (GCA.)

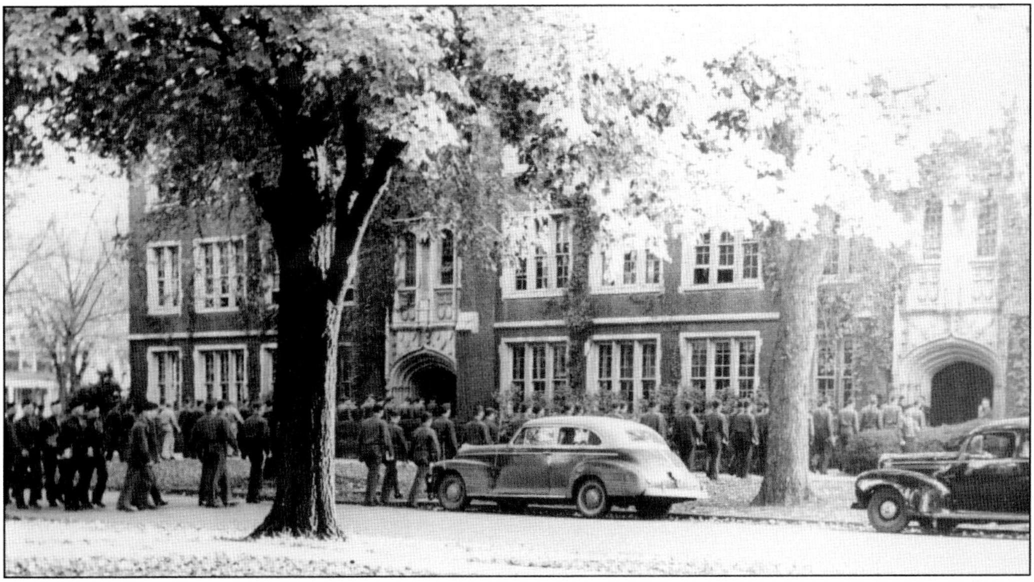

To boost sagging enrollment during World War II, the college recruited military units to make up for the loss of students who were drafted or enlisted. An Officer Candidate School and US Army special training programs brought soldiers in uniform to campus between 1942 and 1944. They lived in the men's residence halls, used Alumni Recitation Hall (ARH) for classrooms, and shared Herrick Chapel and Darby Gymnasium with the student body. (GCA.)

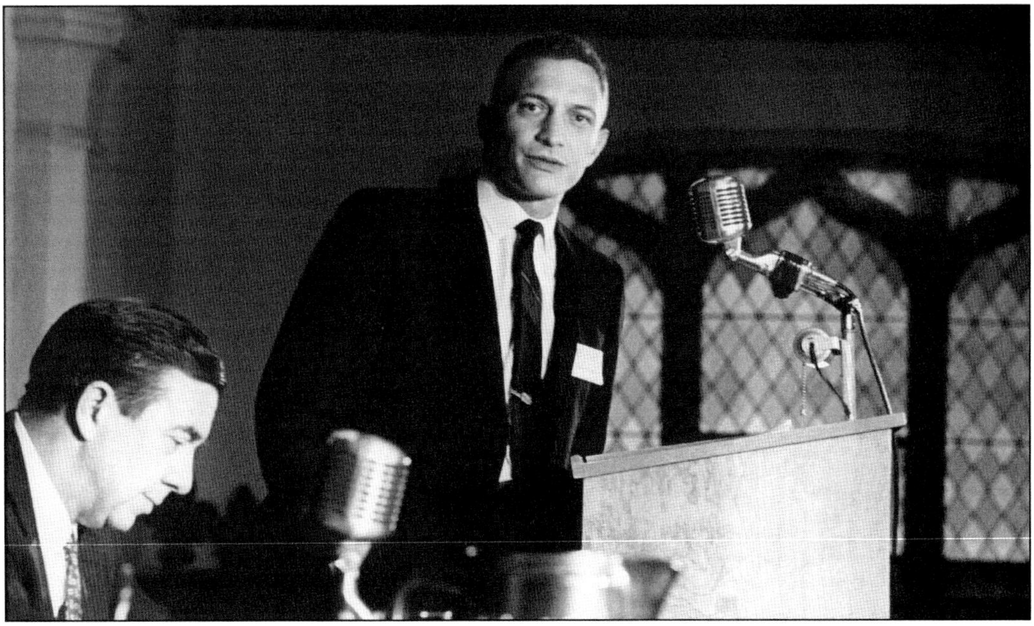

Robert Noyce grew up in Grinnell and took his first physics course from Prof. Grant Gale at the college when he was a senior in high school. He graduated from the college in 1949. Noyce coinvented the integrated circuit and cofounded Intel Corporation, a maker of microchips. He served on the board of trustees and contributed to the Grant O. Gale Observatory by matching a $150,000 Pew Grant. The Robert Noyce '49 Science Center was named in his honor. (GCA.)

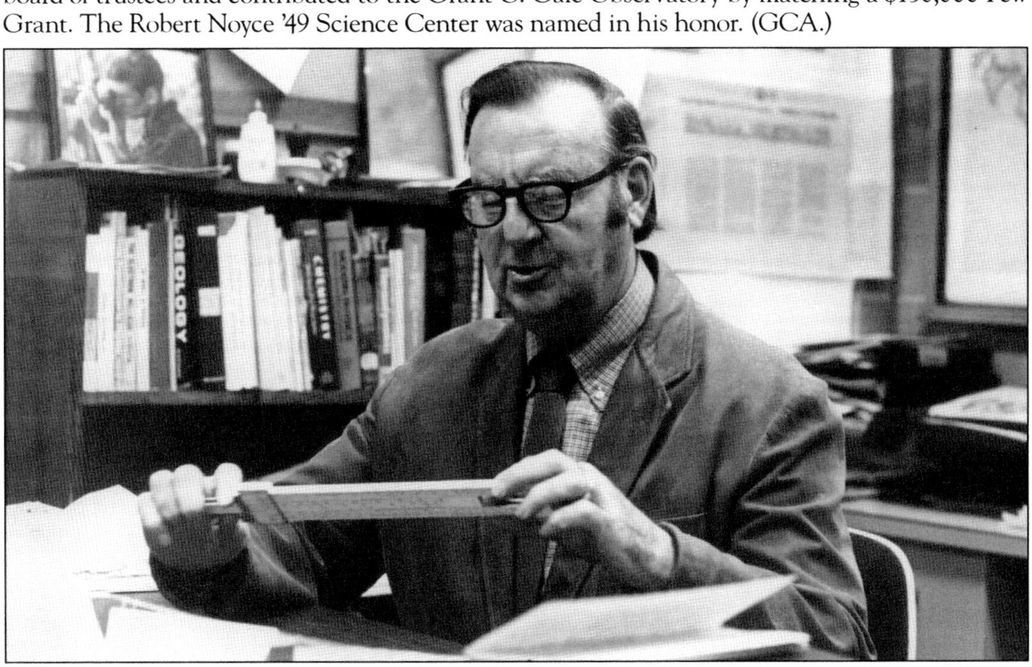

During his 70 years at Grinnell College, physics professor Grant Gale saw the college through the Depression, World War II, and the unrest of the 1960s. Gale collected obsolete science equipment and maintained a series of exhibits, becoming curator of Grinnell's Physics Historical Museum. The observatory at the north end of campus was named the Grant O. Gale Observatory in his honor in 1984. (GCA.)

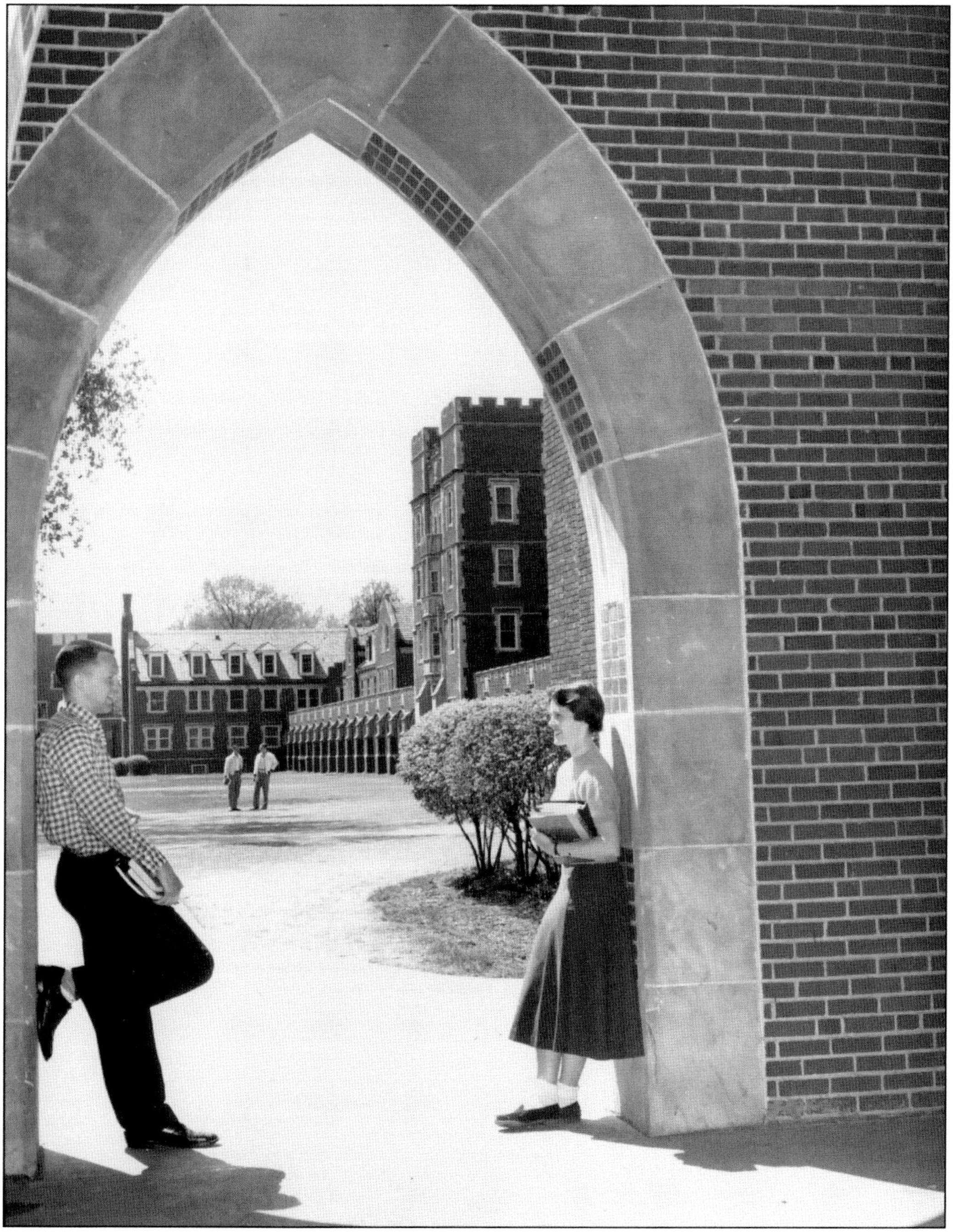

In the spring of 1957, the archway at Cowles Hall provided a meeting point for two students. The campus was in full swing that year, with performances by both Duke Ellington and Louis Armstrong. A *Chicago Tribune* survey ranked Grinnell College sixth among the top 10 liberal arts colleges in the country. The following three graduates of that period were named Rhodes Scholars: George Drake, class of 1956; John Price, class of 1960; and Duane Krohnke, class of 1961. Five members of the class of 1958, Robert and George McJimsey, Tetsuo Najita, Julia Stewart, and Marjorie Wall, were named Woodrow Wilson Fellows. (GCA.)

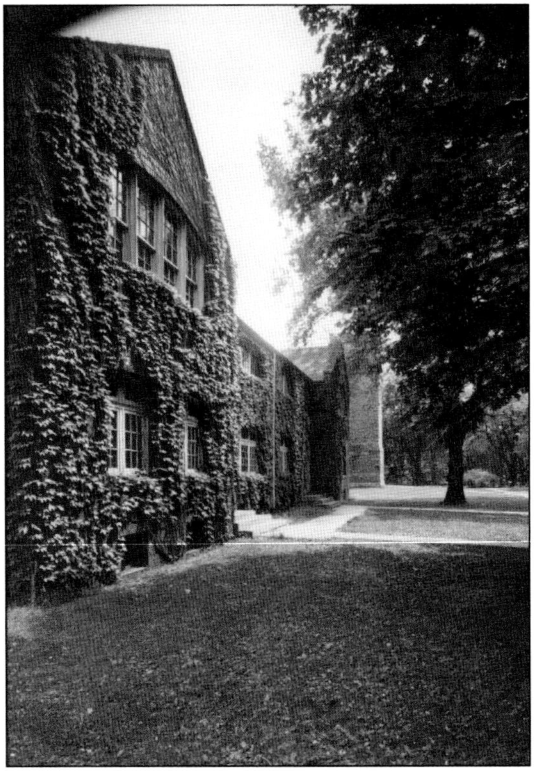

The Christian Association Building was renamed Steiner Hall in a formal ceremony in 1959. Edward A. Steiner, professor of applied Christianity from 1903 to 1941, inspired many students to enter social service work. The college's reputation as an institution with a vigorous public service orientation is based to a great extent on Steiner's work and that of his colleague, Jesse Macy, who founded the nation's first undergraduate political science department. (GCA.)

Students watched the demolition of Alumni Hall (the music building) in May 1958. The structure was the first of three buildings constructed after the 1882 cyclone and had housed the chapel, old gymnasium, and music department over the years. Burling Library was constructed on the same site. (GCA.)

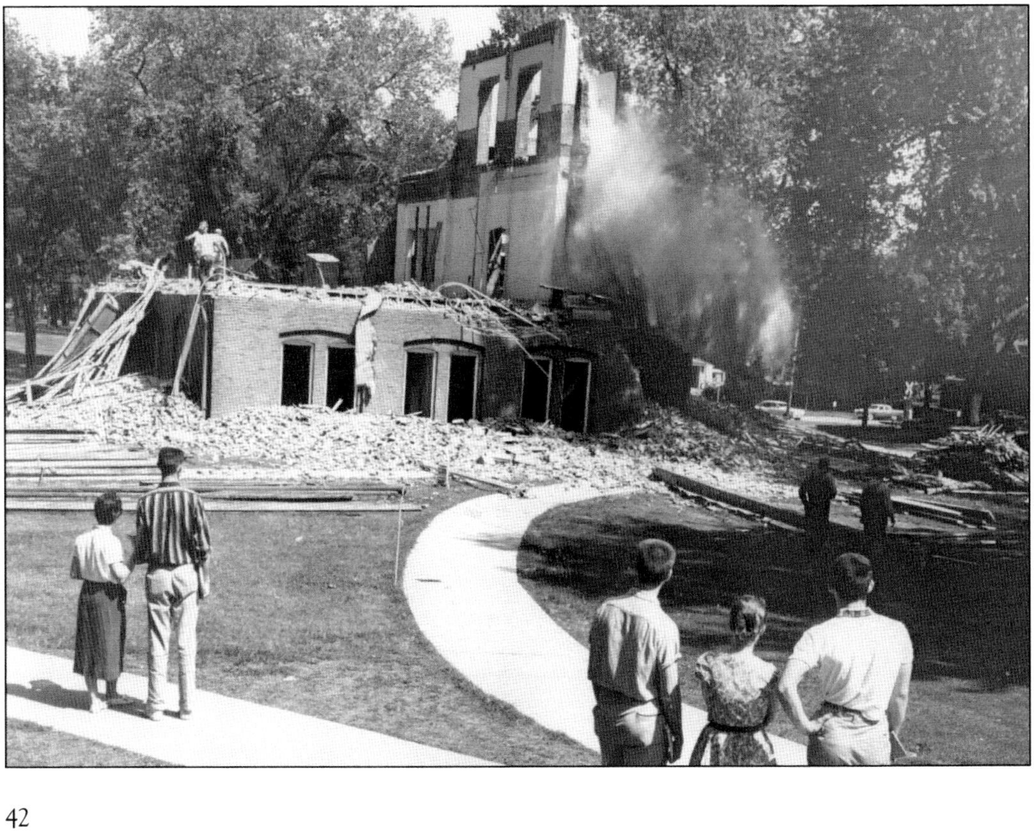

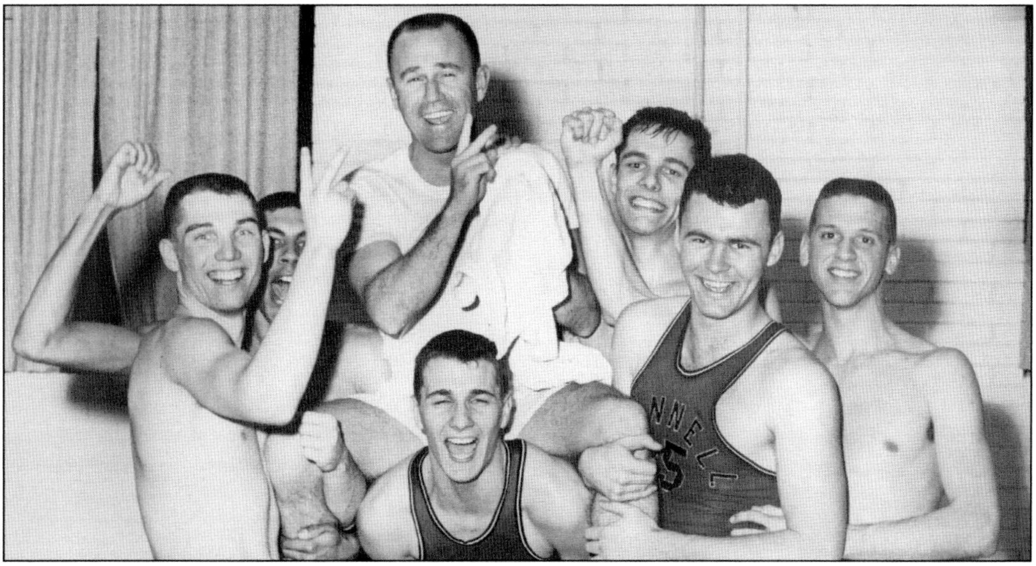

Coach John Pfitsch's 1962 basketball team had a 16-2 record and won the conference title for the first time since 1940. With a career at Grinnell that lasted 47 years, Pfitsch managed to coach almost every sport the college offered as well as serve as athletic director. In discussing his life, Pfitsch said, "One of the big pluses has been my Grinnell experience and the relationships with the thousands of student athletes I've coached." (GCA.)

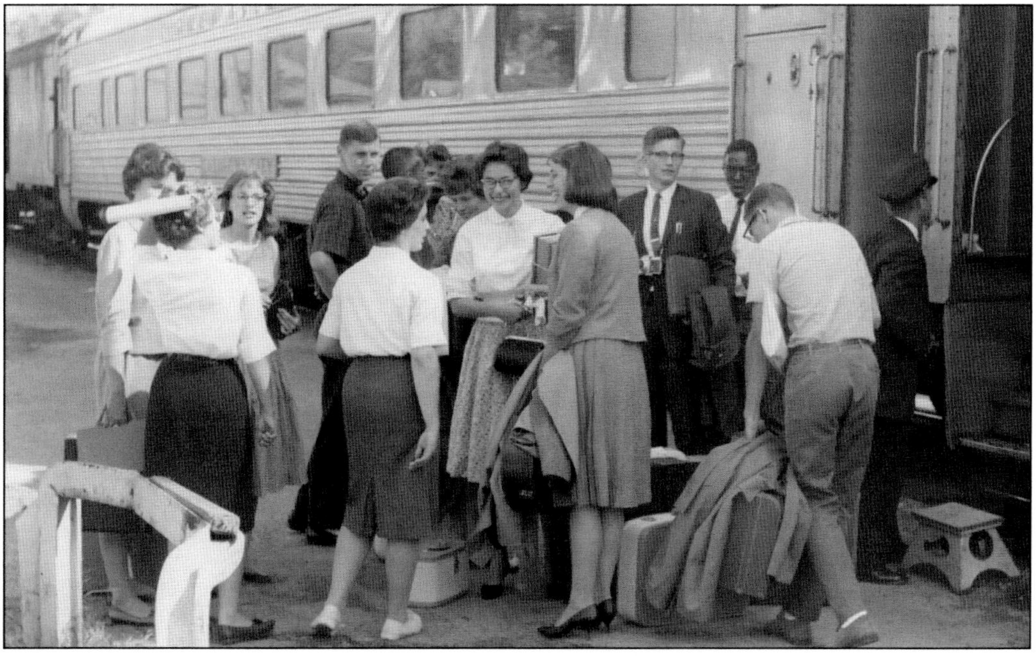

The Rock Island Railroad brought a large number of students to and from the college for many years. Pictured is a group of new students arriving in 1961. With the development of the interstate highway system in the early 1960s, the number of rail passengers declined, and the last passenger train stopped in Grinnell in 1970. Today, the freight-carrying, north-south train tracks still cut through the campus. The long, loud wail of the train horn is a familiar sound to Grinnellians of all ages. (GCA.)

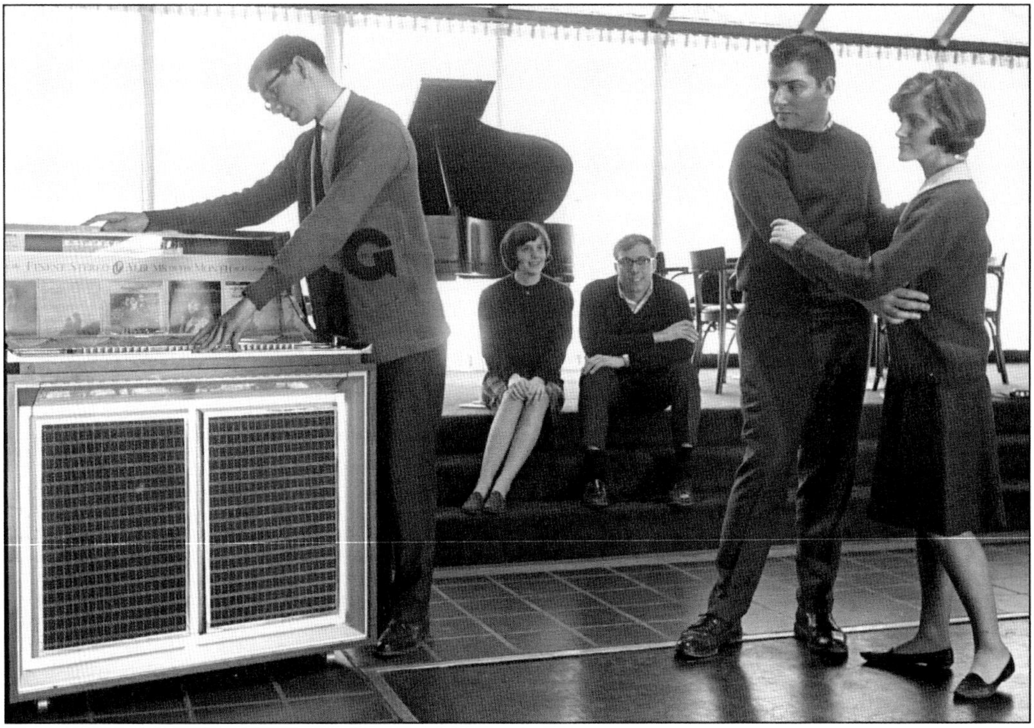

A new student union, completed in the fall of 1964, was called the College Forum. The South Lounge of the College Forum, with floor-to-ceiling windows along both the east and west walls, was a popular spot for lectures, student meetings, and dances. History professor Alan Jones said, "The Forum calls up classical traditions of free inquiry and serious debate." (GCA.)

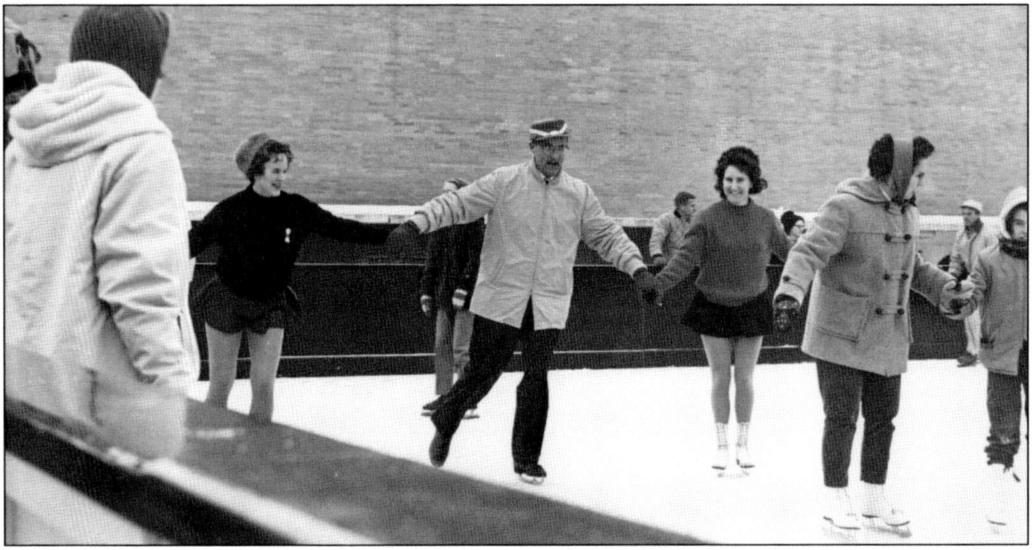

Taking a spin in 1962 at the dedication of the Barber Skating Plaza were Pres. Howard Bowen (center) and students Sue Andersen (left) and Ann Van Guilder (right). Located between Burling Library and what is now the Bucksbaum Center for the Arts, the ice rink attracted students, faculty, and townspeople. It was named for Margaret Kyle Barber, an 1895 graduate who was active in the Young Women's Christian Association. (GCA.)

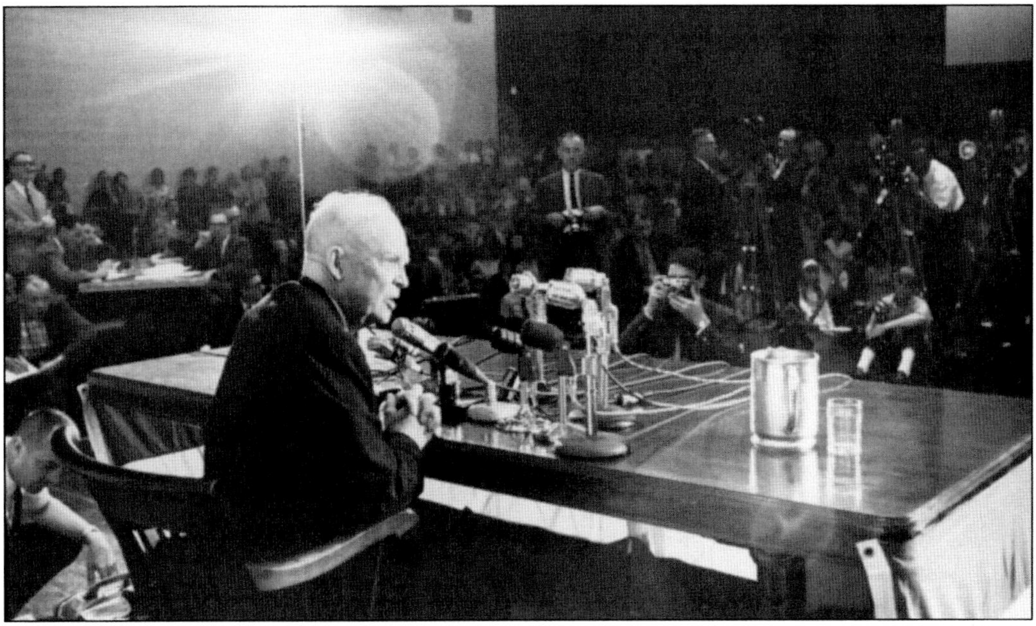

Pres. Dwight D. Eisenhower visited the college as a "Politician in Residence" in 1964–1965. He was brought to campus as part of the Program in Practical Political Education. The program was established in 1957 and had previously sponsored a visit from Pres. Harry Truman. Eisenhower gave a lecture titled "Politics Is Too Important to be Left to the Politicians" and met with classes and informally with students. (GCA.)

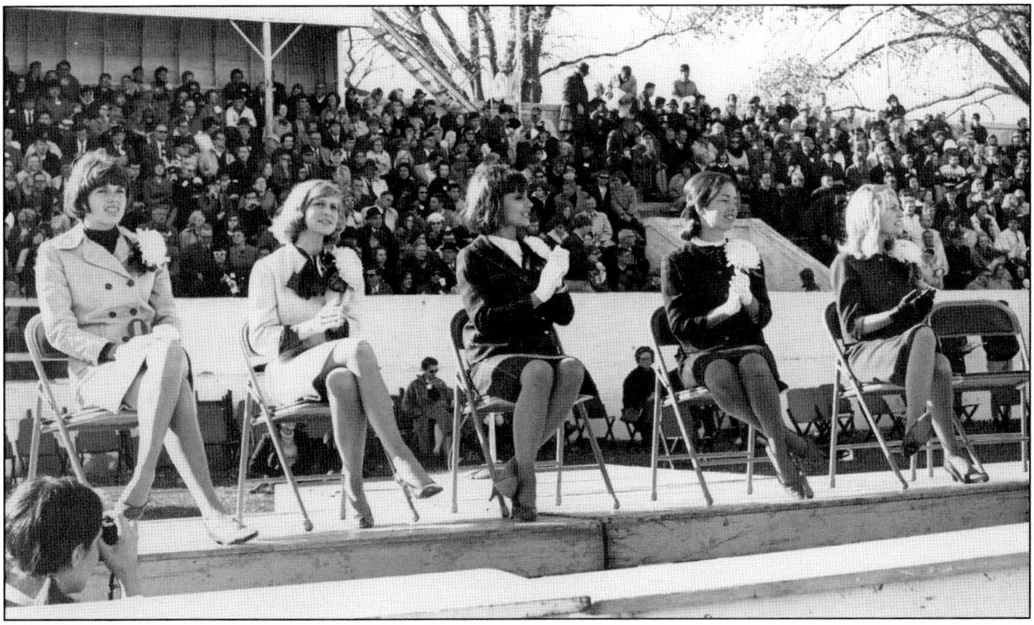

Homecoming queen candidates, from left to right, Cynthia Root, Julie Johnson, Ruthena Sternberg, Kristi Rennebohm, and Nancy Beadslee watched the football game in 1966. Traditions and social life at Grinnell were changing, however. Within the next few years, the curfew for women was eliminated and housemothers were replaced by trained professional resident advisors. In 1971, students voted to abolish homecoming. (GCA.)

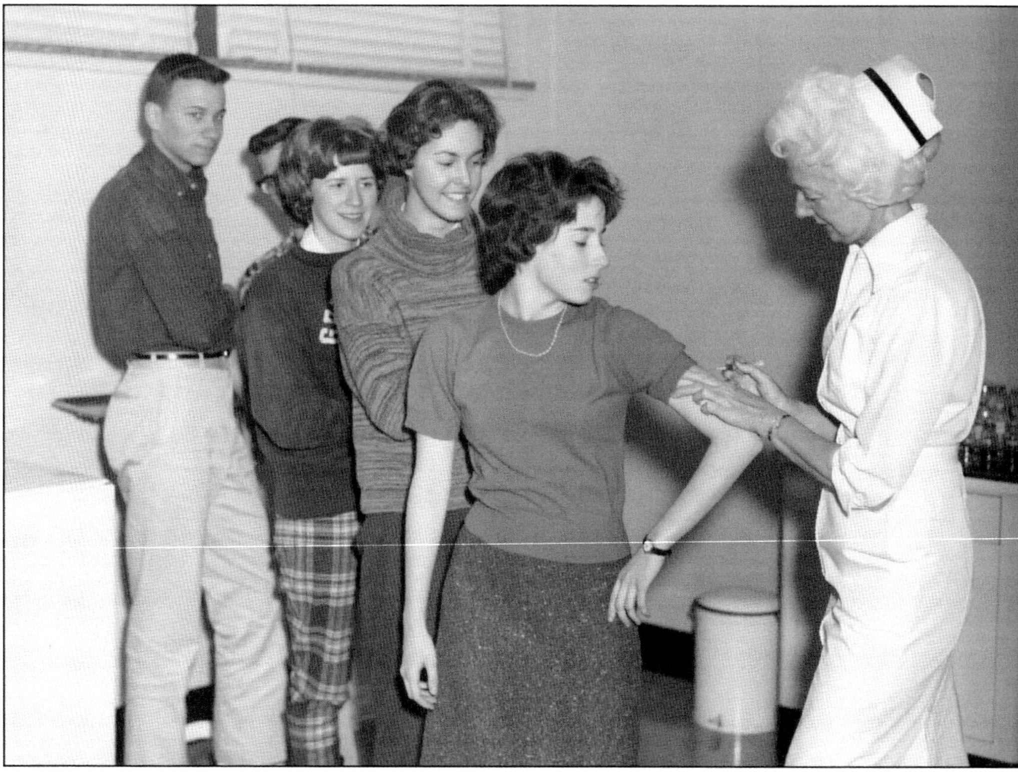

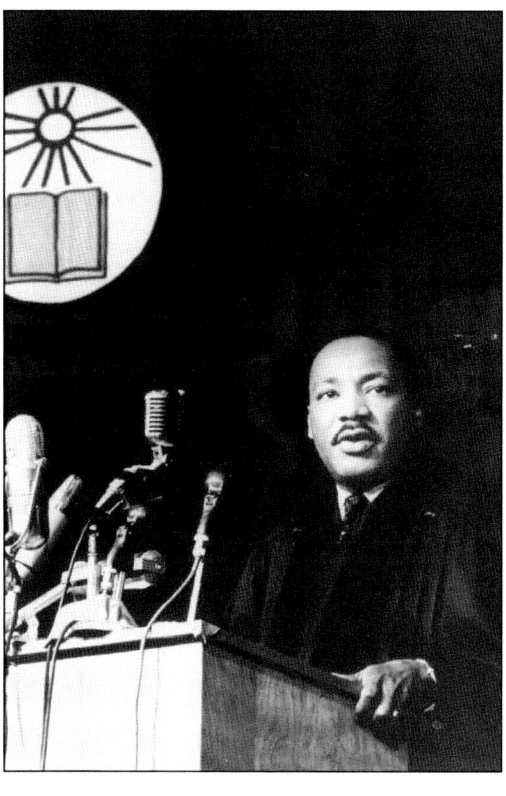

In 1963, students lined up for shots at the Younker Student Health Center. Both the health center and the Younker Residence Hall for men were funded in part by the Younker Foundation and built during 1956 and 1957. The next year, the Asian flu hit campus, affecting more than 400 students. In-patient care of students was dropped in 1977–1978 in favor of using the services of Grinnell General Hospital. (GCA.)

"Remaining Awake Through a Revolution" was the title of the Reverend Dr. Martin Luther King Jr.'s talk to an overflowing audience in Darby Gymnasium on the evening of October 27, 1967. The talk was only months before King's assassination in Memphis. In 1968, the college trustees resolved that the college would be a multiracial society through implementation of an affirmative action policy. (Robert Hodierne, GCA.)

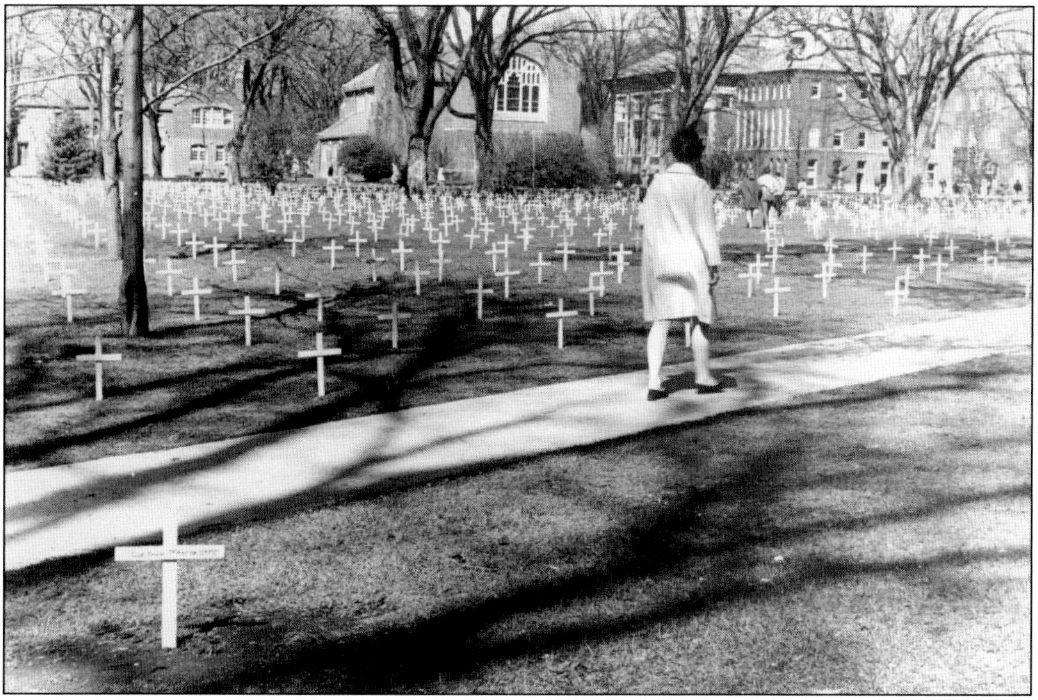

Crosses placed on central campus in the spring of 1971 were sober reminders of the shootings at Kent State University. Student unrest over the Vietnam War, the bombing of Cambodia, and the shooting of Kent State University students by federal troops provoked the college to close two days before finals. Commencement was cancelled. When school opened again in the fall of 1971, students and faculty carried on their extended discussions and peaceful protests about the war. Several peace marches were held through the streets of Grinnell, with townspeople frequently taking part. The rallying cry was, "All we are saying is give peace a chance." (Both, GCA.)

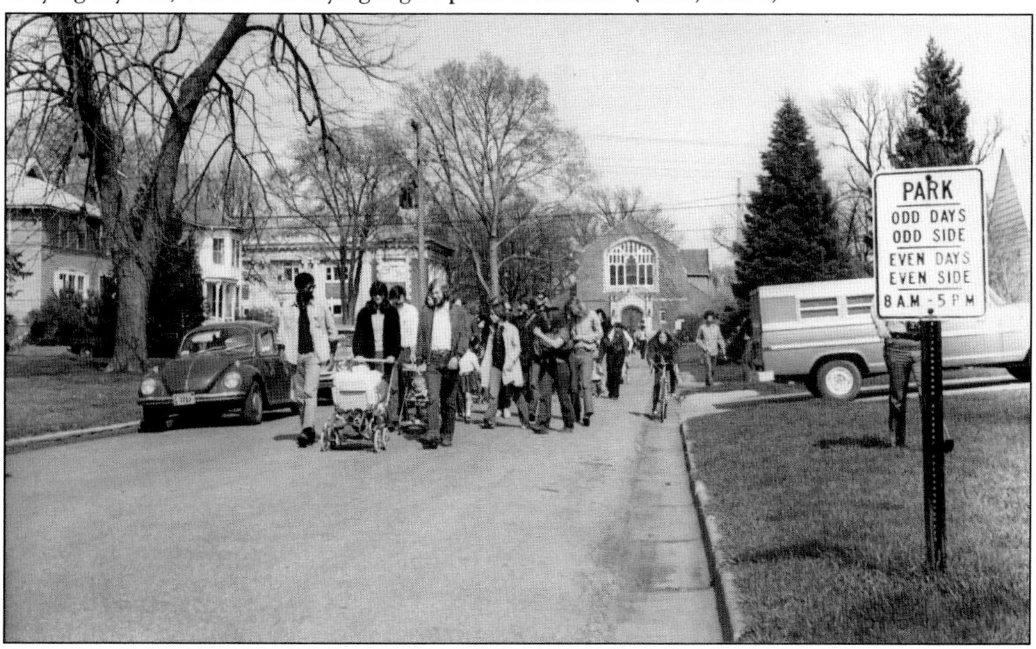

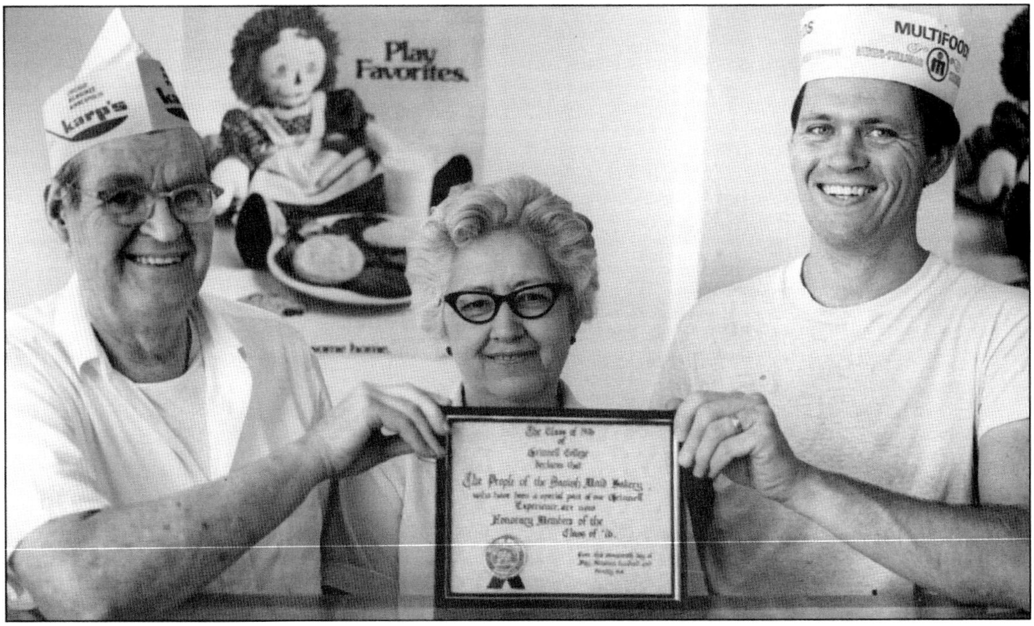

Bakery runs at 2:00 a.m. from the campus to the back door of the Danish Maid Bakery downtown for freshly baked doughnuts were so popular in the 1970s that the bakers, George and Elizabeth Hansen, and their son Bill were given honorary degrees at commencement in 1976. Soft ice cream and corn nuggets from the Dari Barn as well as pizza from Pagliai's have also been popular with students. (GCA.)

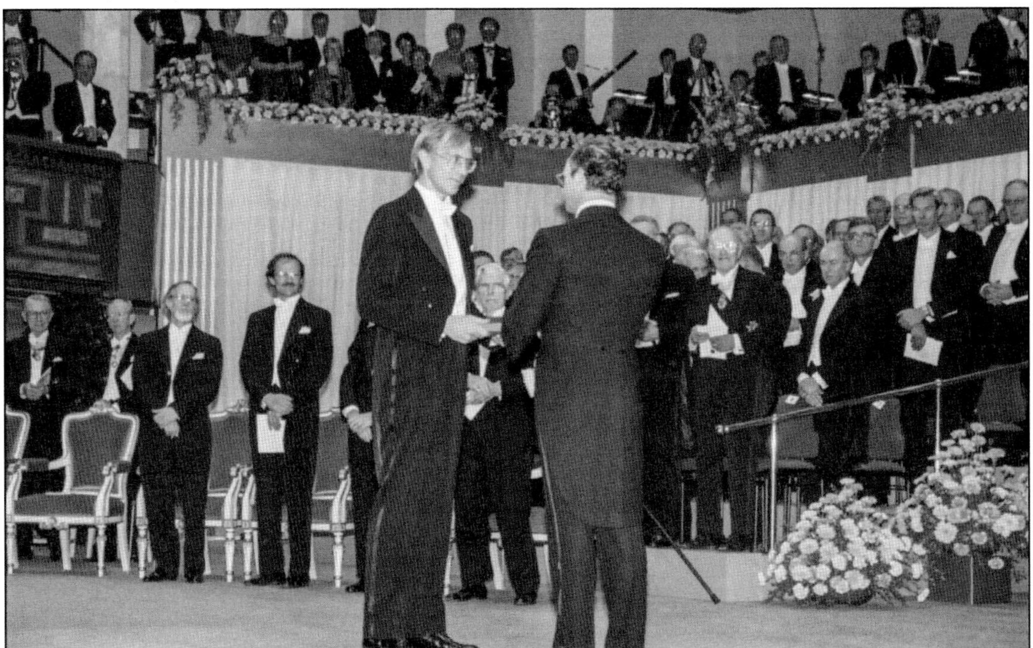

Thomas R. Cech, class of 1970, received the 1989 Nobel Prize in Chemistry for the discovery of catalytic properties of ribonucleic acid (RNA). The prize was presented by King Carl XVI on behalf of the Royal Swedish Academy of Sciences in Stockholm on December 10, 1989. (Cech family.)

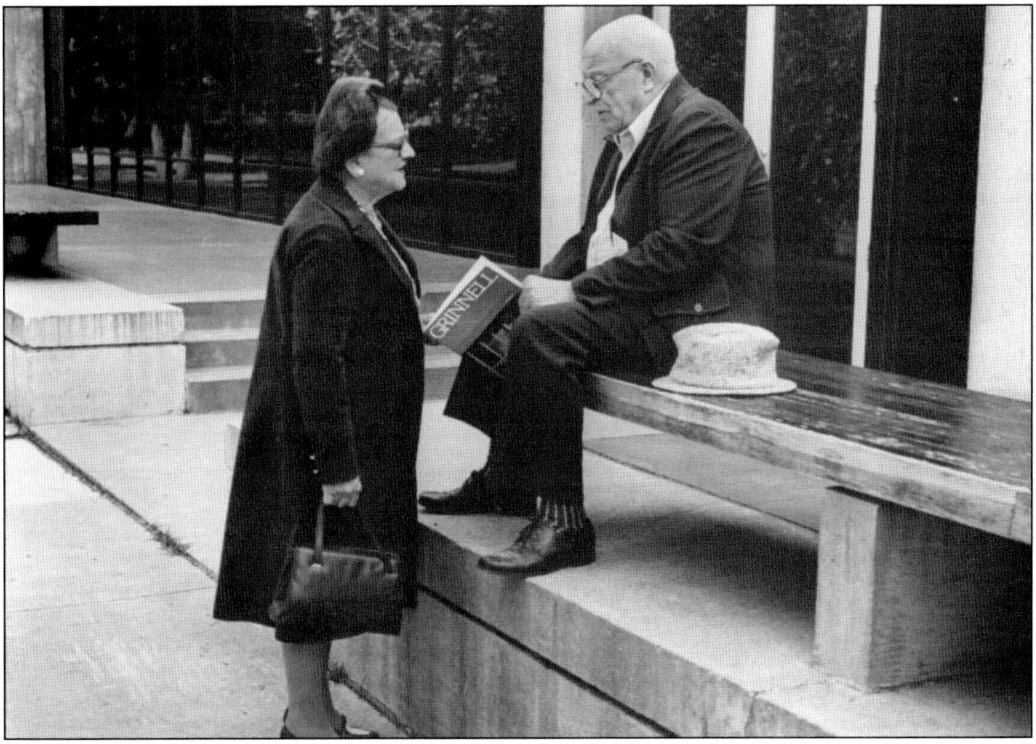

Ruth Neille Roche, class of 1928, and her husband, J.R. Roche, paused in front of the College Forum to discuss their schedule during their busy alumni reunion weekend in 1978. Each year in early June, several thousand graduates and former students return to campus to renew friendships, visit faculty, attend lectures and musical events, and revisit their favorite spots in town. (GCA.)

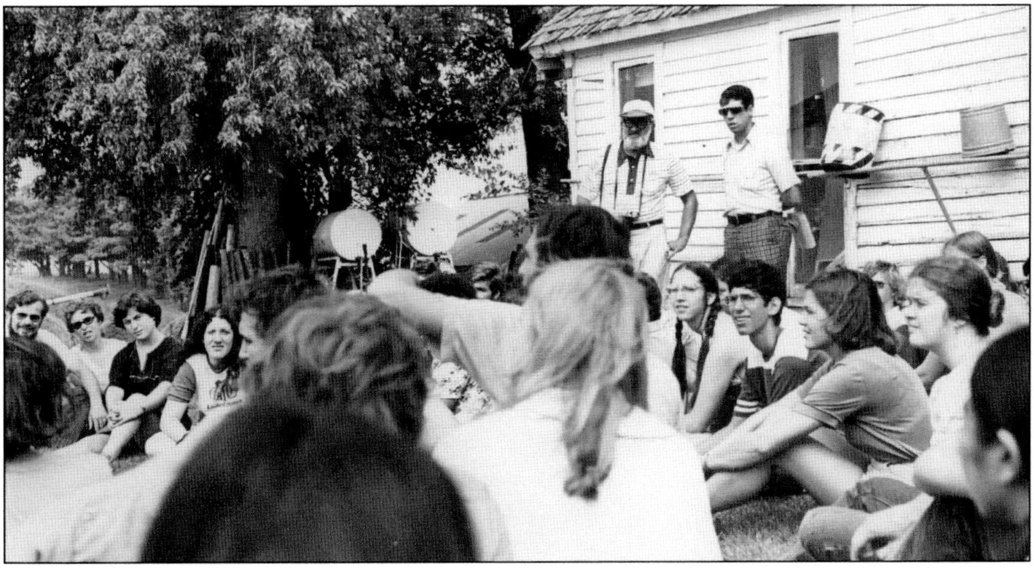

Pres. A. Richard Turner (standing left) and mathematics assistant professor Henry Walker (standing right) joined a group of new students during orientation week in 1975 for a tour of a local farm. From farmers' markets to Ag Days, students have many opportunities to study the rural landscape that surrounds them. (GCA.)

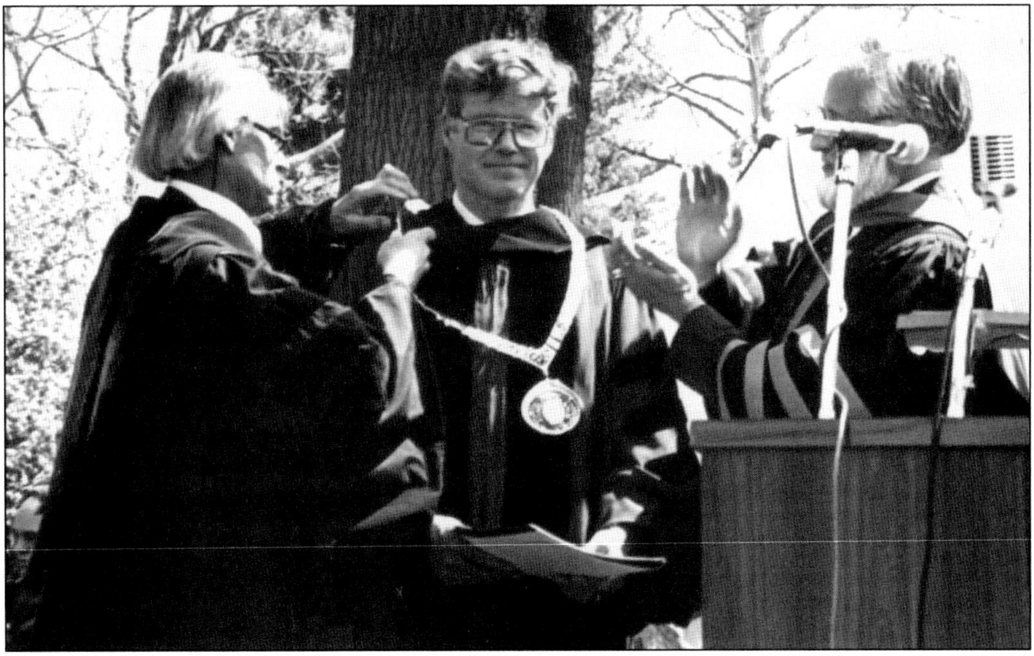

George Drake was inaugurated in 1979 as the 15th president of the college. A 1956 Grinnell graduate and Rhodes Scholar, he headed the college until 1991. After two years in the Peace Corps in Lesotho with his wife, Sue, he returned to the college and community in 1993 as a professor of history. The Drake Community Library is named in honor of the Drakes. (GCA.)

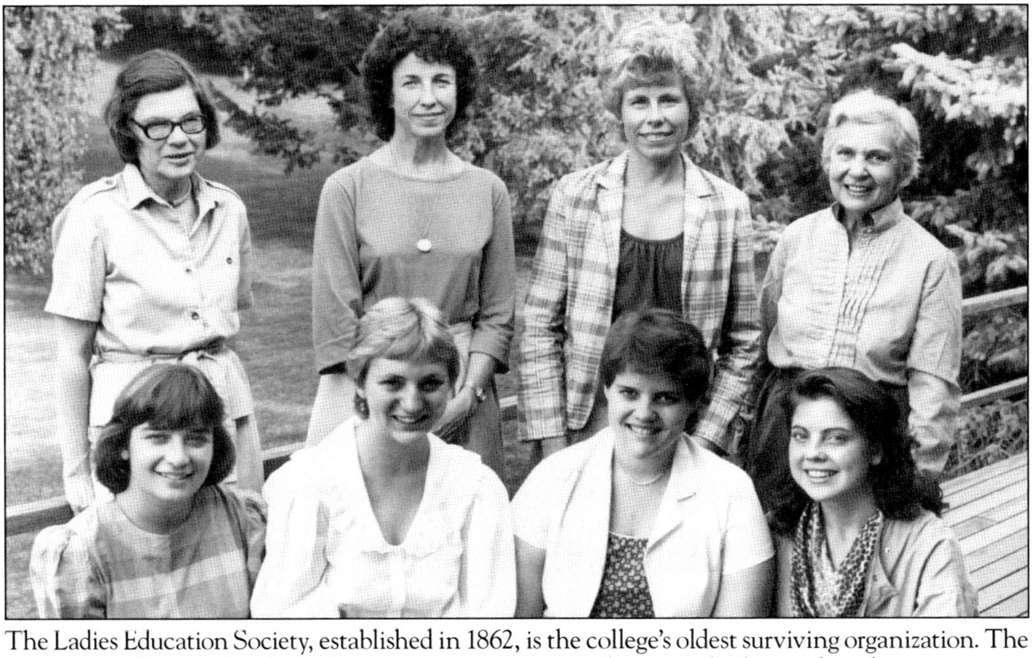

The Ladies Education Society, established in 1862, is the college's oldest surviving organization. The group annually awards scholarships to junior women students on the basis of academics, service, character, leadership, and financial need. Pictured are, from left to right, (seated) the 1983 recipients Anne Bordonaro, Cindy Gilbert, Deanna Snyder, and Bernadette Connors; (standing) officers Jean Jones, Betty Moffett, Sue Drake, and Bea Wall. (GCA.)

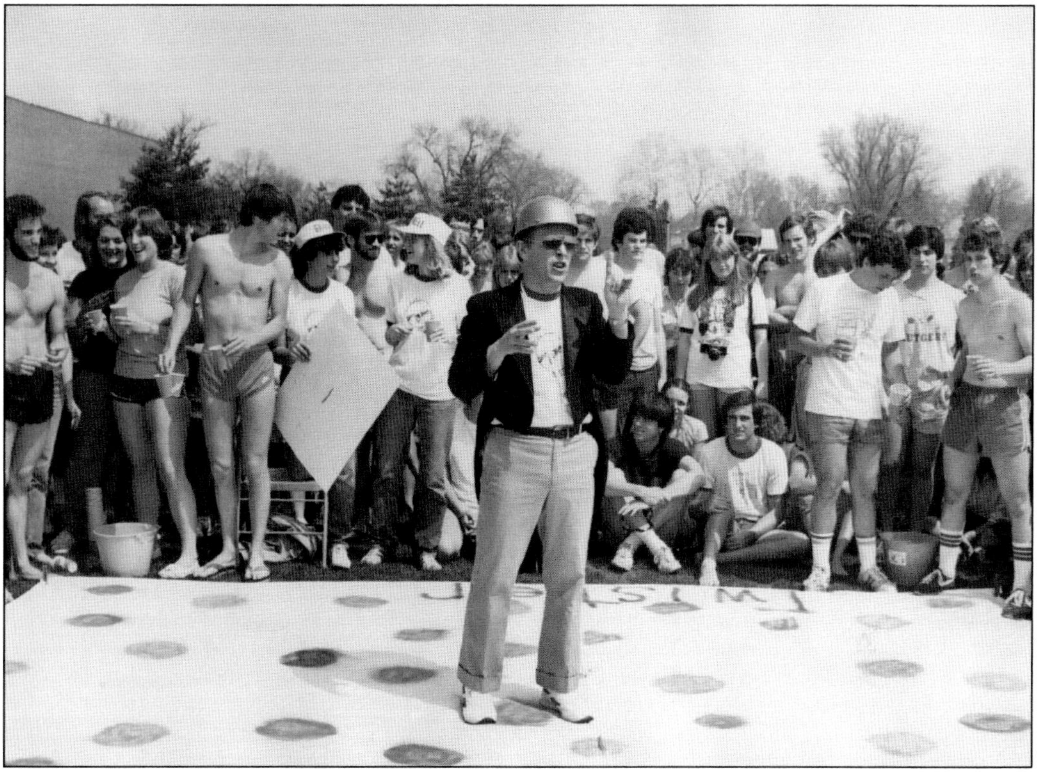

Political science professor Wayne Moyer started the Grinnell Relays in the spring of 1973, hoping to bring a little levity to student life before the crunch of semester finals. He is pictured here in the early 1980s organizing a game of Twister. (GCA.)

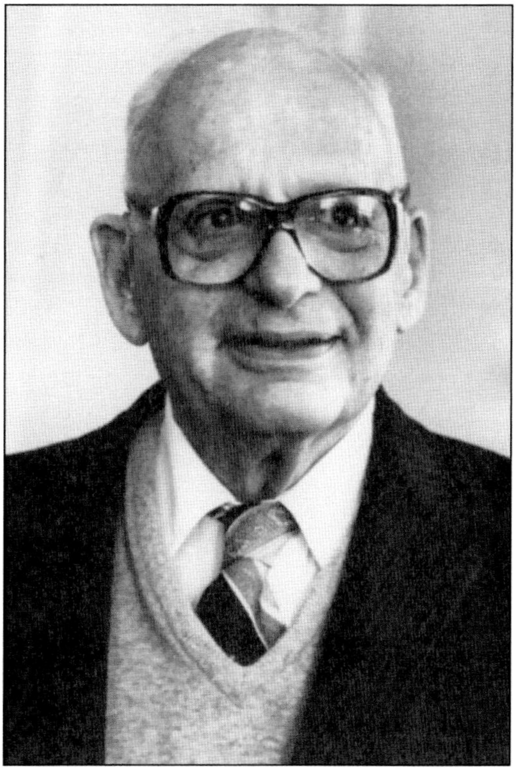

Joe Rosenfield, class of 1925 and college trustee from 1941 to 2000, played a major role in the growth of the college's endowment. A successful lawyer and retailer, he used his financial skills and personal connections to help the college create one of the country's largest college endowments. The Joe Rosenfield '25 Center, built in 2005, was named in his honor. It is the general campus center, containing dining services, a post office, meeting and lecture spaces, and some administrative offices. (GCA.)

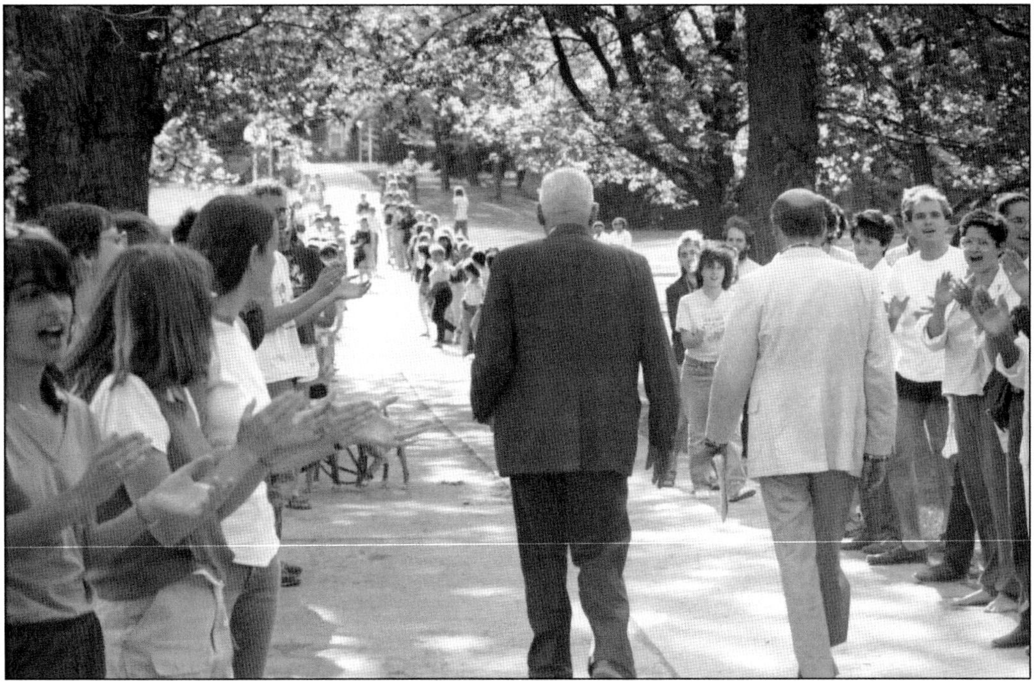

At a May 1985 meeting of the board of trustees, students protested the trustees' refusal to divest the college portfolio of South African securities. The following year, the trustees voted to sell the college's portfolio of several stocks of corporations with business interests in South Africa. (GCA.)

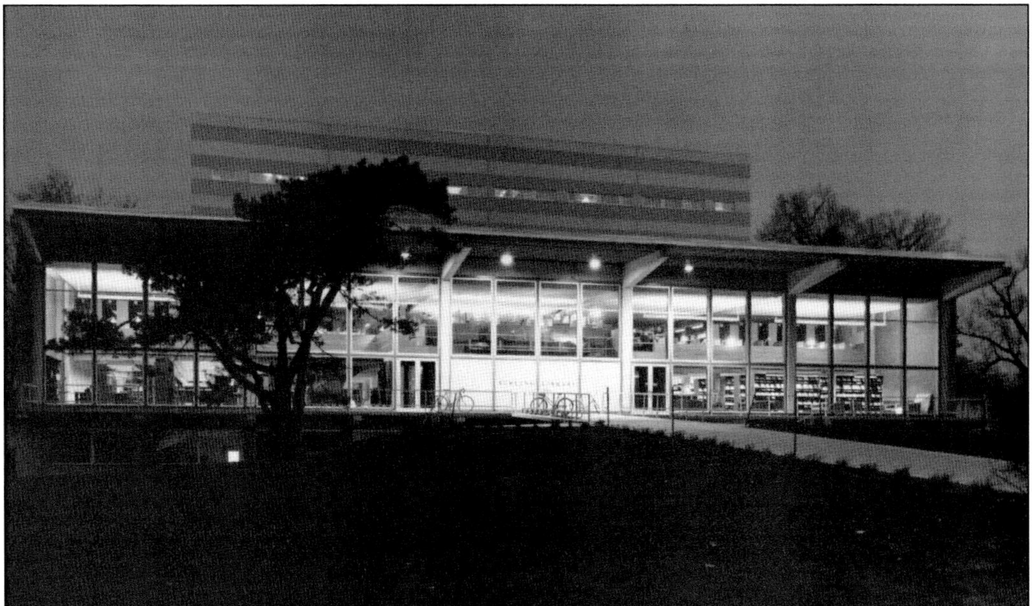

Built in 1959 on the south edge of campus, Burling Library was designed by its architects so that the interior would be seen from the exterior as a single large room. Renovations in 1982 added a third and fourth floor. The project increased the number of student study spaces, which included "study jungle gyms," armchairs, and study carrels, to a total of 402. Book holdings grew to more than half a million volumes. (GCA.)

Three

Making a Living

Work twice as hard as you think you ought to, save something out of every piece of money you get, live quietly and regularly, don't buy anything without seeing it, and get a good wife.

—Henry W. Spaulding

Surrounded by the vast fertile prairie, Grinnell built its foundation on farming and farm-related businesses. The arrival of the railroad in 1863 launched manufacturing and commercial development by providing an efficient way to bring in raw materials and send out finished products. The passenger trains also encouraged population growth and increased communication with other parts of the country.

One of the first businesses was a tanning operation started by Frederick W. Morrison, a native of New Hampshire who came with his family to Grinnell in 1855. Before long, he began to use the tanned skins to make gloves. The company, known as Morrison & McIntosh, and later as Morrison-Ricker, eventually expanded to be a major producer of leather gloves and mittens that were sold nationwide.

The largest and best-known early business was the Spaulding Manufacturing Company, established by blacksmith Henry W. Spaulding. He started in 1876 by making buggies and then began to manufacture automobiles in 1909. The assembly line of Henry Ford put an end to the Spaulding automobile in 1916.

Even before the streets in Grinnell began to be paved in 1909, the downtown was filled with small shops (street level) and offices (above). Fourth Avenue between Broad and Main Streets was the center of commercial activity for many years. Early retail businesses in Grinnell included Grant Ramsey Groceries, McNally's Meat Market, Bates Rexall Drugs, H.R. Ritter Hardware, Child Studio and Art Store, Preston's Clothing Store, and Arnold and Rivers Shoes.

Today, Grinnell's three largest employers are Grinnell Mutual Reinsurance Company, Grinnell College, and Jeld-Wen, which manufactures windows and doors.

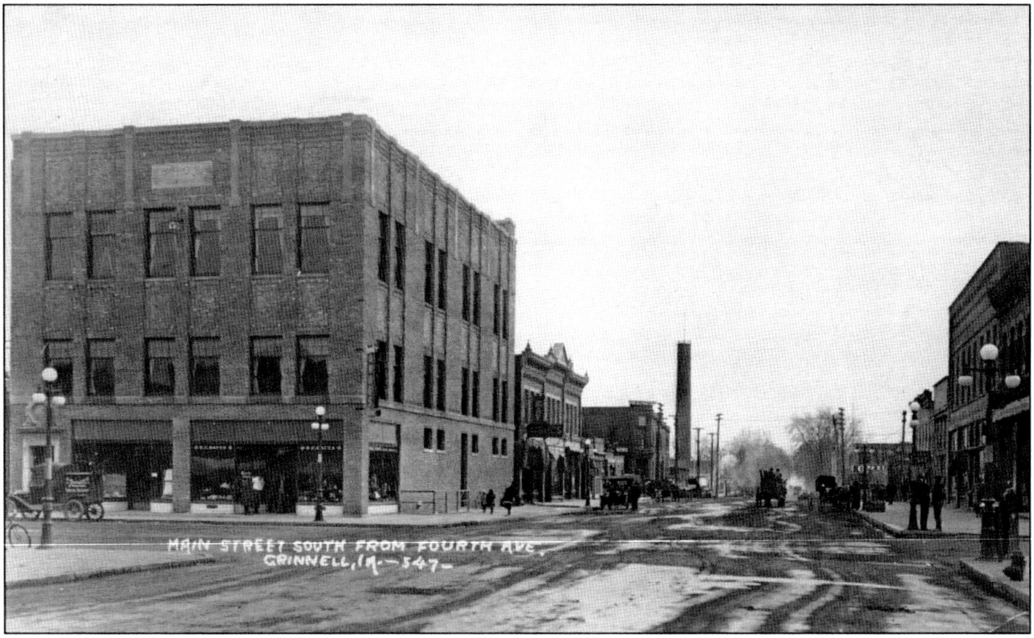

Roy Bates's Rexall Drugstore anchored the southeast corner of Fourth Avenue and Main Street about 1920. Note the store's delivery vehicle in front of the building. In the background is the city's first water tower, a 116-foot structure built in 1894. (Blankenfeld family.)

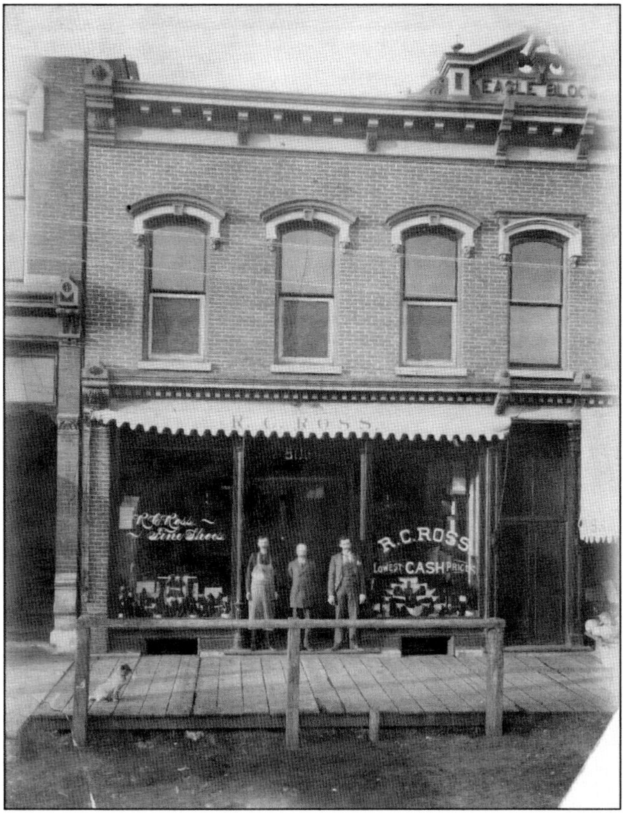

R.C. Ross Shoes opened in 1881. In this 1897 photograph in front of the store at 803 Fourth Avenue, owner Richard C. Ross (center) is shown with a shoe repair man, a clerk, and a dog. Note the sturdy wooden sidewalk. Ross went on to own and operate Grinnell Stone Company, which manufactured red-tinted blocks that were used for several homes in Grinnell, including Ross's own home at 1114 Broad Street. (GHM.)

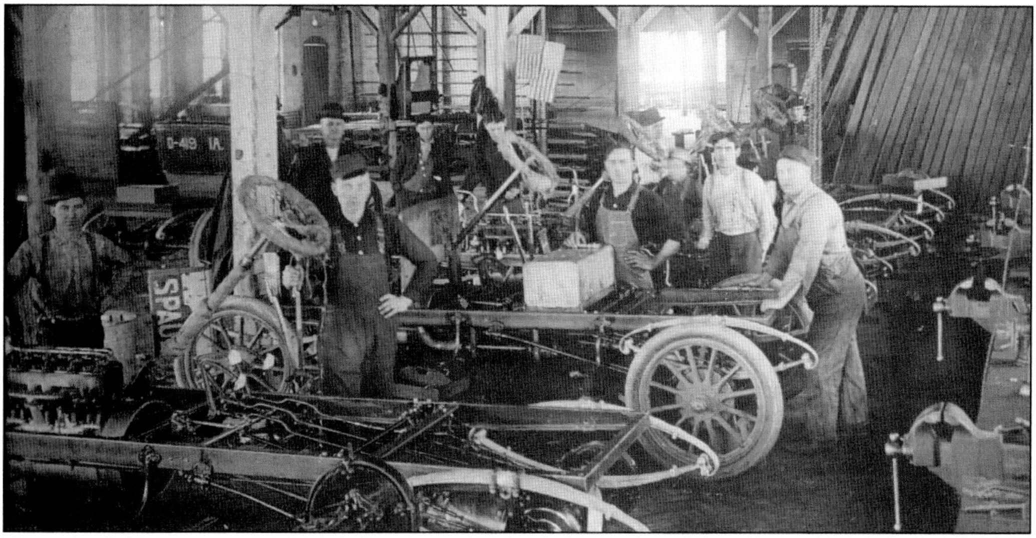

The Spaulding Manufacturing Company, founded in 1876 by blacksmith Henry W. Spaulding, had already made a name for itself with buggies and wagons (10,000 buggies a year by 1905) when it began producing automobiles. The sprawling factory (above) was located at Fourth Avenue and Spring Street. Approximately 5,000 Spaulding automobiles were manufactured in Grinnell between 1909 and 1916. Most were so-called touring cars, like the two pictured below, but the company also produced a racing model that set a world dirt-road speed record in 1913. (The average speed was 39 miles per hour.) Underfinancing and competition from the Model T assembly line of Henry Ford put an end to the Spaulding operation. The company's former office building is now the Iowa Transportation Museum. (Both, DCL.)

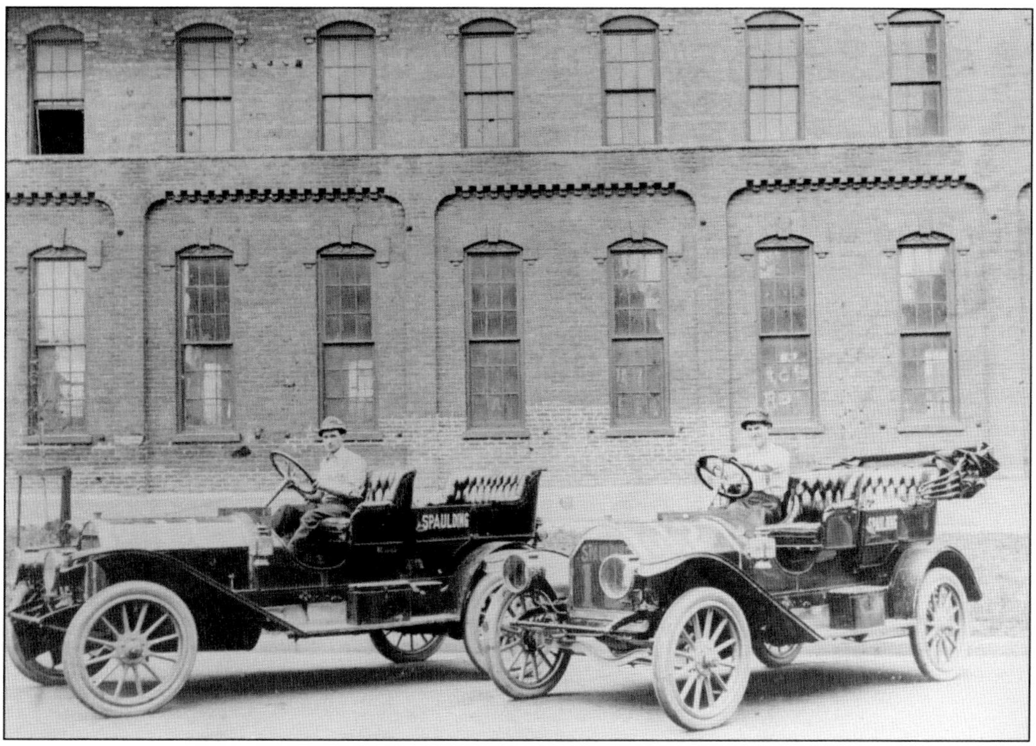

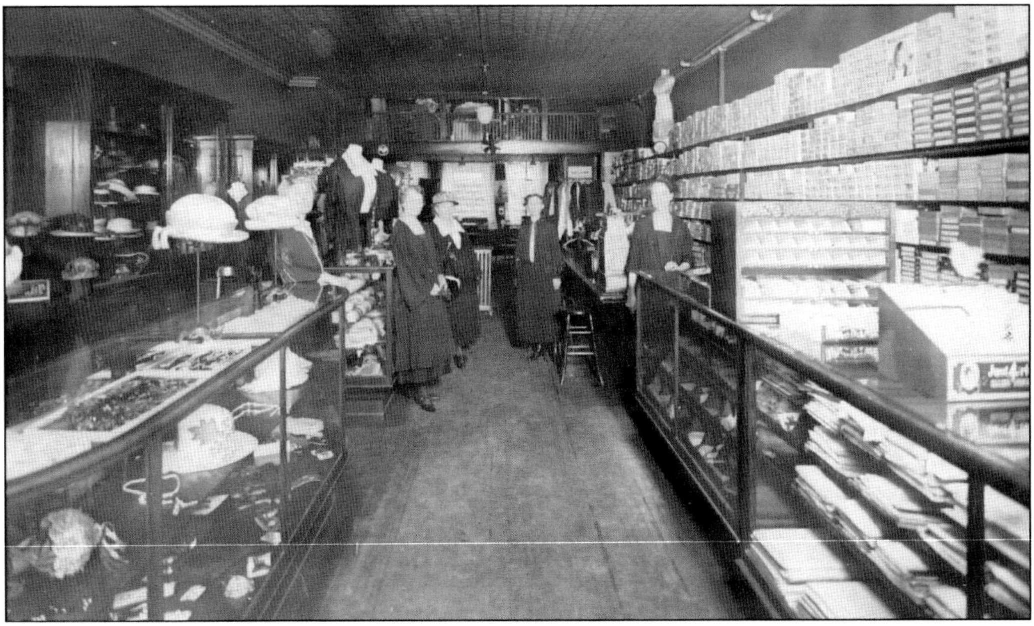

Among a handful of women business owners in Grinnell in the early 1900s was Emily Manatt, who owned a women's clothing and millinery shop at 805 Fourth Avenue. She came to Grinnell from Brooklyn in the 1890s as a store clerk, then acquired and operated her own dry goods store. When she died in 1933, she had been in business for 38 years, 25 of which were in the same location. She was still making hats a week before her death. (GHM.)

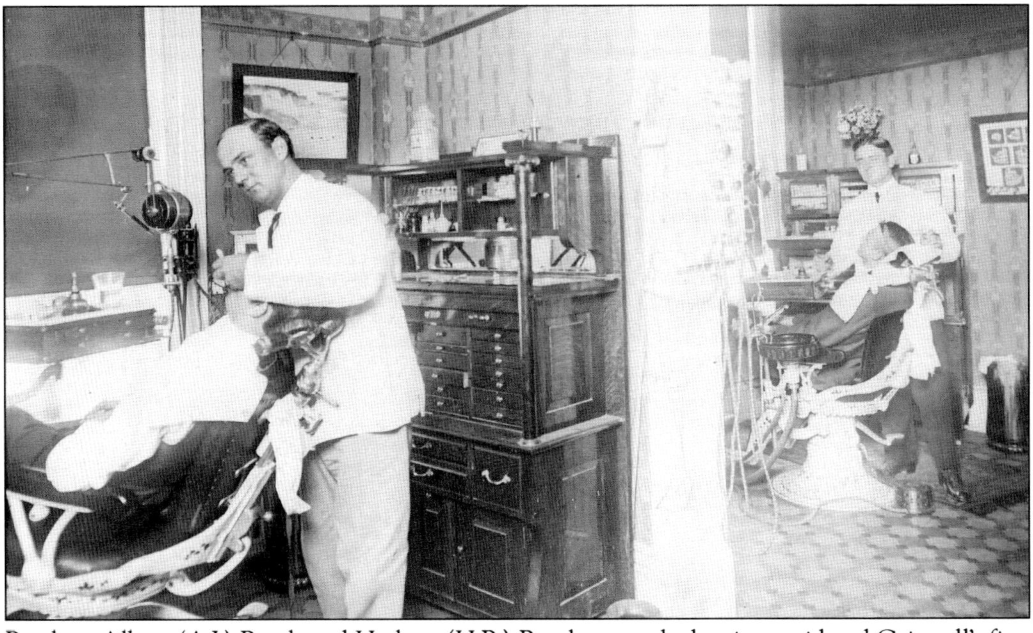

Brothers Albert (A.J.) Brock and Herbert (H.B.) Brock opened what is considered Grinnell's first dental clinic in 1909 at Fourth Avenue and Broad Street. The two Brock families lived around the corner from one another—A.J. at 917 Tenth Avenue and H.B. at 1503 Park Street. H.B. moved to Des Moines in 1927. A.J. continued in practice in Grinnell until his death in 1940. The photograph is dated 1912. (GHM.)

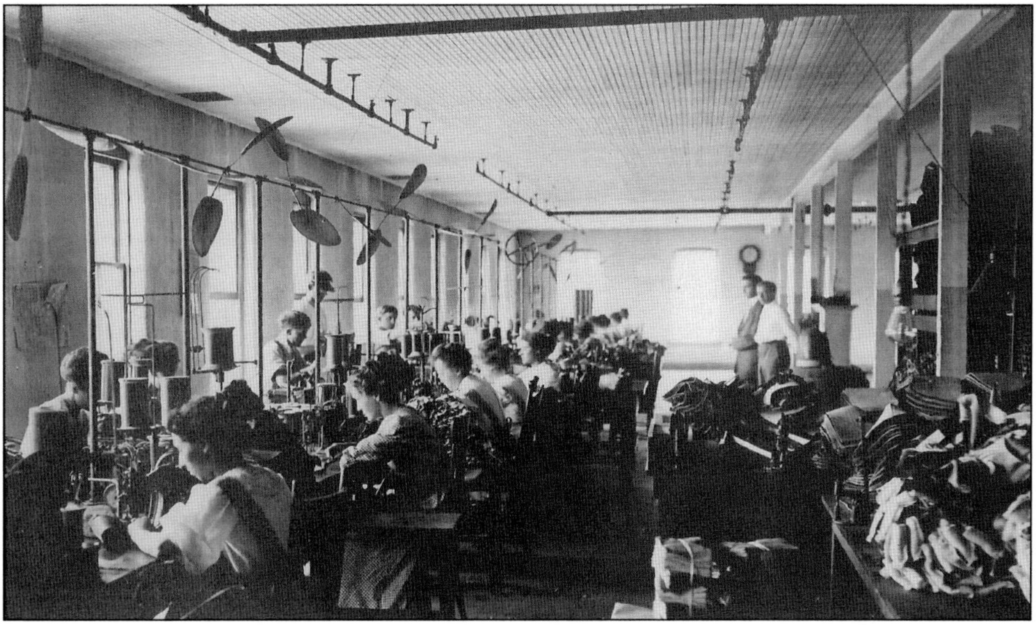

The "sewing girls" at the Morrison-Ricker Manufacturing Company turned out leather gloves by the thousands in the early 1900s. The company was no sweatshop. In a 1919 newspaper advertisement aimed at women, it claimed to be Grinnell's "best place to work," with perks such as "refined surroundings, a recess period, welfare manager, and personal sewing instruction." The average pay was $12 a week. (GHM.)

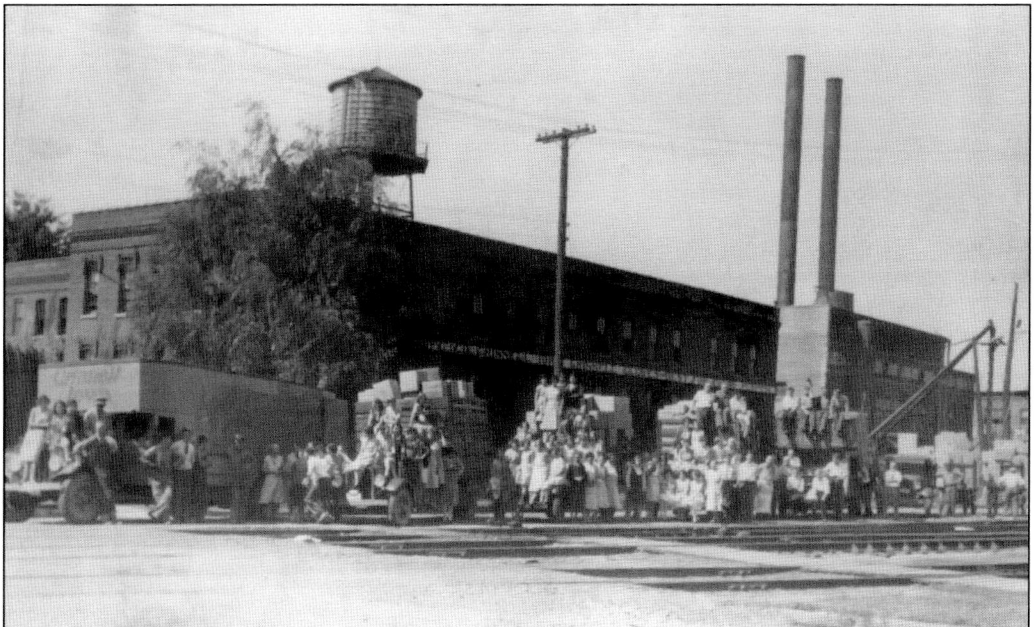

Employees of Morrison & McIntosh (later Morrison-Ricker) Manufacturing Company displayed their production of gloves outside the factory at Third Avenue and Broad Street. The building, constructed in 1895, was later owned by DeLong Sportswear. In the 1990s, it was purchased and renovated by Grinnell College for office space. It is now called, appropriately, the Old Glove Factory. (GCA.)

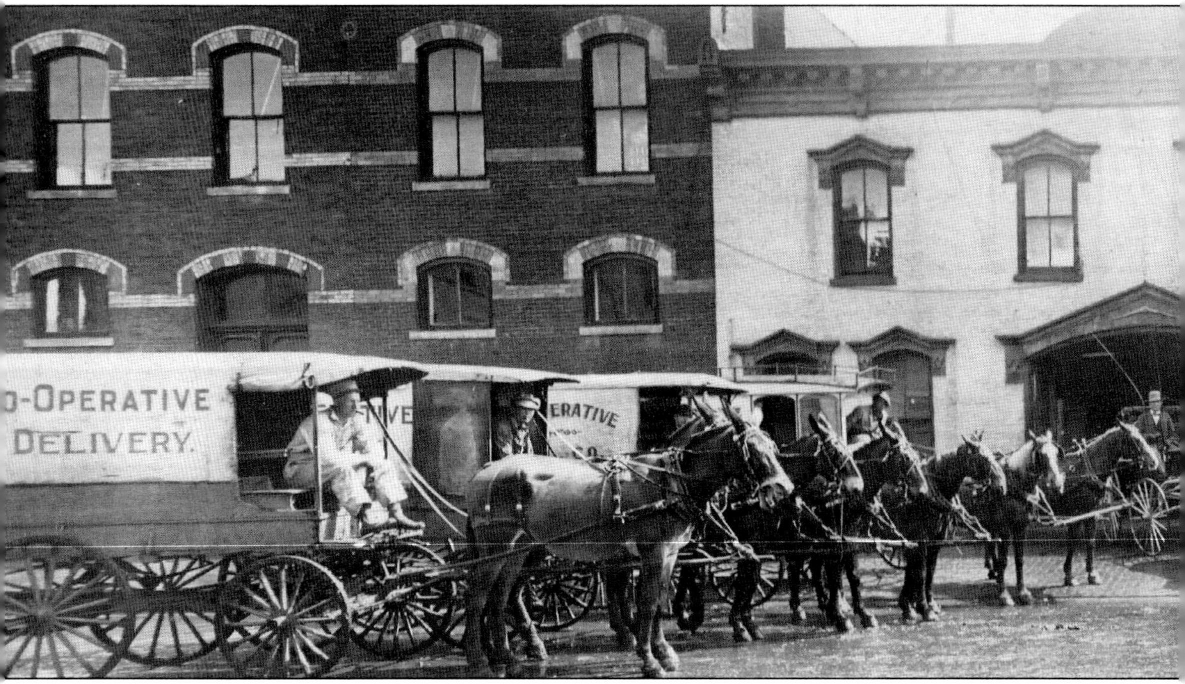

The Cooperative Delivery Co. used mule-drawn wagons to make home deliveries of groceries from several local stores. Its headquarters was on Fourth Avenue between Main and West Streets. Note the promotional slogan on a wagon at the top right—"Help to Make a Beautiful Grinnell."

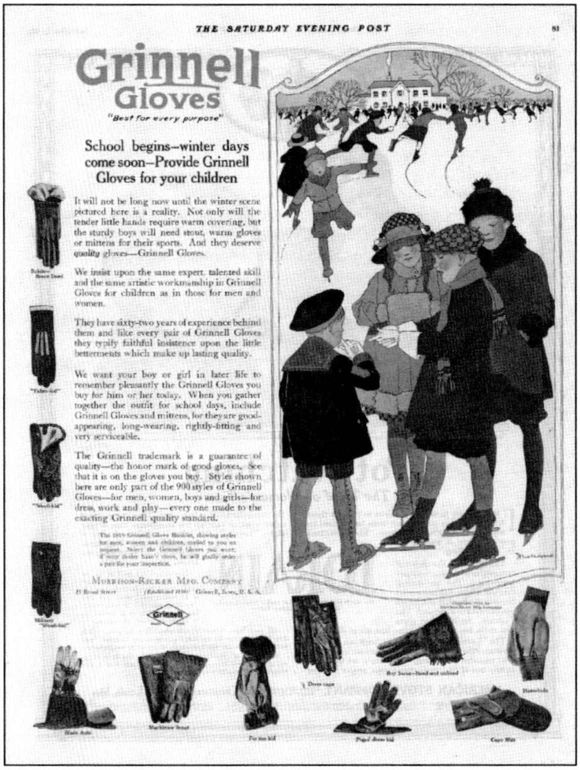

The success of Grinnell Gloves made the Morrison-Ricker Manufacturing Company one of the state's best-known corporations in the early 1900s. The company prospered in part because of a national sales force and national advertising such as this full-page advertisement that appeared in the September 6, 1919, issue of the *Saturday Evening Post.* (GHM.)

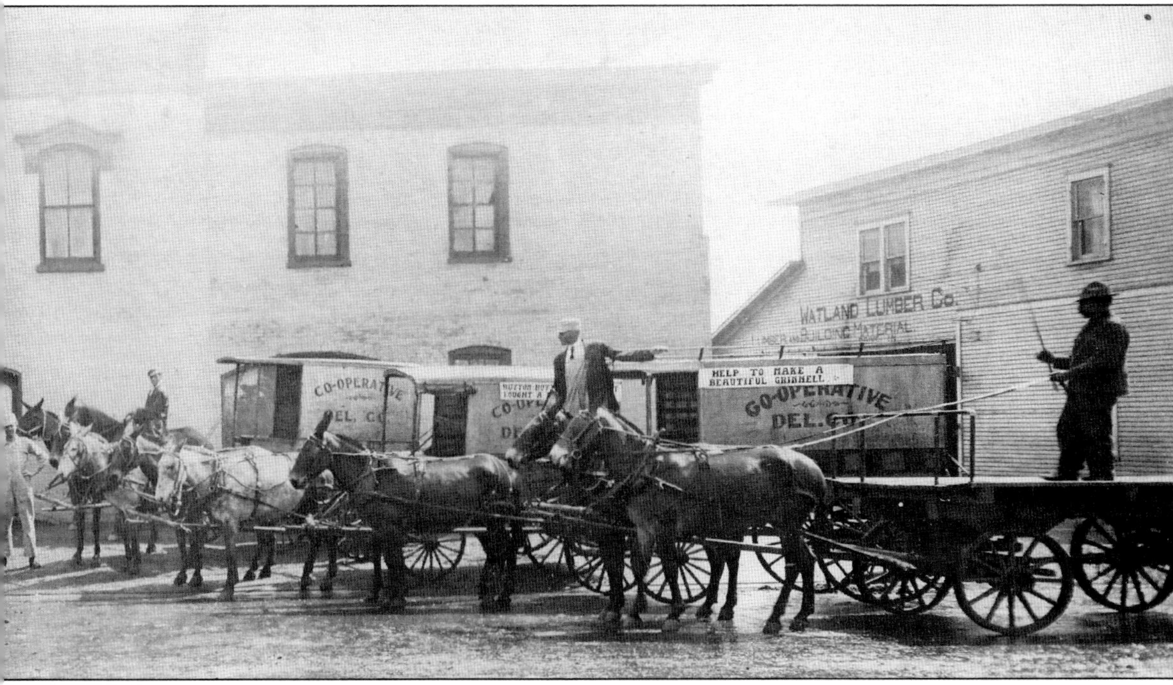

The beginning of self-service grocery stores put the wagons, and the mules, out of business. The photograph is dated 1919. (GHM.)

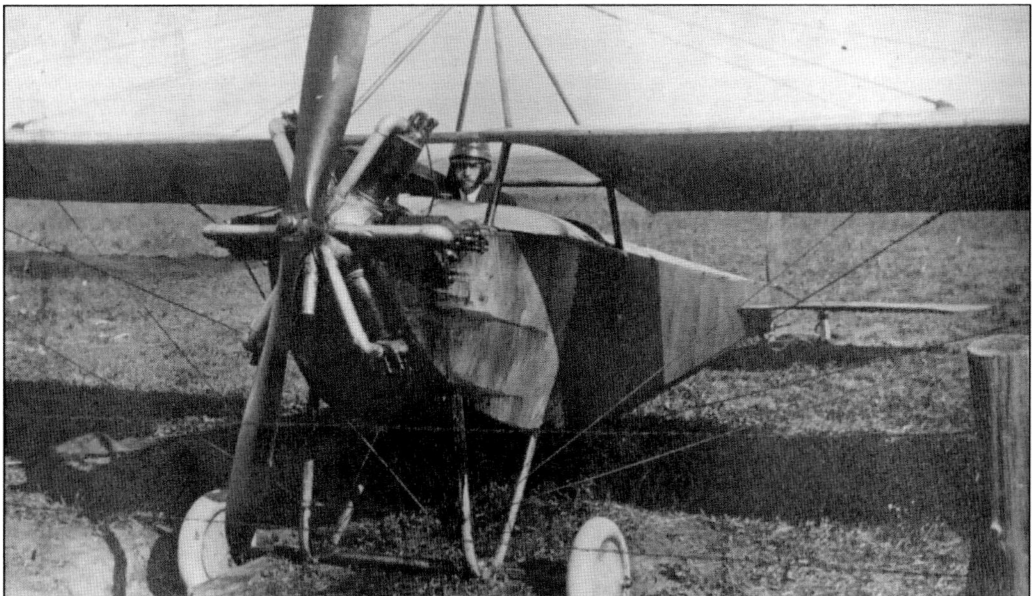

Grinnell's pioneer aviator, Billy Robinson, enlisted financial support from his hometown in 1913 to start the Grinnell Aeroplane Company. It was here that he designed and built his monoplane, *Scout*. The aircraft was powered by an innovative radial engine that he and his friend Charley Hink had designed in 1909. Robinson broke the US nonstop long-distance flight record in 1914 by piloting his plane from Des Moines to Chicago. Robinson died in 1916 over Grinnell attempting to break the altitude record of 17,000 feet. (DCL.)

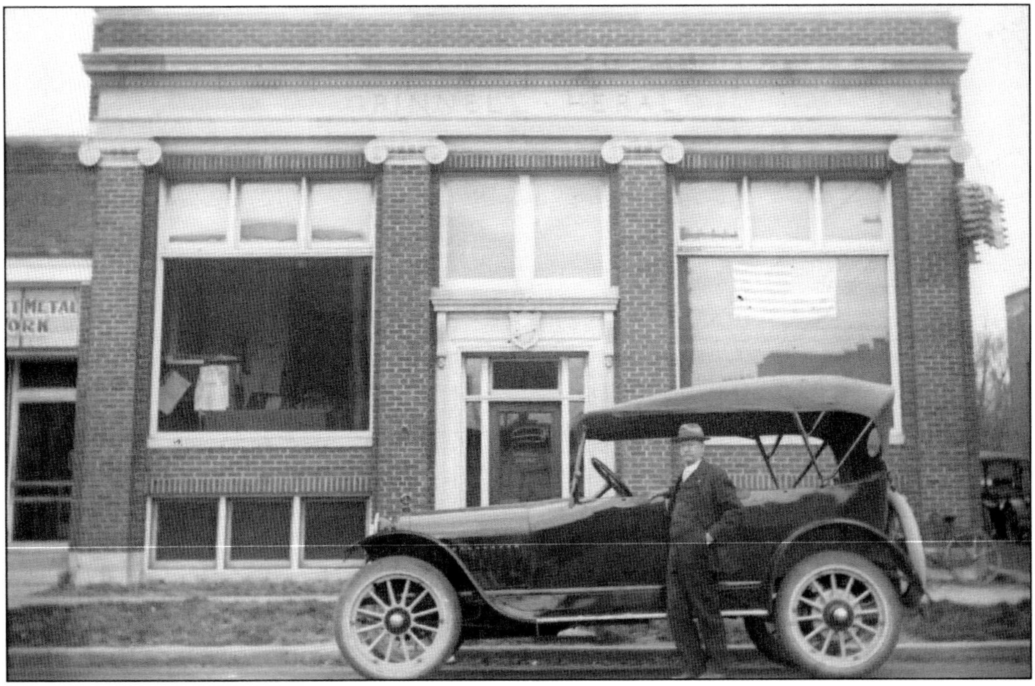

W.G. Ray with his 1913 Spaulding posed for a picture in 1916 in front of the new Grinnell Herald Building at 813 Fifth Avenue. Ray came to the *Grinnell Herald* (one of two newspapers in Grinnell at the time) as copublisher in 1890 and worked at the paper until his death in 1936. In addition, Ray was Grinnell's postmaster, superintendent of schools, and mayor; he also served two terms in the state legislature. (DCL.)

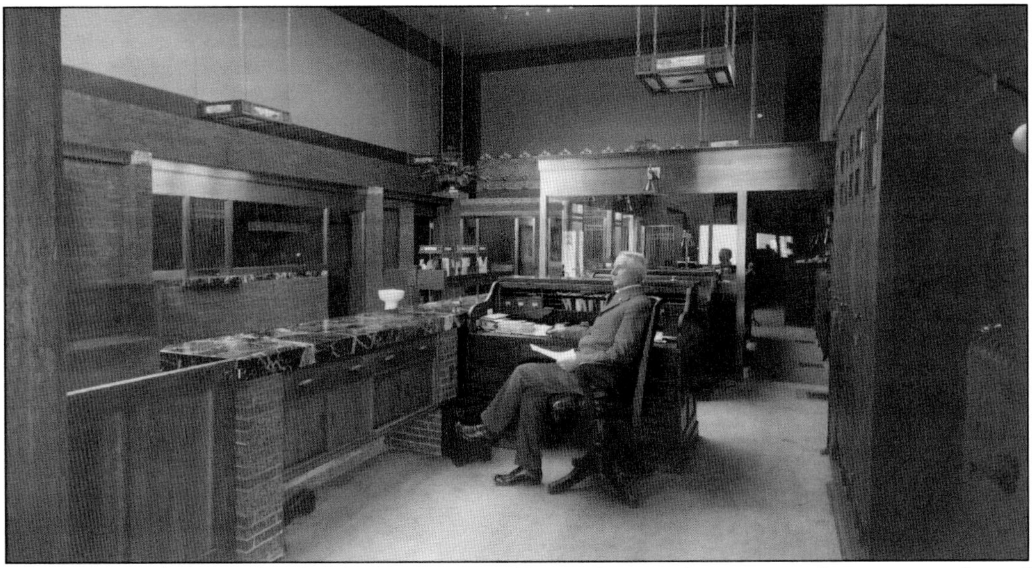

George F. Hamlin started in banking as an errand boy at $4 a week. He rose to become president of Merchants National Bank (pictured here), the "Jewel Box" bank designed by Louis Sullivan that is now a National Historic Landmark. The bank's interior contains brick, terra-cotta tile, and marble. Natural light enters the building through a skylight, a rose window above the entrance, and an east-facing bank of stained-glass windows 40 feet wide. (GHM.)

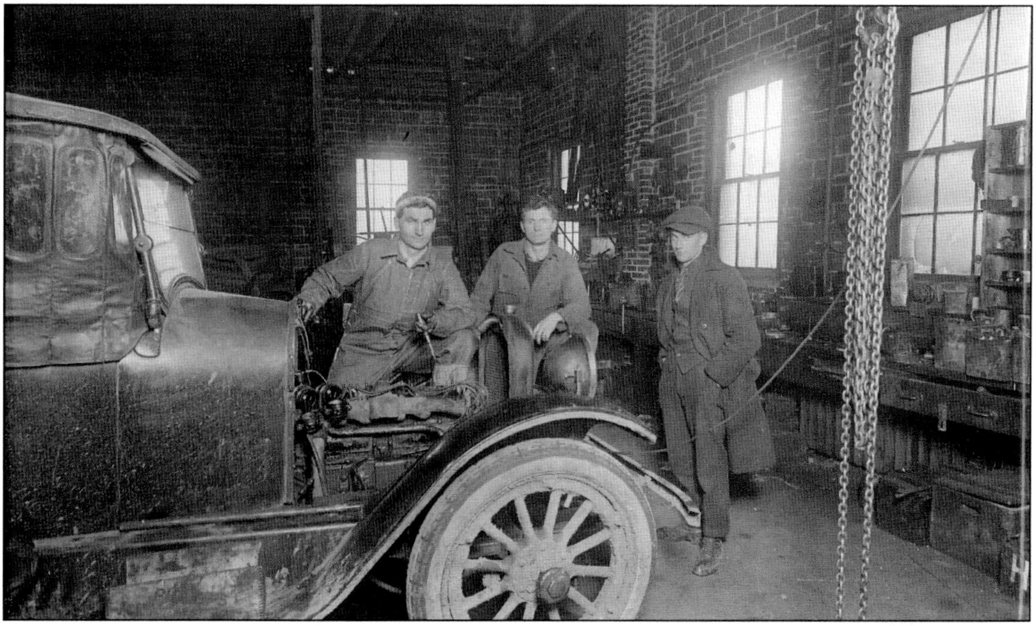

Mechanics and brothers Phil Hagen (left) and George Hagen (center) and an unidentified customer paused for a photograph in 1922 at Hagen Brothers Garage, located at 1013 Broad Street. The structure, which the Hagens built, is now the St. Mary's Religious Education Center. Phil and George, along with two other brothers and a step-brother, started in business with a garage located three blocks south on Broad Street. (Jerry Hagen.)

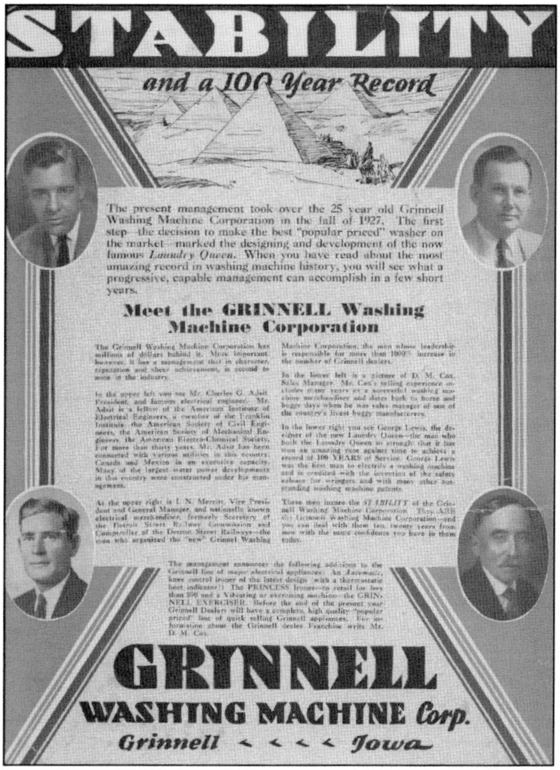

Grinnell Washing Machine Corporation touted the reliability of its Laundry Queen model in this 1920s advertisement. The company started in Newton in 1908 but moved to Grinnell within a few months. The factory was located at Third Avenue and Main Street. Business thrived for a time, reaching a peak in the early 1920s. It soured within a few years, however, forcing a reorganization in 1926 and ultimately bankruptcy in 1937. (Ramsey family.)

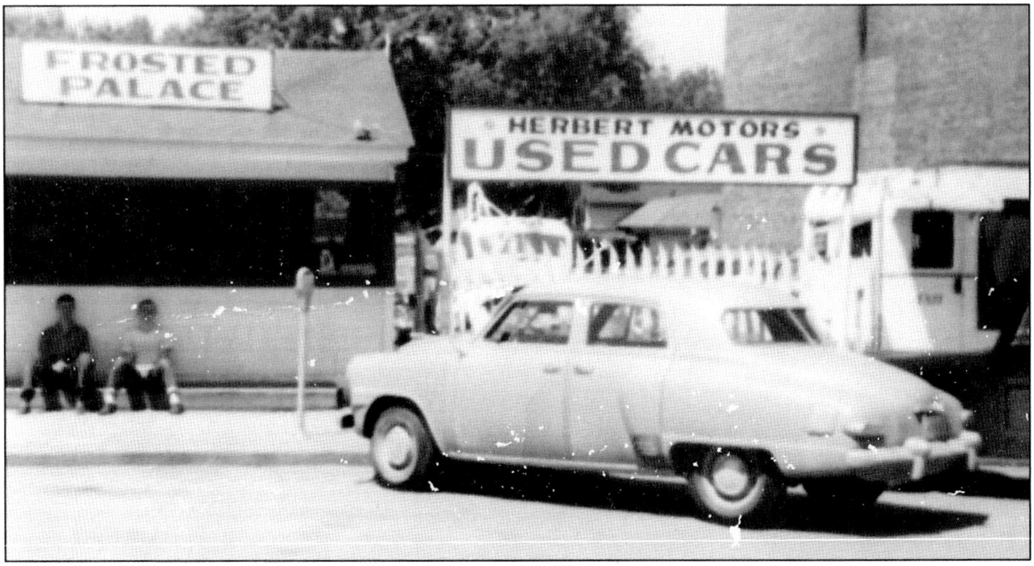

A pair of ambitious teenagers, Jerry Hagen (left) and Lyman Walter, operated Grinnell's first soft-serve ice cream stand during the summer of 1951. Called the Frosted Palace, the stand was a wood-frame structure located in the 900 block of Main Street. The most popular item was a vanilla cone, in either a 5¢ or 10¢ size. The stand was later hauled to Rock Creek Lake and used as a cabin. (Jerry Hagen.)

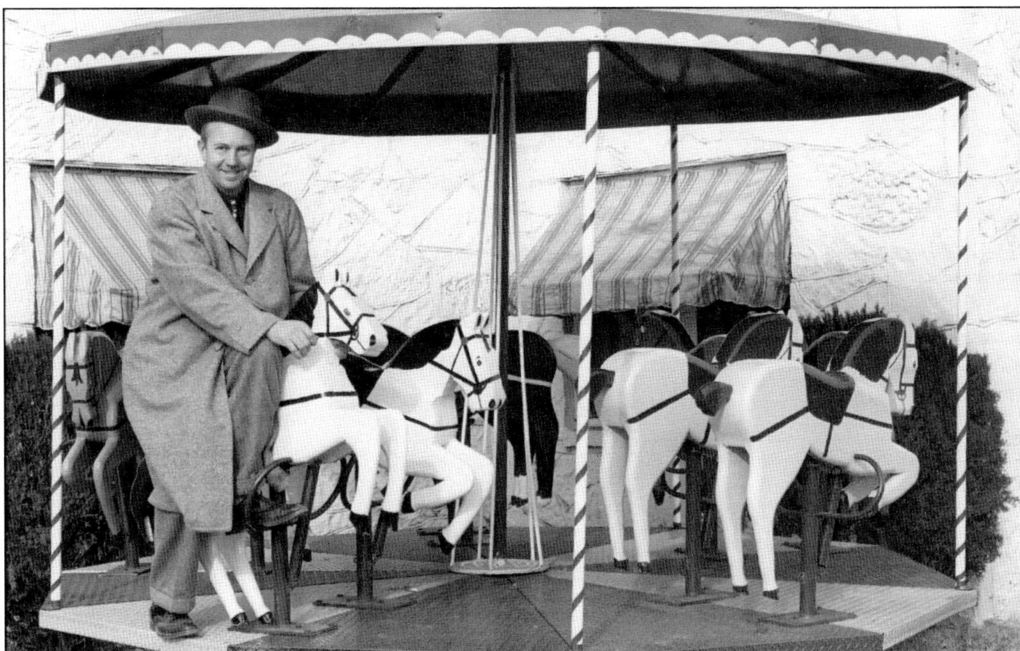

Entrepreneur Claude W. Ahrens started out in the hybrid seed corn business, then took over his father's playground equipment operation. The Miracle Recreation Company began with a merry-go-round and later added swings, teeter-totters, jungle gyms, and eventually stadium seating. Ahrens and his wife, Dolly, established a family foundation in 1993 that has supported a variety of quality-of-life projects in the area. The photograph is from the 1950s. (Claude W. and Dolly Ahrens Foundation.)

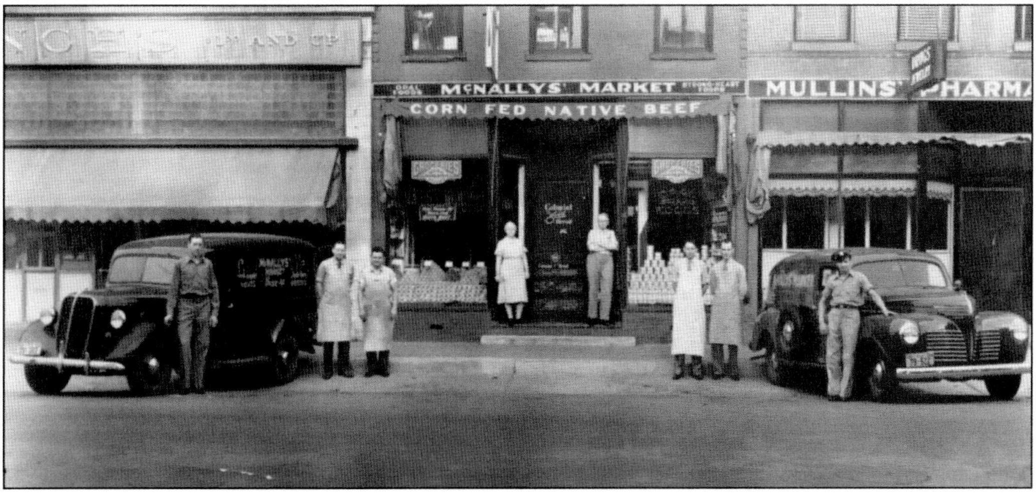

McNally's, one of Grinnell's oldest businesses, was started in 1902 by C.L. (Chris) McNally as a meat market at 915 Main Street. The store was expanded and grocery items were added in 1923. High-quality beef, raised locally and processed in McNally's own plant, continued to be a specialty. In 1935, orders could be placed by telephone (phone number 44) and delivered by store vehicles. (Bill McNally.)

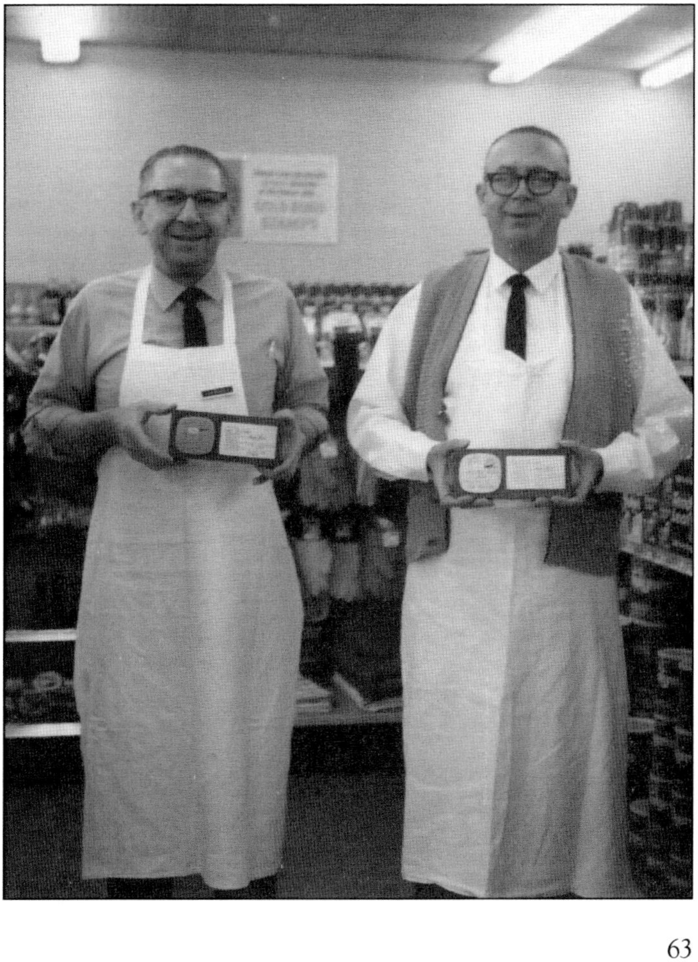
Jim (left) and Ed (right) McNally purchased McNally's in 1947 from their father, C.L. (Chris) McNally, renaming it McNally's SuperValu. Jim and Ed were active in their church and in the community. Both served terms on the city council. (Bill McNally.)

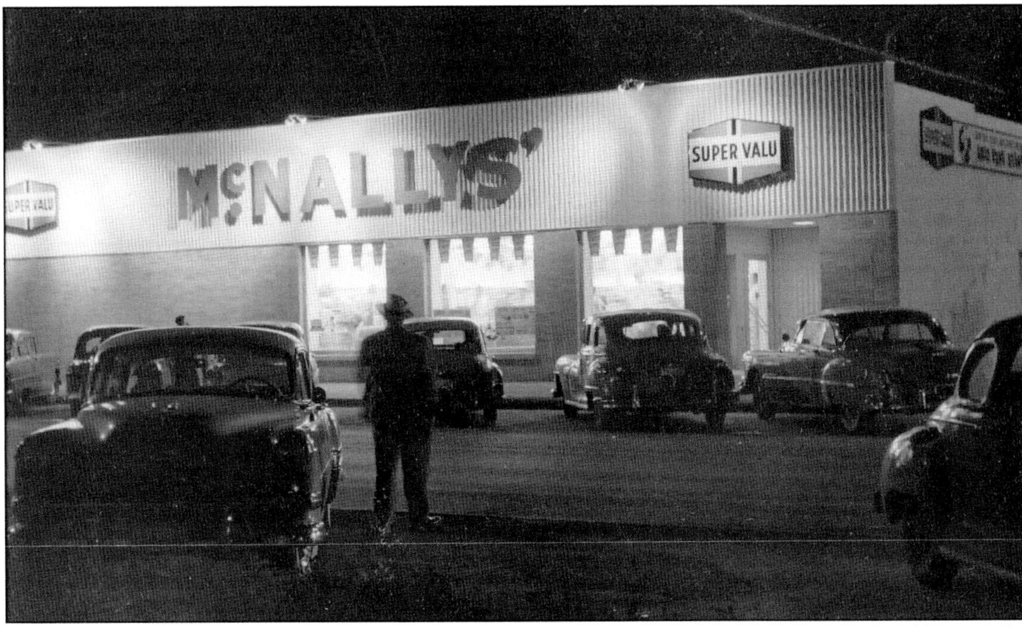

McNally's relocated in 1955 to a new building at 1021 Main Street. A newspaper headline at the time credited the move to the owners' faith in the community. The new store's innovations included Stanley "Magic Doors," automatic doors that promised "no more juggling . . . to make marketing easier than ever." The building served McNally's until 2013, when the store, now owned by Randy and Julie Smith, moved across the street. (Bill McNally.)

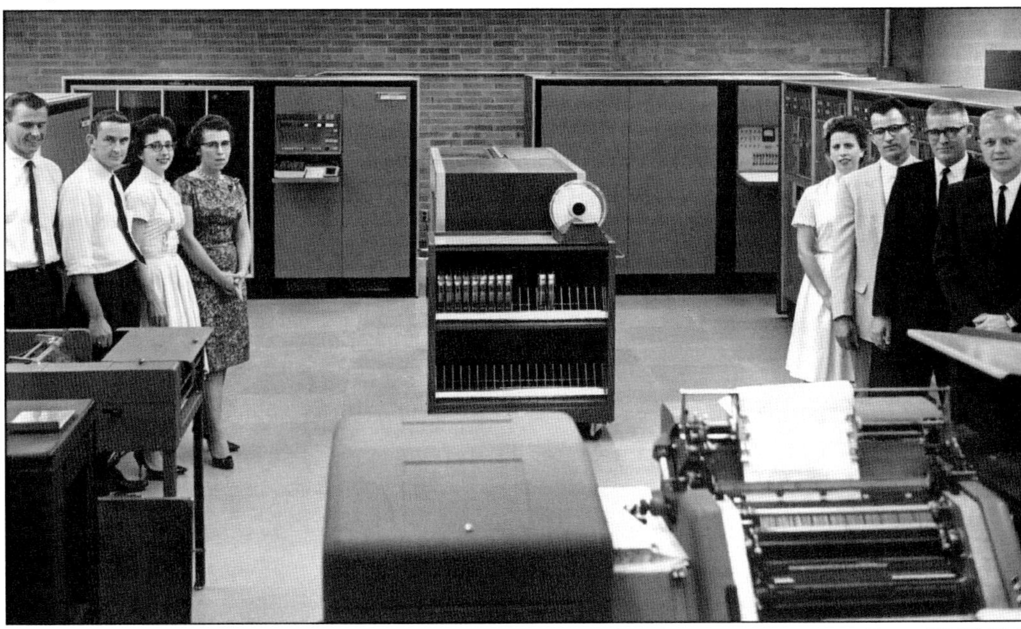

Grinnell Mutual Reinsurance Company (GMRC) acquired its first computer in 1963—a UNIVAC system pictured here with the company's data processing staff. GMRC was founded in Greenfield in 1907 as Iowa Farmers Mutual Reinsurance Association. The company moved to Grinnell in 1933. Now located on Highway 146 south of town, GMRC is the largest employer in Poweshiek County. (Grinnell Mutual Reinsurance Company.)

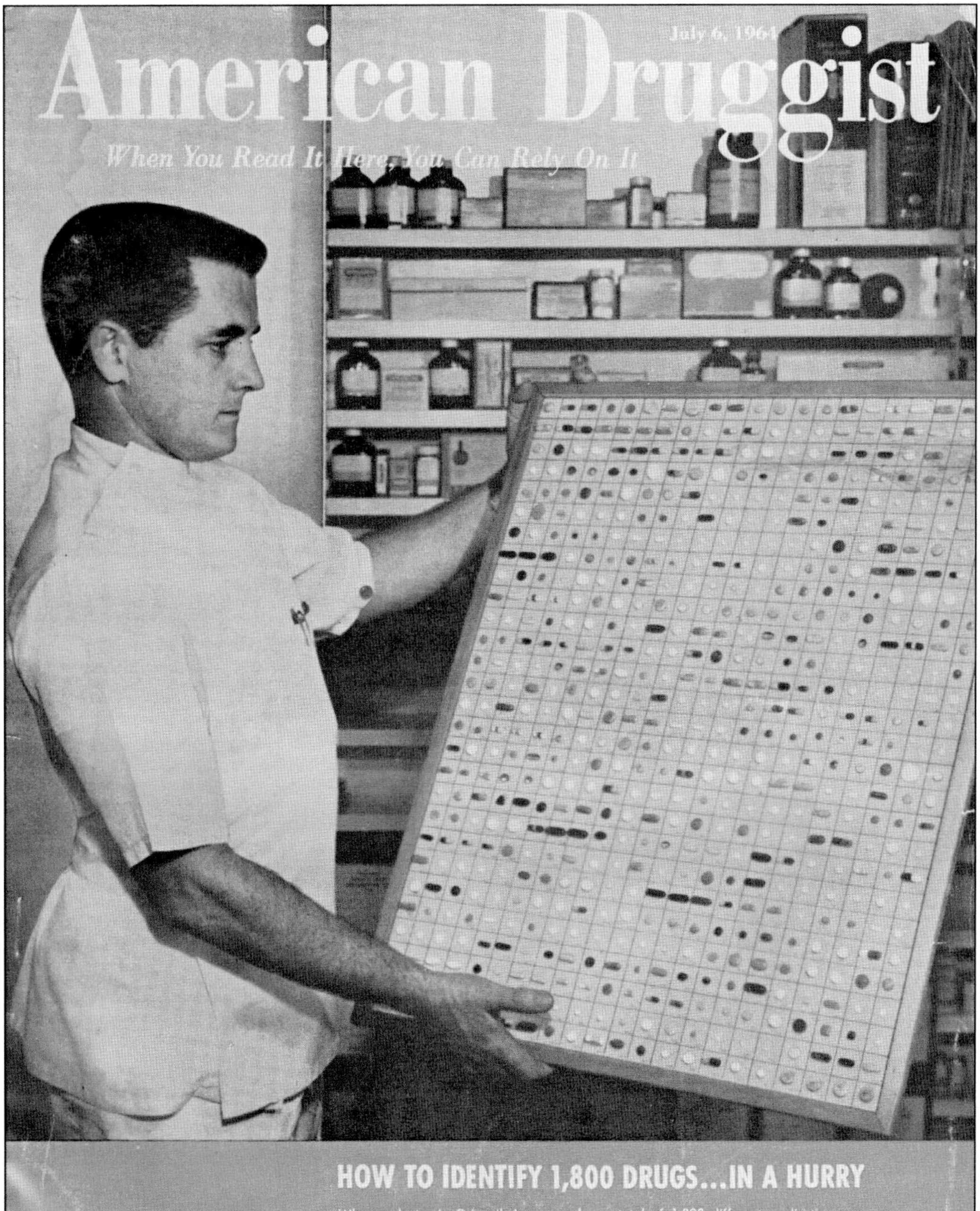

Pharmacist Mike Hotchkin and Cunningham Drug were featured on the cover of the July 1964 issue of the *American Druggist* magazine for an innovative way to identify capsules and tablets available at the pharmacy. Owner Don Cunningham, his son Jim, and Hotchkin put together display boards showing an example of each of the 1,800 prescription pills the pharmacy carried. Cunningham's was in business at 827 Fourth Avenue from 1938, when Don Cunningham bought an existing drugstore, until 2003, when it closed. It was a community gathering spot (coffee for 5¢ a cup) as well as a full-service drugstore that provided 24-hour emergency service. The delivery vehicle was a Volkswagen Beetle with a pillbox on top. (Jim Cunningham.)

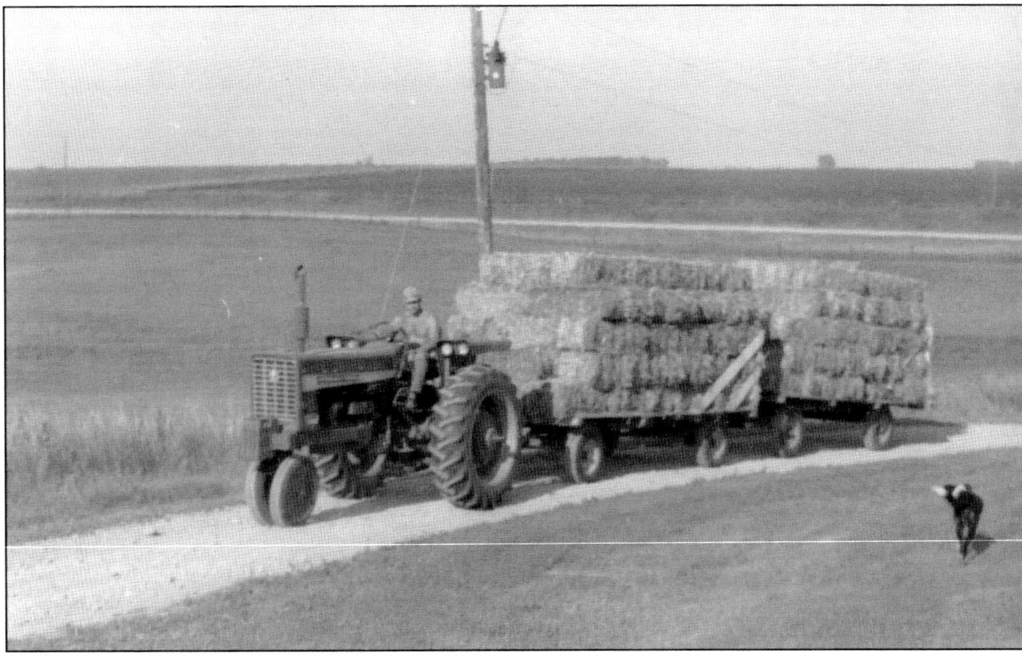

Gordon Louden, a third-generation farmer, used his International 656 tractor on a hot summer day in 1970 to haul bales of hay from the field to the barn on his 640-acre property northwest of Grinnell. His son Ben now farms that land plus additional acres. The farm dog, Pepper, is remembered for his habit of shredding plastic Frisbees. (Dorothy Louden.)

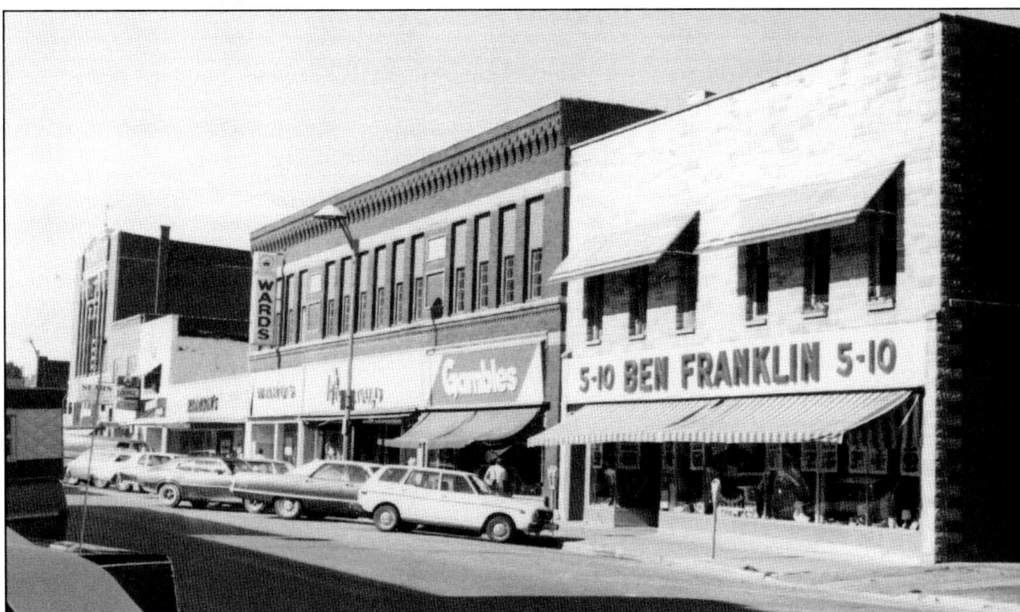

J.C. Penney, Gambles, and Ben Franklin helped satisfy the needs of Grinnell shoppers for many years. Increased mobility and the popularity of suburban shopping malls contributed to the closing of the three stores starting in the 1980s, significantly changing the character of Grinnell's downtown. The arrival of Walmart in 1985 further altered the local retail scene. The photograph of the 900 block of Main Street was taken in 1978. (GCA.)

Four

Teaching and Preaching

At the foundation of this town are religion, intelligence, and enthusiasm for education. These were all typified in him from whom the town gets its name—the lion of the tribe.

—Rev. James L. Hill, Iowa College trustee

J.B. Grinnell was passionate in his belief that a community should be focused on religion and education. Less than a year after the first settlers arrived, a combination church-school was constructed north of Fourth Avenue and Broad Street. To build the 16-by-24-foot structure, 10 settlers contributed $15 each. J.B. was the contractor. It is said that the building was put up so quickly that the lumber used for the structure was standing as trees only a week earlier. It was no surprise, then, that the green wood warped and the roof leaked. A separate school and a separate church were built nearby a few years later. The school burned in 1871 but was replaced on the site by a new school called Center School.

In the late 1800s, four schools were built in different parts of town. One of them was replaced in 1918 by the present Davis School. A high school was built in 1904 on the site of Center School. It was expanded in 1921 to include a junior high school.

In response to the state's mandate to close small school districts, the nearby Newburg schools merged with the Grinnell schools in 1958, creating the present Grinnell-Newburg Community School District.

Bailey Park Elementary School was built in 1957, and Fairview Elementary School was built in 1960. The present Grinnell High School opened in 1961. Grinnell Middle School was built in 1979.

Although Grinnell was founded by Congregationalists, the first building constructed solely for religious purposes was built by the Baptists in 1859. The Methodists and Catholics soon followed. Today, more than 20 religious denominations are represented in Grinnell. The college, with a diverse student body from around the world, gives the town a glimpse of the even broader faith community.

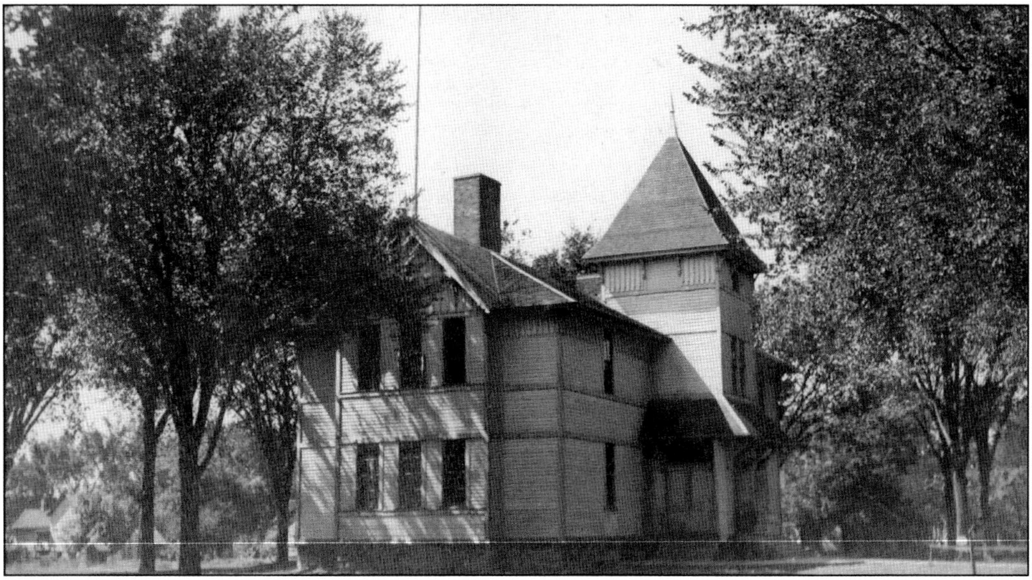

The first school to be built outside the heart of town was South School, constructed in 1877 at Hamilton and Broad Streets. (Grinnell's first three schools had practical names—Center, South, and Northwest.) South School was replaced in 1918 by the present Davis School, named in honor of Edna and Lizzie Davis, who graduated from the Grinnell schools in the 1870s and spent their working lives teaching in the local schools. (GHM.)

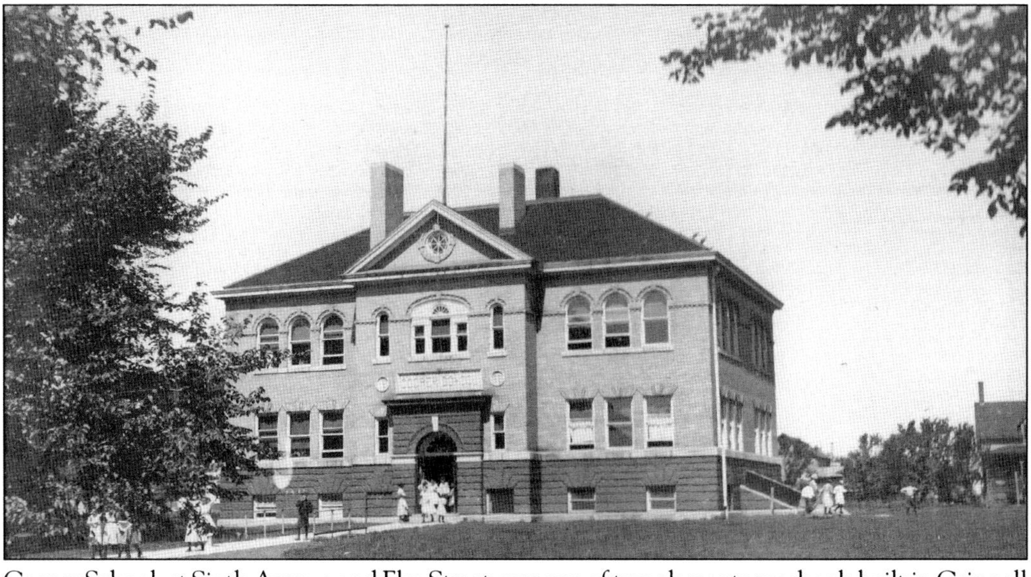

Cooper School, at Sixth Avenue and Elm Street, was one of two elementary schools built in Grinnell in the late 1890s. It was named for Col. S.F. Cooper, an early teacher who had served as commandant of the local troops during the Civil War. The school was closed in 1974 and sold to neighboring Grinnell College, which used it for storage before razing it in 1983. (GHM.)

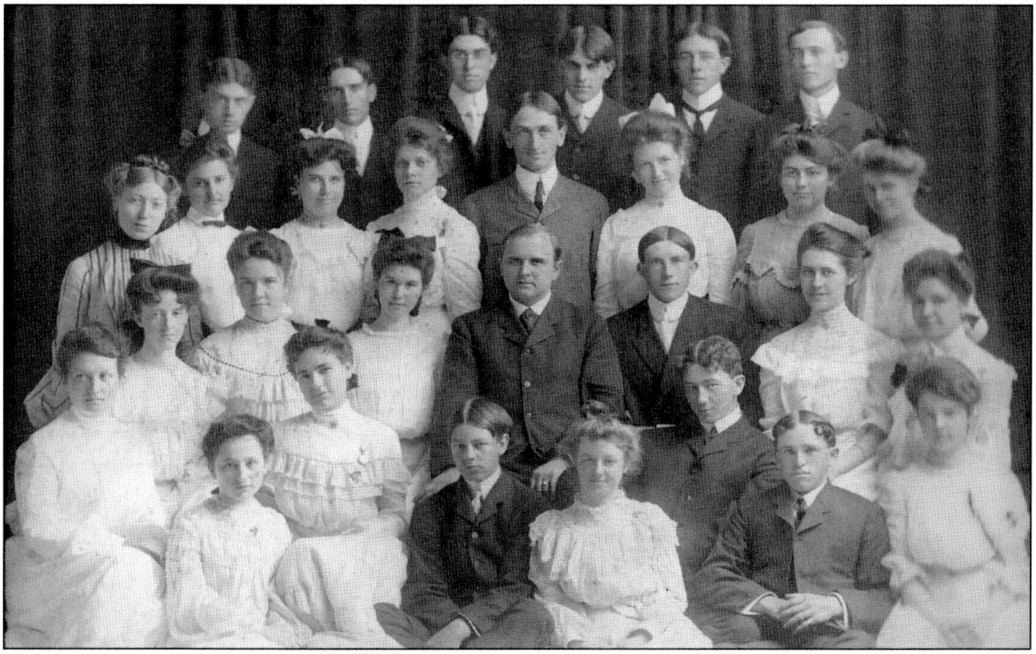

Members of the Grinnell High School class of 1903 arranged themselves for a photograph at graduation time. A separate high school building was a year away, but the school was already accredited by the North Central Association of Colleges and Schools—the first school in Iowa to be so recognized. (GHM.)

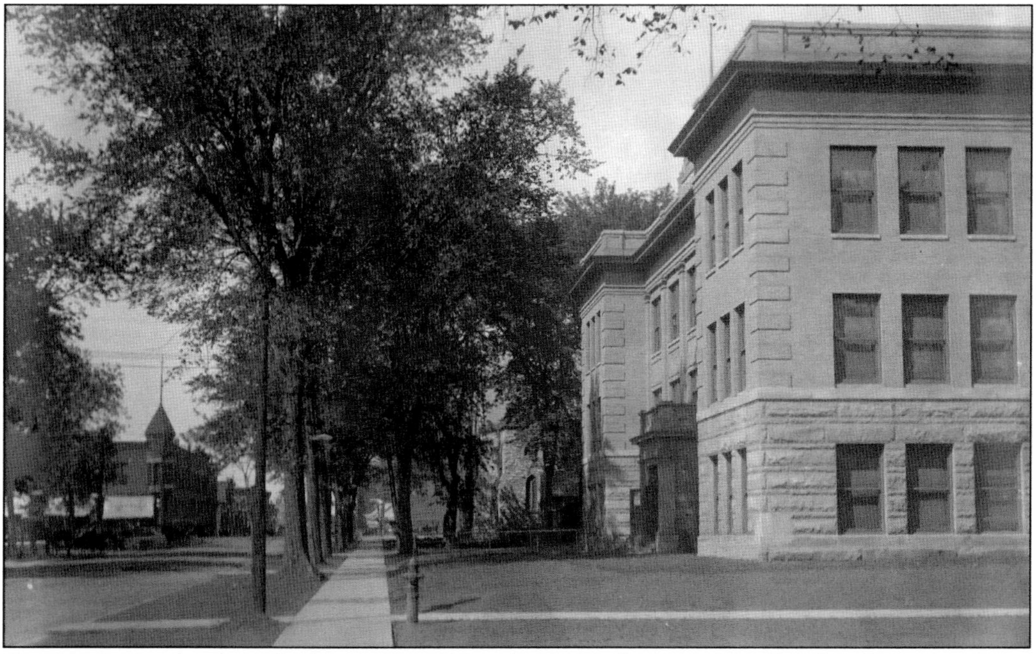

The first high school was built in 1904 on Fourth Avenue between Broad and Park Streets. It was expanded in 1921 to include a junior high. The building was used for the high school until 1961 and for the junior high until 1978. The present community center, which includes city and school district offices, incorporates the former junior high. (GHM.)

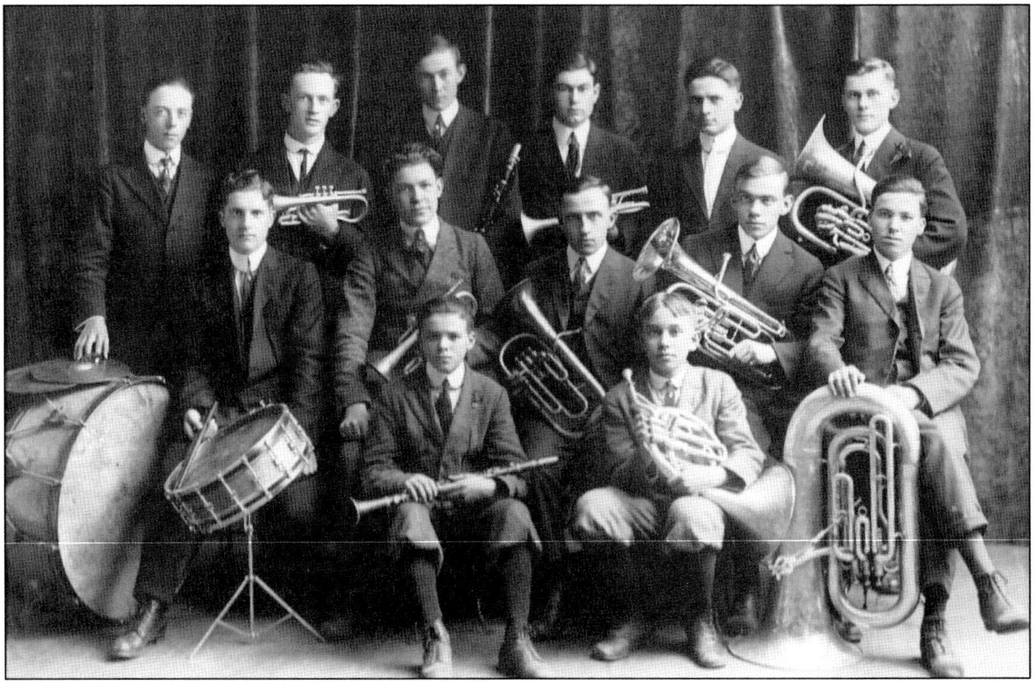

The high school put together its first band in 1915. The yearbook for that year praised the group's ability and enthusiasm, noting that it was formed in early November and performed for the first time later that month. The band is "loyally doing its part to promote the high school spirit," the photograph caption in the yearbook said. (GHM.)

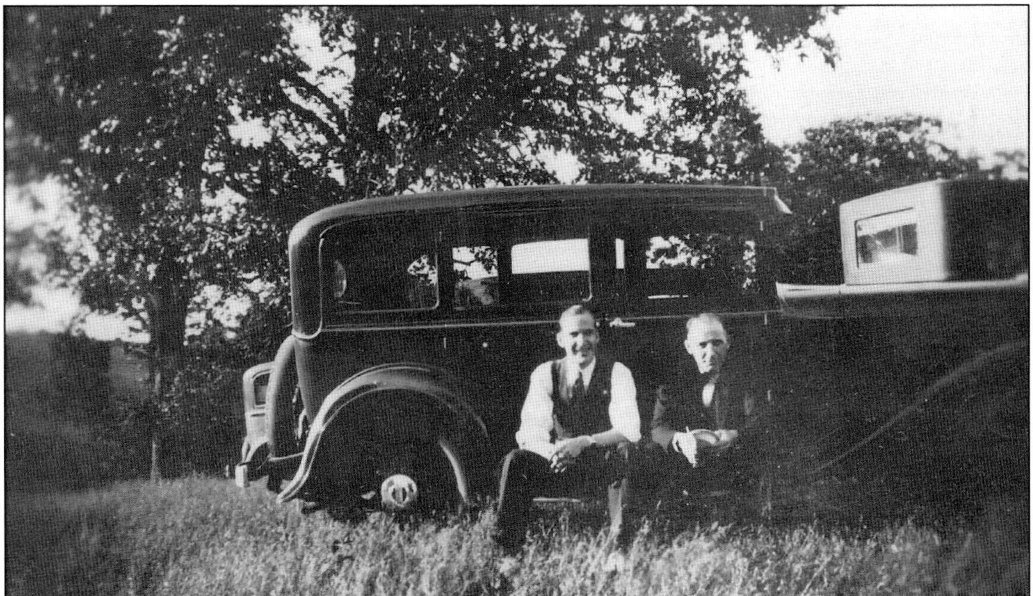

Grinnell High School principal T.T. Cranny (left) and teacher Francis (Tommy) Hawk (right) took a break at the Senior Days picnic in 1933. Cranny came to the school in 1915 as a physics and debate teacher and then served as principal from 1922 to 1953. He was on hand when the high school athletic field was dedicated in his honor in 1961. (Karen Groves.)

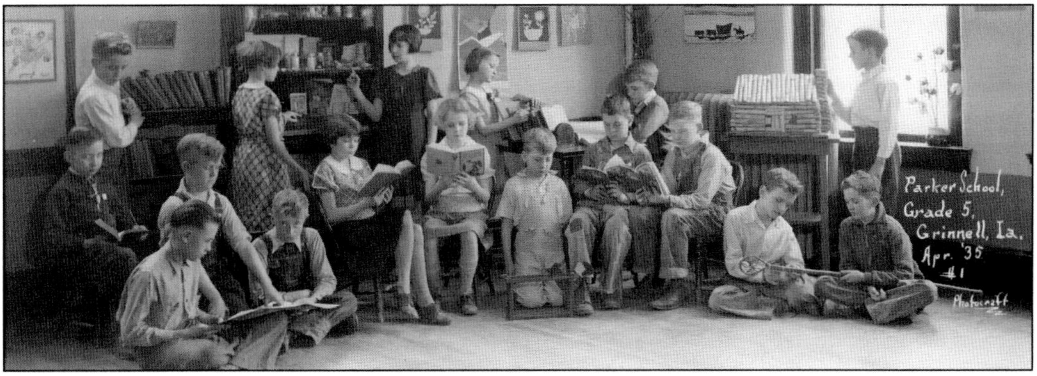

A photographer likely encouraged these fifth-graders at Parker School to read, or at least to appear as if they were reading, when this picture was taken in 1935. Parker School was named for L.F. Parker, the first superintendent, who taught at both Grinnell College and in the public schools and managed also to write a detailed history of Poweshiek County. Note the cabin made of Lincoln Logs on the table in the background. (GHM.)

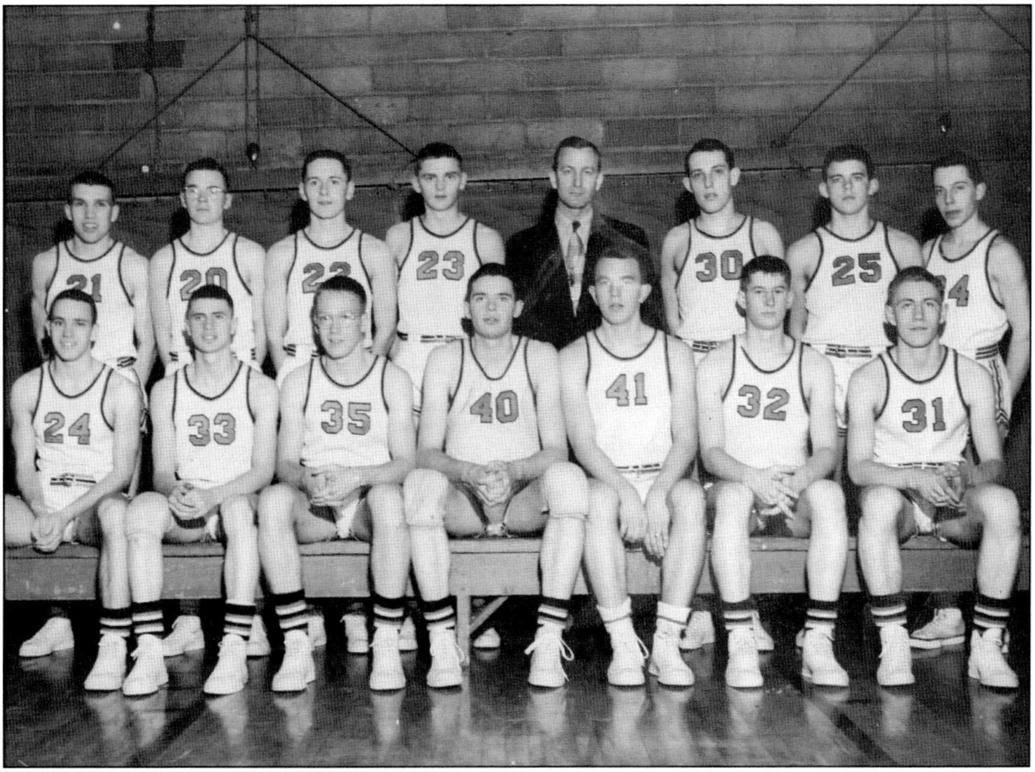

In 1951, the Grinnell High School boys' basketball team compiled a 23-2 record, the second-best record in school history. The team was undefeated in conference play and advanced to the quarterfinals of the state tournament before losing to Keokuk. At that time, the high school used the athletic facilities of Grinnell College, playing its home basketball games at Darby Gym and its home football games at Ward Field. (Jerry Hagen.)

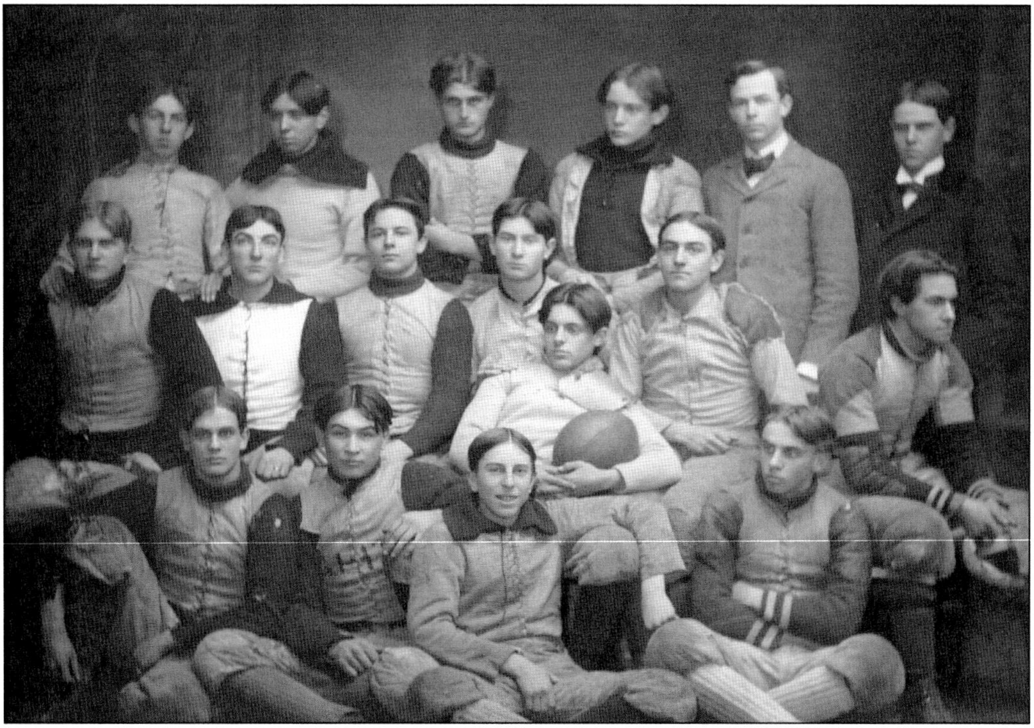

Four generations of the Ramsey family were quarterbacks on the Grinnell High School football team—Grant, Fred, Rick, and Jim. The teams of two of the four generations are pictured here. In 1894 (above), Grant Ramsey (first row, second from left) was part of a 15-member squad shown with Principal Ernest Fellows and coach Charles Haines (in suits at right in the third row). The 1954 team (below) included Rick Ramsey (first row, far right). Fred Ramsey was part of the 1923–1925 teams. Jim Ramsey played in 1981–1983. Other Ramseys—Fred's brother John and Jim's brother Mike—also played football but at other positions. (Both, Ramsey family.)

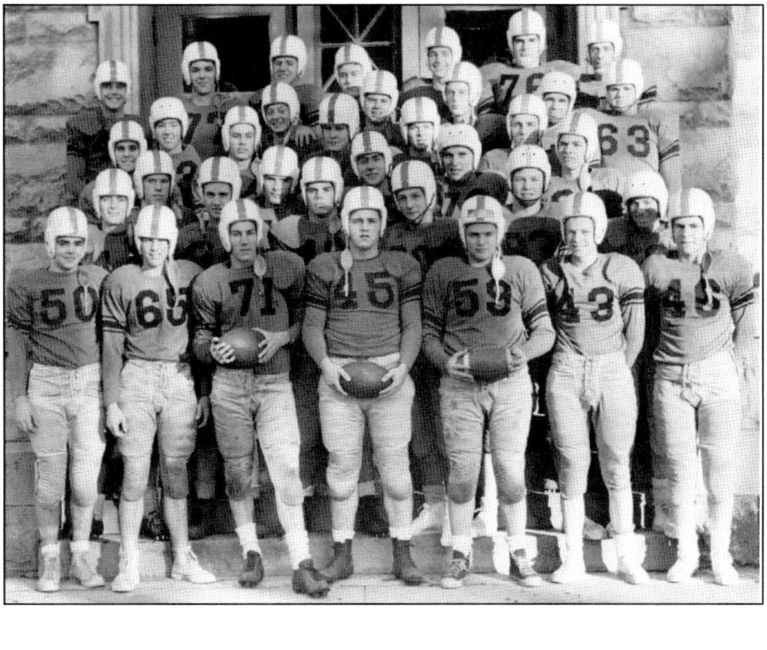

Boys arranged themselves on the slide while, presumably, the girls were off at another activity during recess at Cooper School in 1955. Avis Tone was a longtime teacher and principal at the school. When space became tight in the 1950s because of increasing enrollment, her principal's desk was located in the hallway. (Karen Packard.)

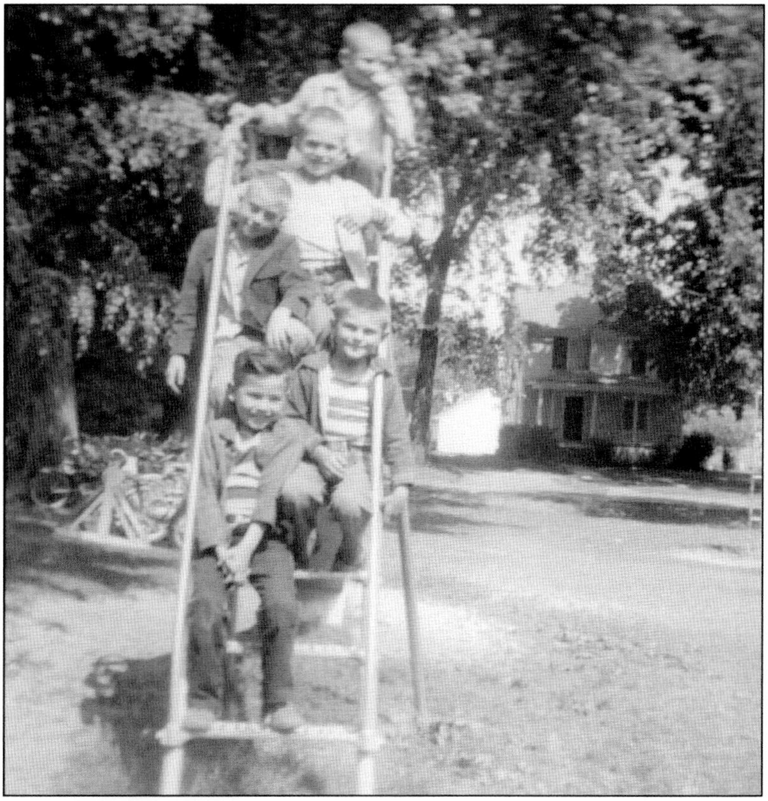

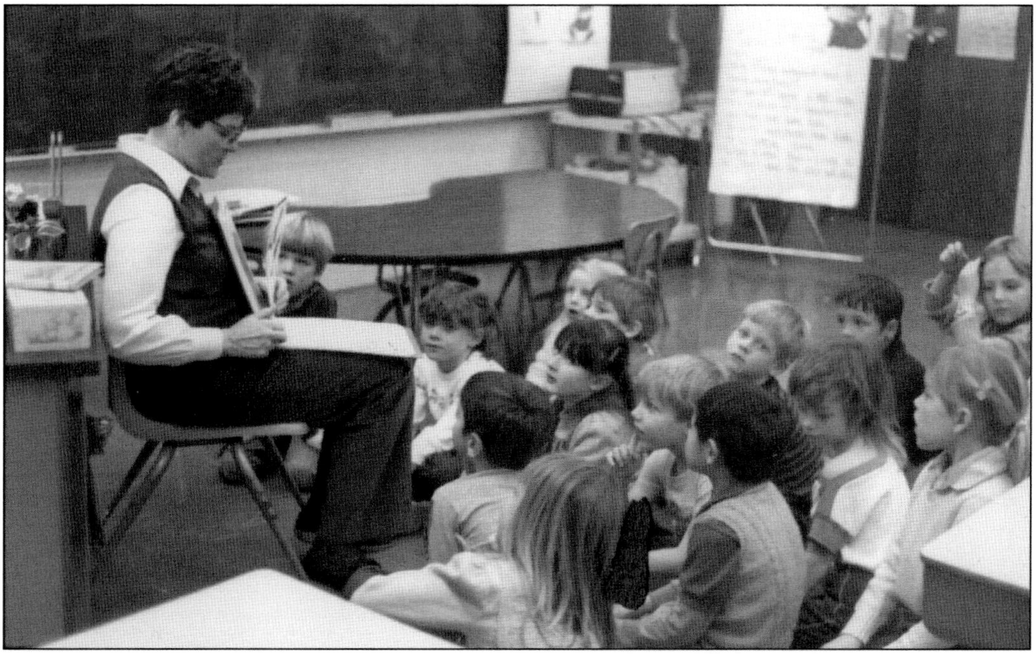

Teacher Thomsa Haas led a language arts lesson for a class of first graders at Davis School in the early 1980s. Haas did her student teaching through Grinnell College and worked both at Newburg School and Grinnell Middle School before the position at Davis. (DCL.)

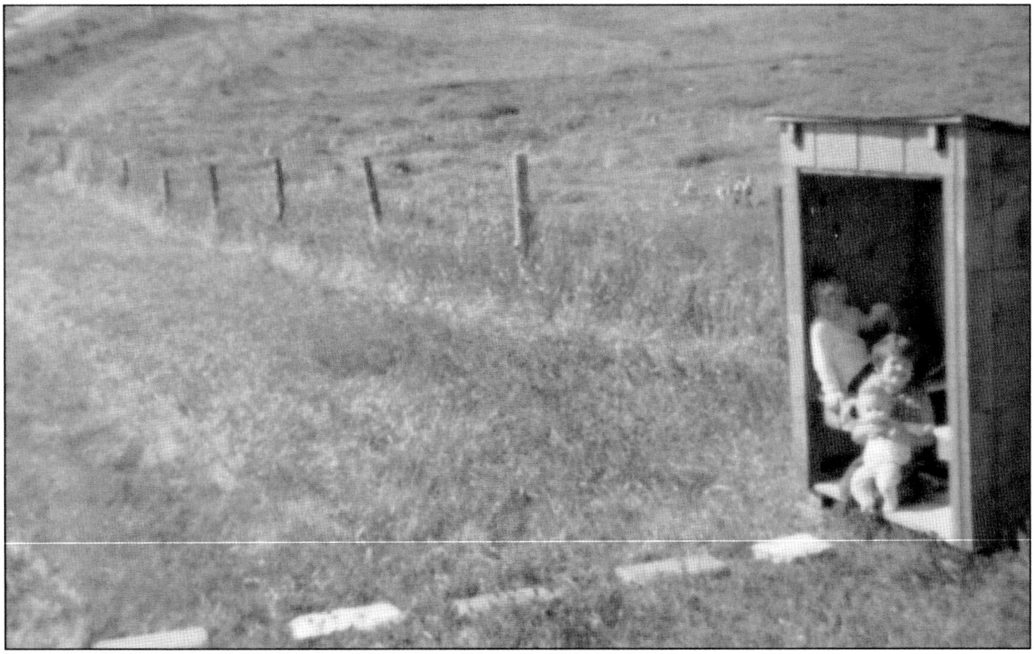

Enrollment in the Grinnell schools for many years included a large number of rural children who rode the school bus each day. Waiting for the bus in the shelter near the road on their farm northwest of Grinnell in 1976 were Emily and Ben Louden. The number of rural students has decreased as farms have become larger and fewer families are farming. (Dorothy Louden.)

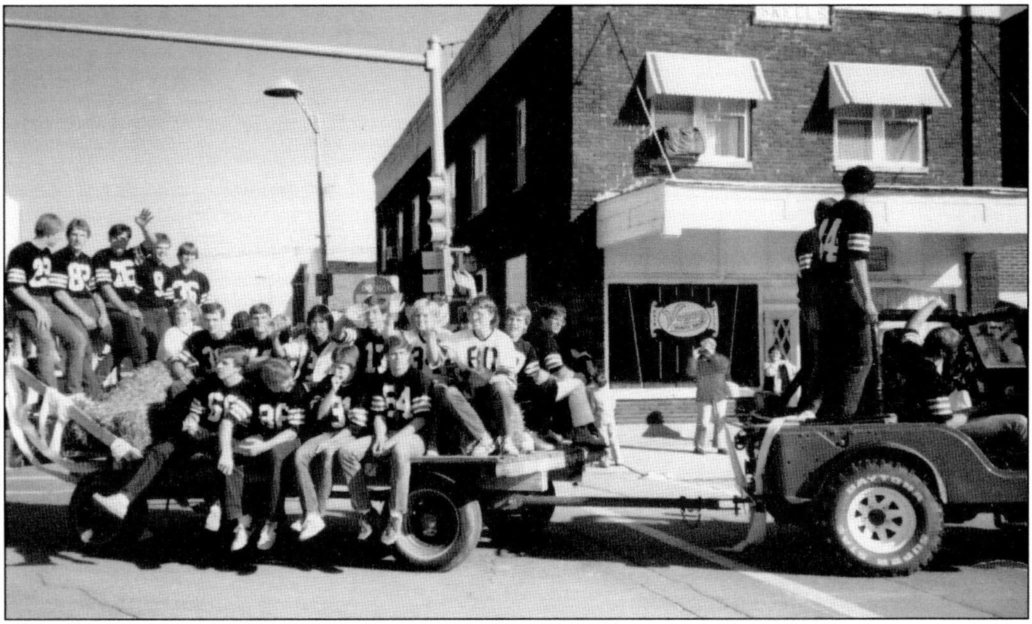

Homecoming at Grinnell High School is celebrated each fall with a parade through the central business district, followed by a pep rally in Central Park. In this 1983 photograph, the football team and team managers enjoyed their ride on a flatbed truck as they turned the corner of Fifth Avenue and headed down Main Street. At that time, the downtown streets were one way, and intersections were controlled by traffic signals. (Ramsey family.)

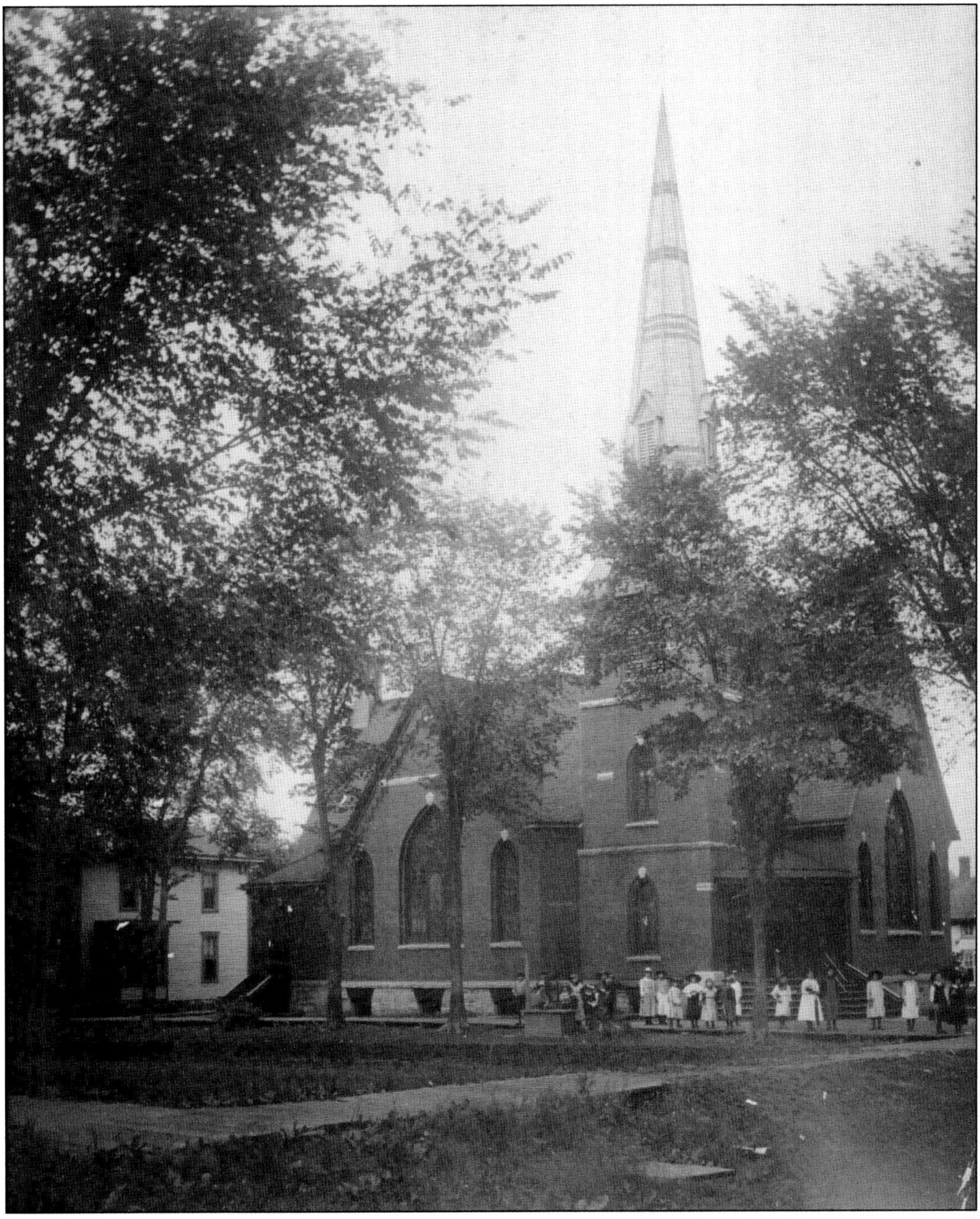

Although Congregationalists founded the town, the Baptists constructed the first building in Grinnell used purely for church purposes in 1858 and 1859. The first baptisms were conducted in what was known as the college botanical garden, now the site of St. Paul's Episcopal Church. The first church building was replaced between 1889 and 1890 by a new church (shown here) at Fourth Avenue and Park Street. The photograph was taken sometime before 1906, when the Brande Apartments were built next door. Note the wooden sidewalk. Paving of streets and sidewalks in Grinnell started in 1909. When the Baptists built a new church at another location in 1951, the building at Fourth Avenue and Park Street was sold to Glad Tidings Assembly of God Church, which used it for the next several years. (Ruth Greenwald.)

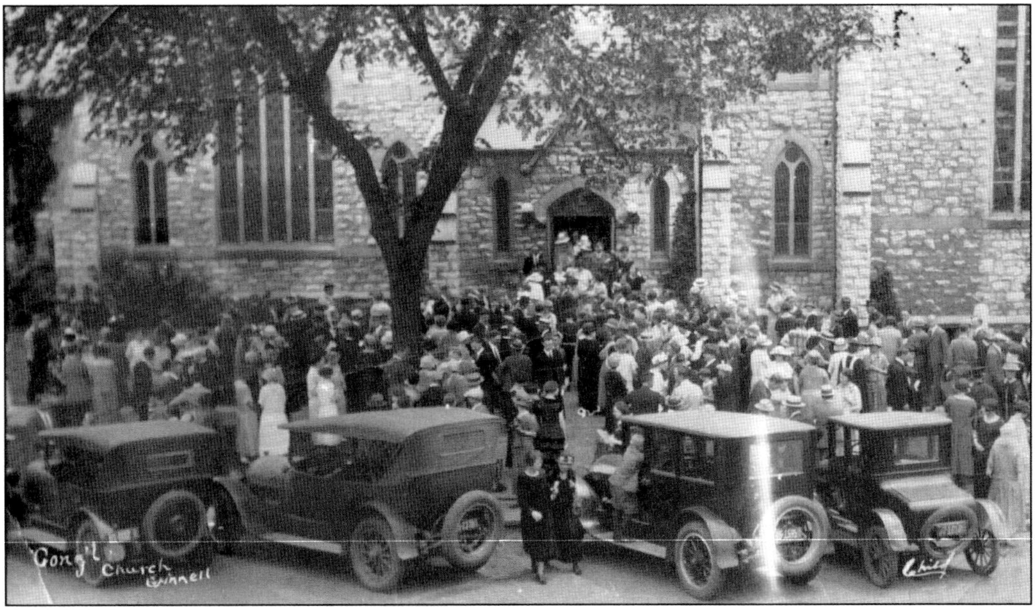

The Congregationalist church at the corner of Fourth Avenue and Broad Street was used for a variety of civic, social, and educational purposes as well as for worship services. Built in 1878 and known as the Old Stone Church, it was constructed to seat 800, then expanded to accommodate 1,500. (Mickey Munley.)

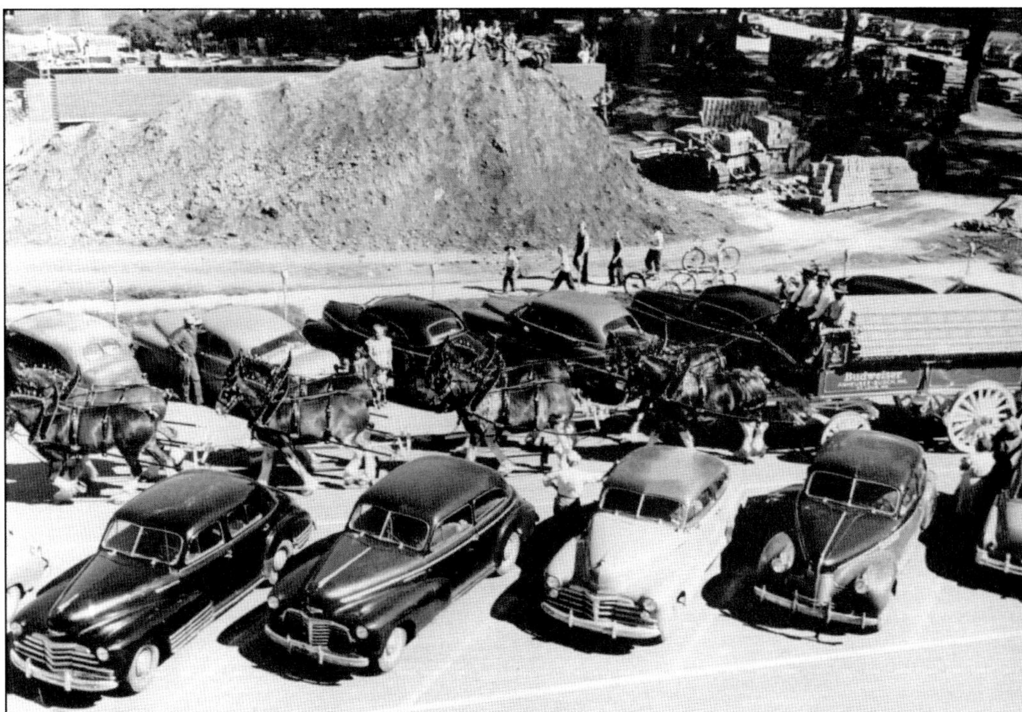

The Old Stone Church was demolished in 1951 to make room for a smaller, more usable building on the site. The demolition project was a major community attraction for weeks. On this day, the Budweiser Clydesdales were also in town. (DCL.)

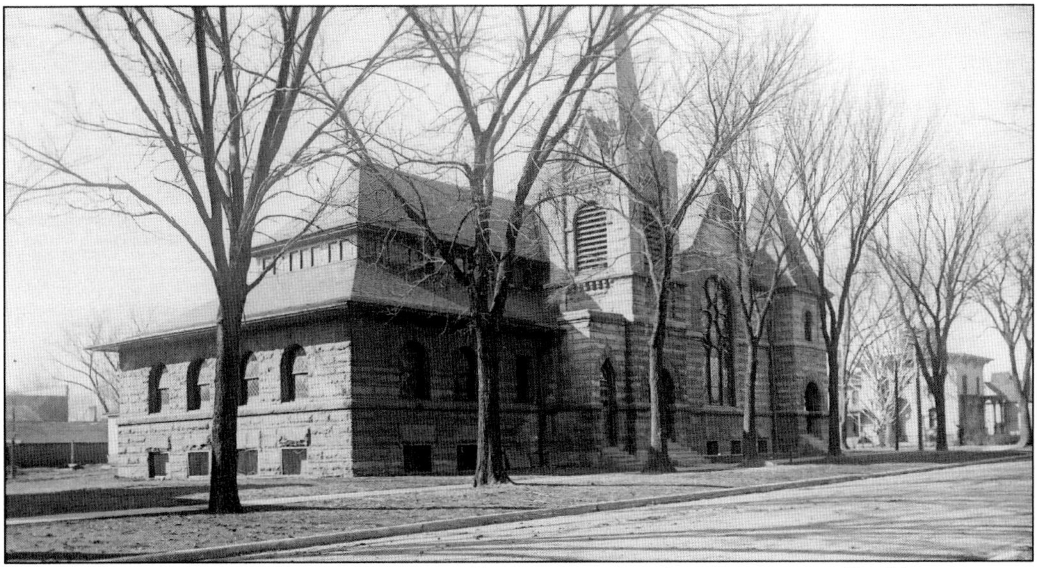

The Grinnell United Methodist Church at Fifth Avenue and Park Street is Grinnell's oldest surviving church building. It was designed and built of Indiana limestone by Robert G. Coutts, a well-known mason who was also president of the church's board of trustees. An education wing was added in 1966. The photograph shows the southeast corner of the church prior to 1921, when the junior high school was added to the high school building next door. (Mickey Munley.)

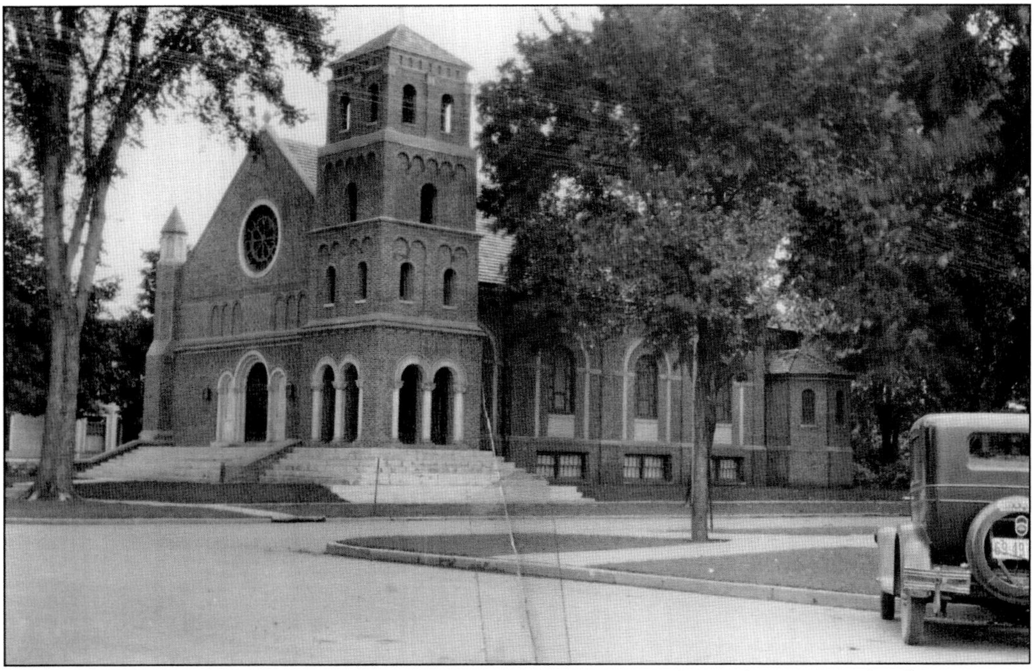

St. Mary's Catholic Church was built in 1927 at Fifth Avenue and Broad Street, under the pastorate of the first resident priest. The first Catholic Mass in Grinnell was celebrated in the sitting room of a private home in 1870. The first Catholic church, called St. Columbanus, was erected in 1883 at Washington Avenue and Main Street. The photograph is dated 1930. (GCA.)

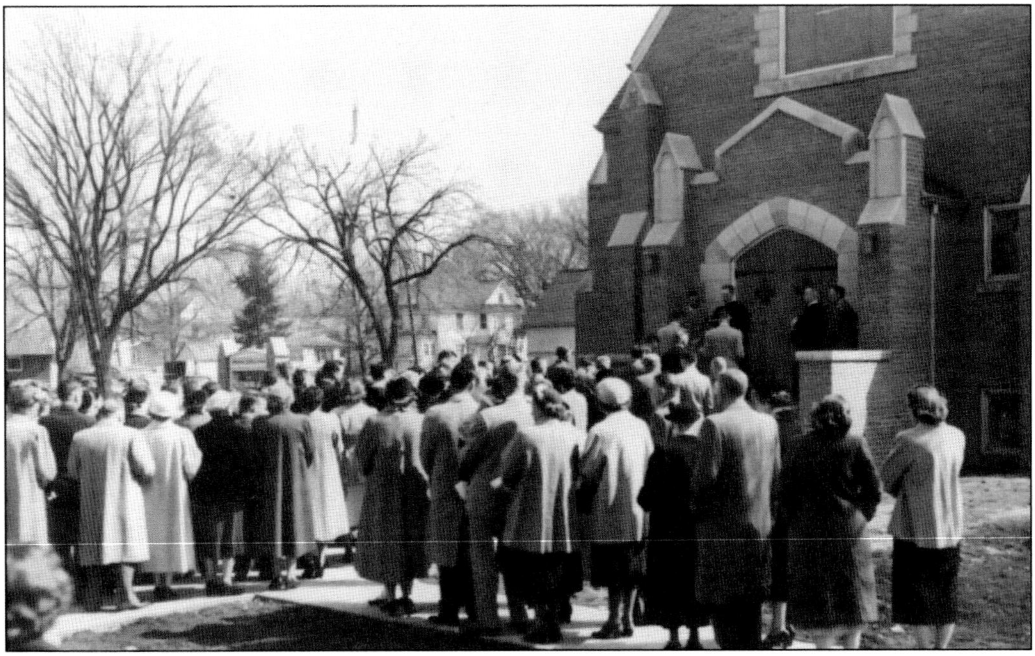

St. John's Lutheran Church dedicated a new church building on April 4, 1954—two weeks before Easter Sunday. The observance included a procession from its previous location, a small chapel a block away on Elm Street (now a private home at 1309 Elm Street). Church records state that volunteers contributed thousands of hours to the building project. (St. John's Lutheran Church.)

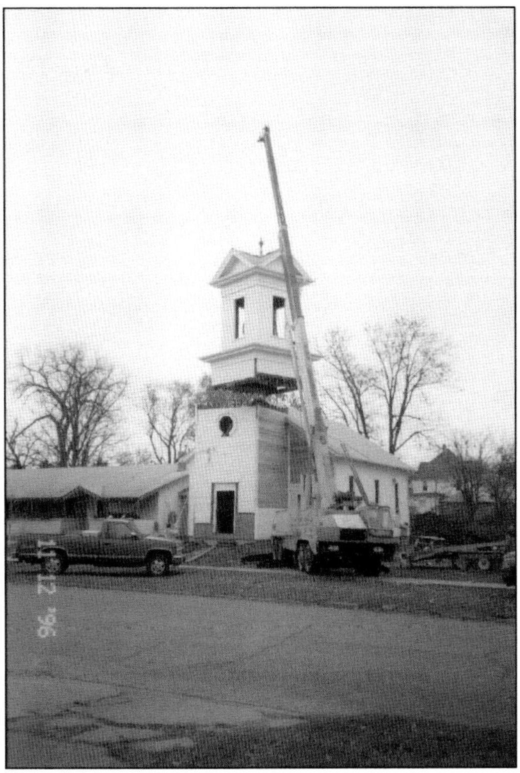

Adding the steeple was the final step when the Chester Church (United Church of Christ Congregational of Chester Township) was moved in 1996 from its rural location to become the sanctuary for St. Paul's Episcopal Church at Sixth Avenue and State Street—a seven-mile trip. The wood-frame building was constructed in 1868. St. Paul's had its beginnings in Grinnell in 1872. (DCL.)

Five

LIVING IN COMMUNITY

Come right in and stop with me till you find a place. We are going to have a good town right here.

—Loyal Phelps, early settler

J.B. Grinnell set an activist tone for his new community that has continued to the present day. Desiring a town that followed his devotion to church and school and supported his antislavery and temperance beliefs, J.B. encouraged civic involvement.

In 1856, the town organized a lyceum "to take mental measure of one another and of their neighbors . . . both men and women participated and took active roles."

From the beginning, organizations have played a large part in community life. The initial structure was provided by the church, specifically the Congregational church, which was the center of civic and social activity for more than 100 years.

Early women's organizations included the Elizabeth Earle Magoun Club, established in 1870 and named after the wife of the first president of Grinnell College; Historical and Literary Club, started in 1881; Drummond Club (1886); Priscilla Club (1892); Entre Nous (1898); and Tuesday Club (1898). All are active today.

Men had their organizations too: the Masonic Lodge, formed locally in 1869, and business-oriented groups such as the Franklin Club (1887) and the Poweshiek Club (1903).

The arts have always been important in Grinnell. The college offers a variety of arts experiences, most of them free of charge and open to the public. A local theater group, the Grinnell Community Theater, was organized in 1972. When a new library was built in 2009, the old library was turned into the Grinnell Arts Center.

For many years, residents have banded together for political purposes and community service. In the late 1960s and early 1970s, many townspeople became involved in the college's antiwar protests and peace marches. The famed Iowa caucuses bring political hopefuls to town every four years. Volunteers currently help in the schools, assist at the library and the hospital, clean up the parks, and work to aid those in need in the community.

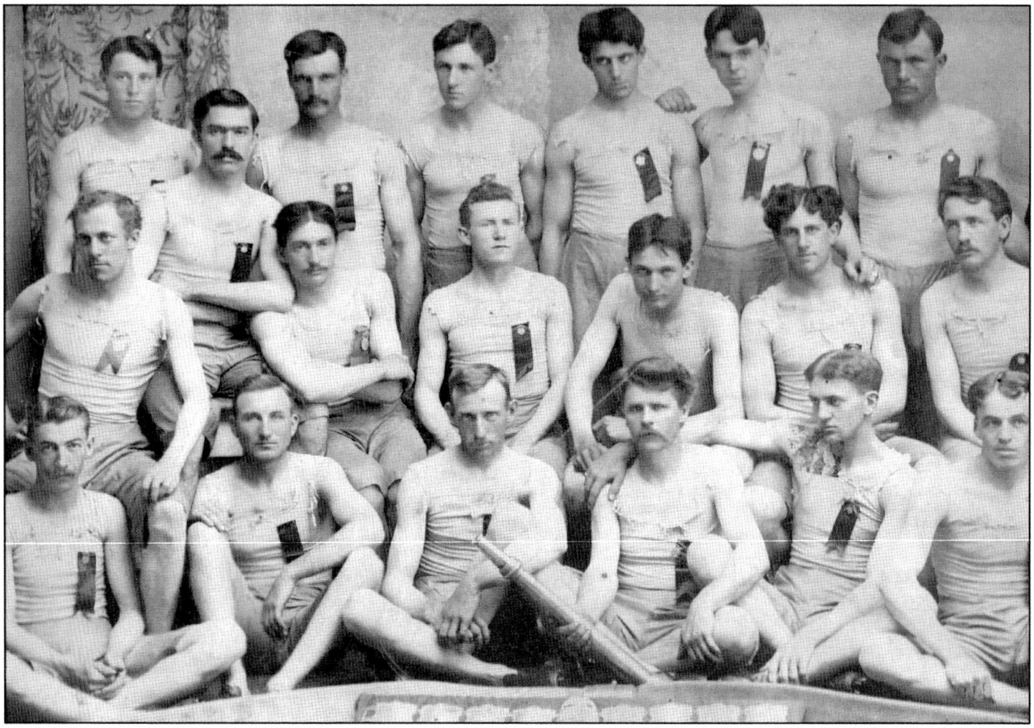

The Fire Department was known in the late 1890s as the E.W. Clark Hose Team, named for Dr. E.W. Clark, physician and mayor who took an active interest in the department. Besides fighting fires, the hose team won a state championship in 1895 for speed in pulling a hose cart. The department history acknowledges, however, that the team was fortified for the competition with a number of recruits, including several well-known college athletes. (GHM.)

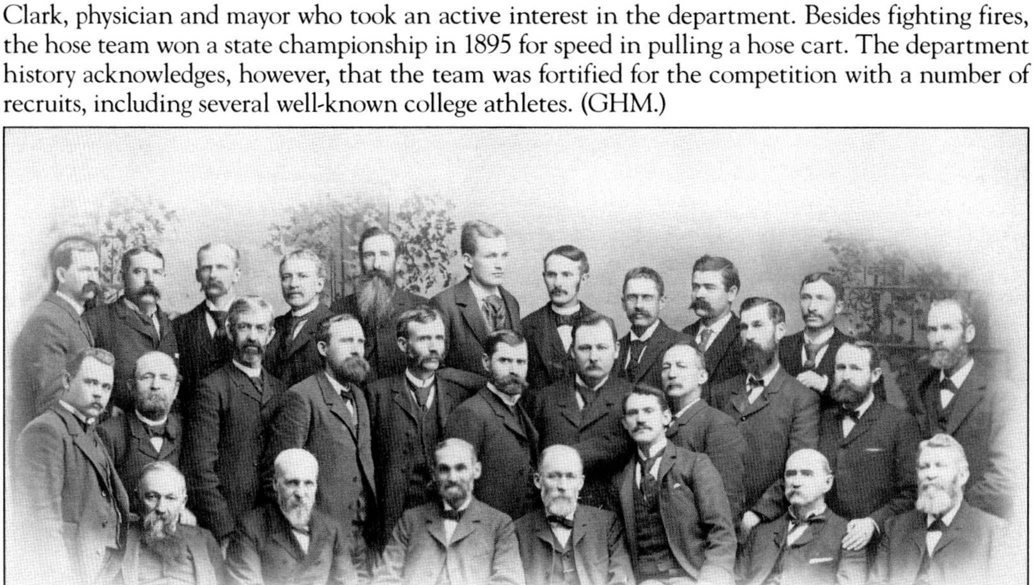

Before there was a local chamber of commerce there was the Franklin Club, organized in 1887 for the purpose of "social and intellectual improvement of the members and the advantages of the business interests of the city of Grinnell." Members in this 1893 photograph were familiar names in early Grinnell—C.R. Morse, E.W. Clark, George H. Hamlin, Arthur Child, and J.H. McMurray. (GHM.)

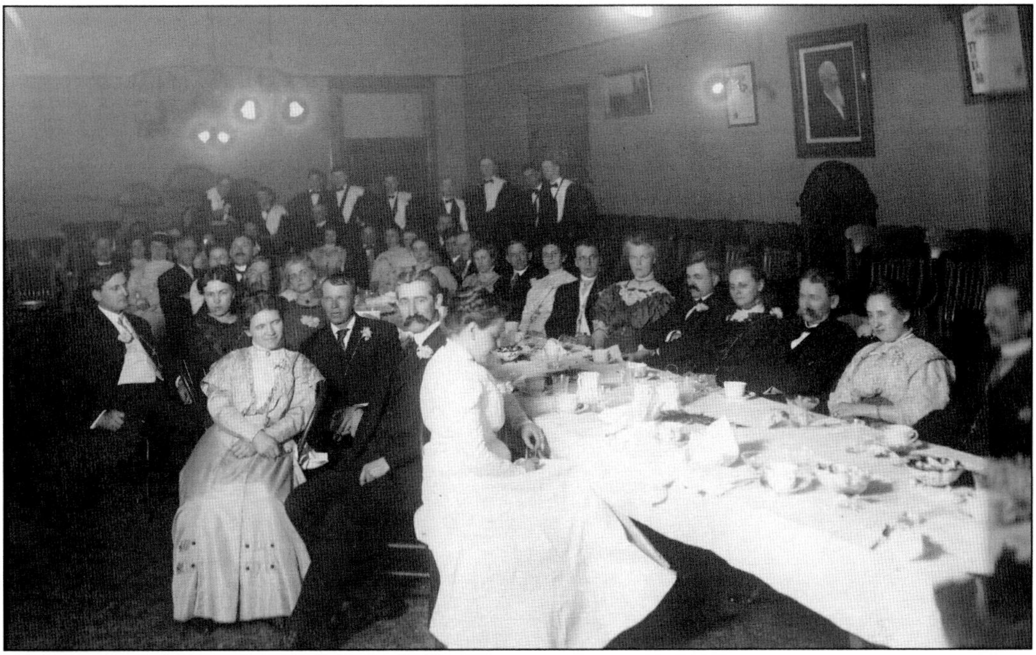

The Tuesday Club gathered with husbands for a special dinner in 1910. The club was organized in 1898 for the purpose of "a good time generally." Programs included book reviews, travelogues, and discussions of civic problems. The club was the first to suggest the idea of a local historical museum. More than a century later, the group still meets monthly—on Tuesdays, of course. (DCL.)

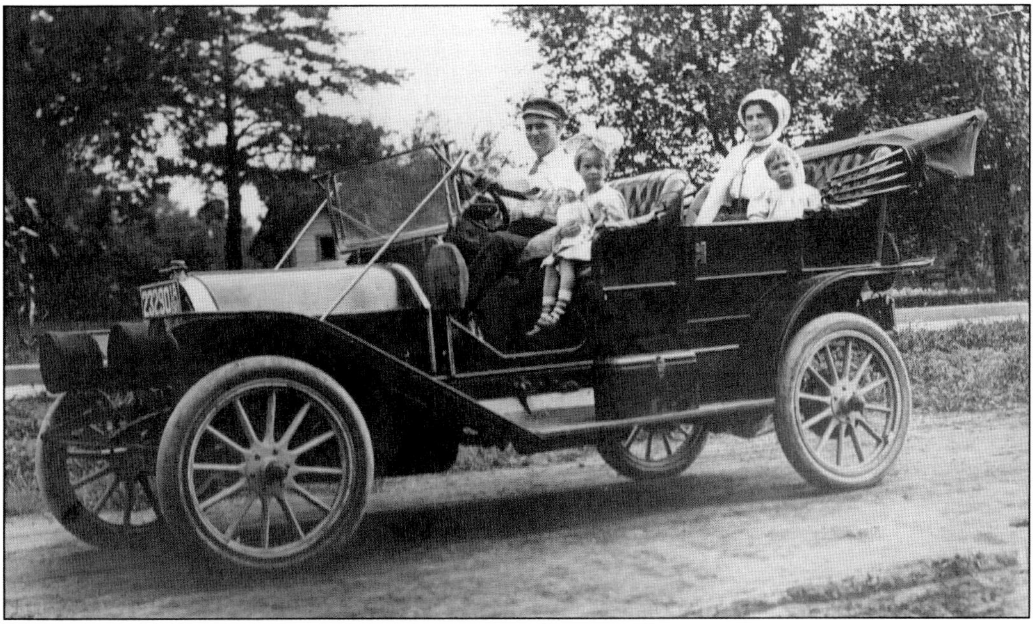

Grinnell dentist A.J. Brock; his wife, Edith; daughter Beatrice, three and a half years old; and son Atwood, one and a half years old, were photographed in their Spaulding automobile in 1911 in front of their home at 917 Tenth Avenue. Atwood grew up to become a dentist like his father. When A.J. died in 1940, Atwood took over his father's practice and continued in dentistry until 1973. (DCL.)

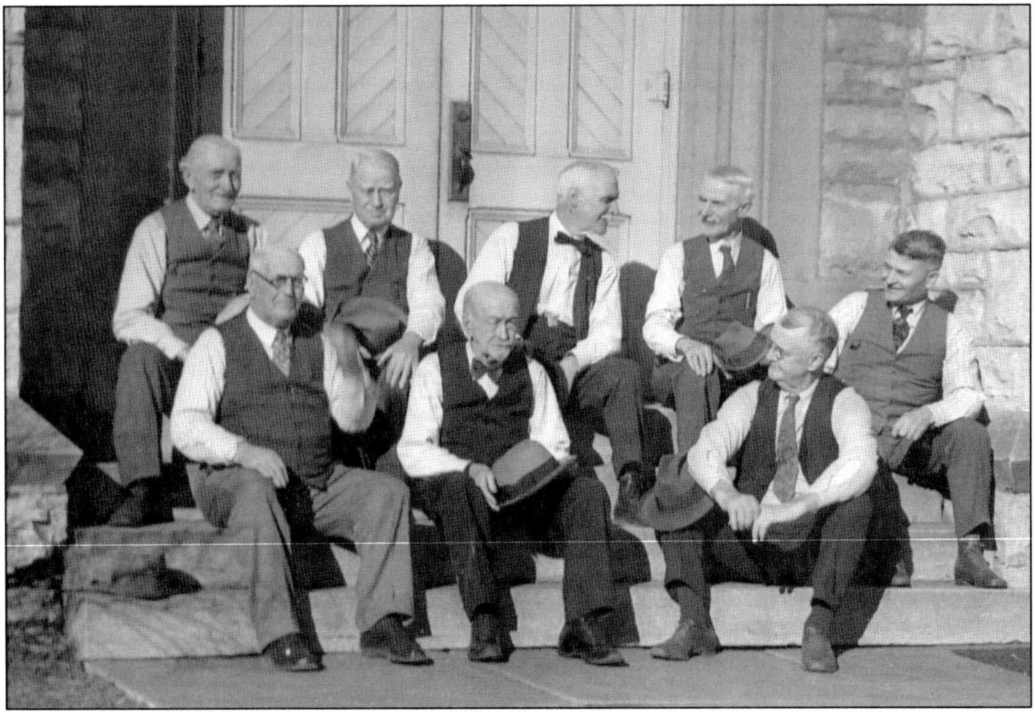

Years ago, turning age 70 must have been the equivalent of reaching age 90 today. In a photograph labeled "70 and over Men," a group of friends or perhaps business associates celebrated their longevity with a gathering and a portrait. Note the hats in hand. (GHM.)

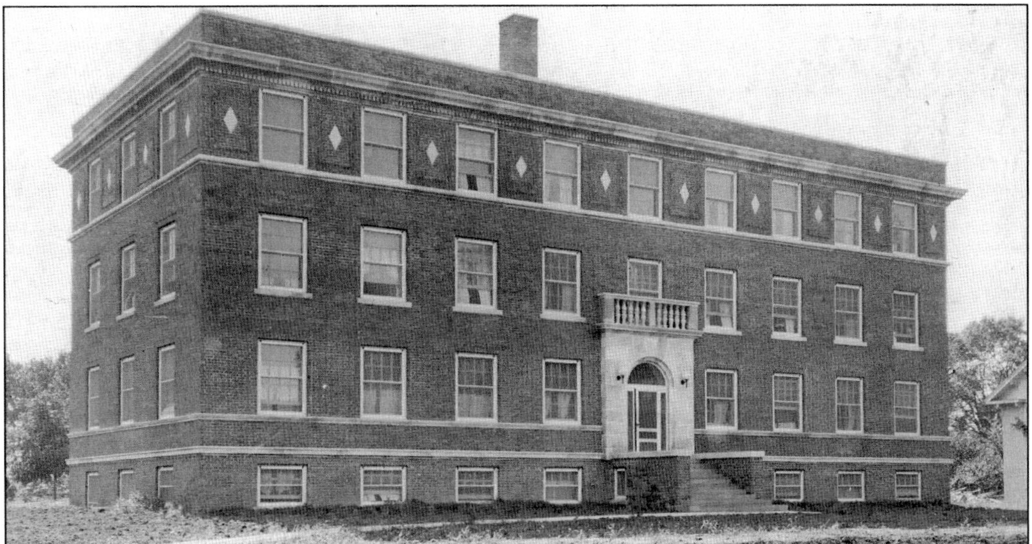

Community Hospital opened in 1919 at Fourth Avenue and Reed Street, on the west side of town, the same year St. Francis Hospital opened on the east side. When it became clear in the early 1960s that two hospitals were not cost-effective, a merger took place in 1967. The new hospital, called Grinnell General Hospital, was located on the former Community Hospital site. In 1994, it was renamed Grinnell Regional Medical Center. St. Francis Hospital became St. Francis Manor. (GHM.)

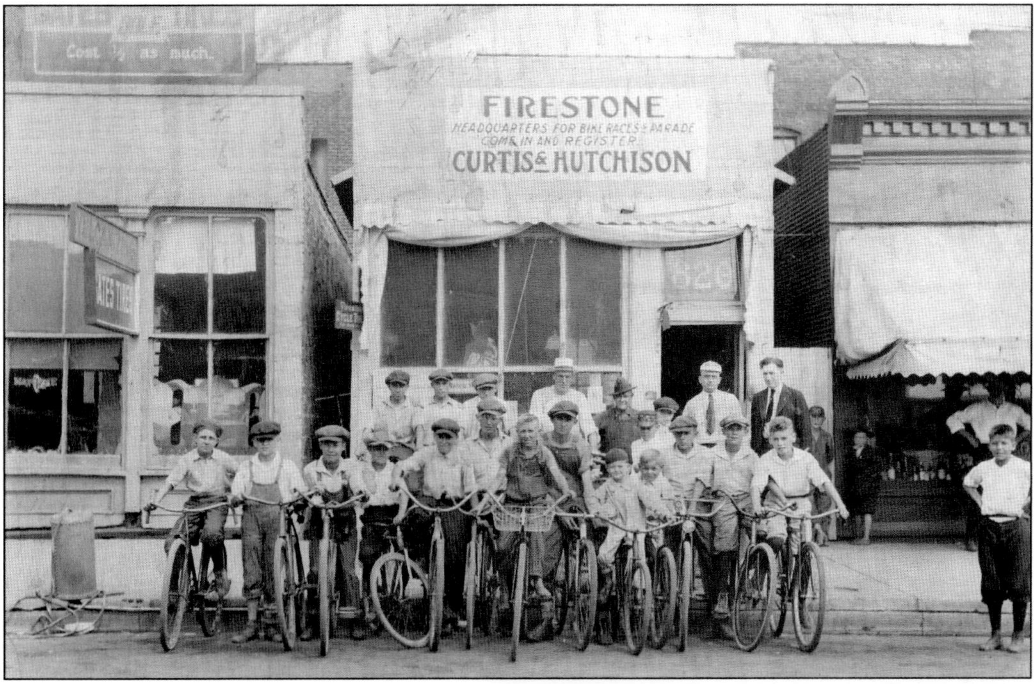

Young men and boys gathered with their bicycles around 1919 in front of Curtis & Hutchison, 820 Main Street, perhaps for the start of a bike race. The sign describes the store as the "Headquarters for races and parades. Come in and register." (Ramsey family.)

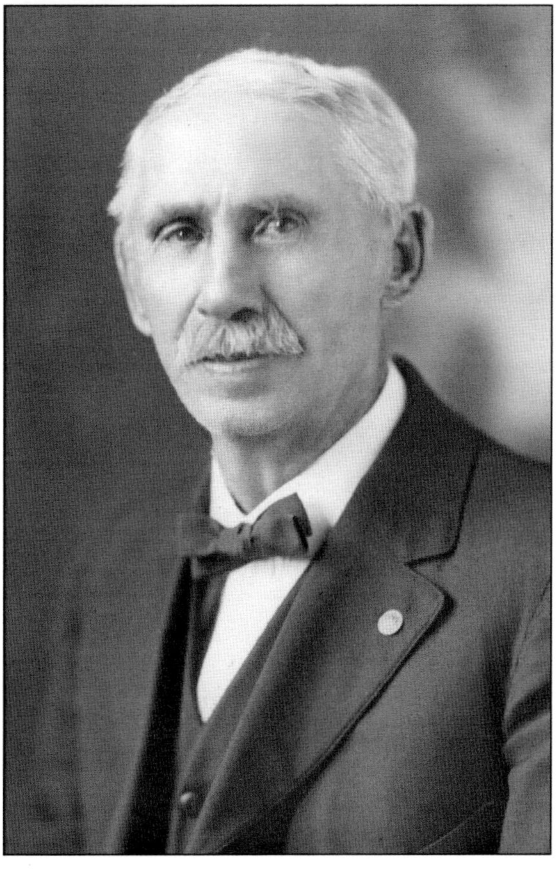

Retired farmer John Campbell in 1931 bequeathed the income from his five farms to the City of Grinnell for the benefit of what he called the "worthy poor." Since 1953, when the provisions of Campbell's will went into effect, several million dollars has been distributed through the Campbell Fund to individuals in need as well as to social agencies that serve them. (GHM.)

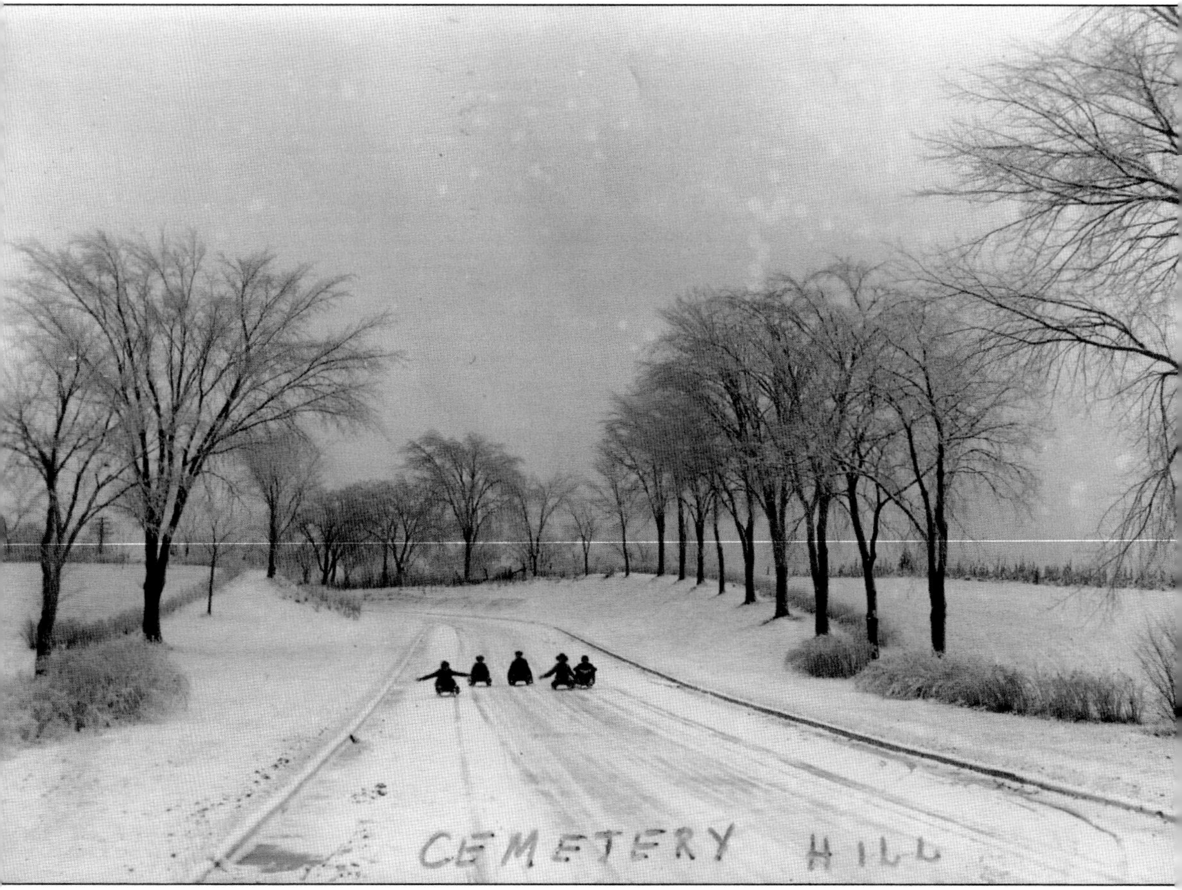

The rolling hills of Hazelwood Cemetery—so different from the relatively flat terrain of the rest of the town—provided sledding opportunities for generations of Grinnell children. Although a location for the cemetery was a subject of brief debate in the beginning, the final choice had unanimous support. J.B. Grinnell wrote the following in his autobiographical reminiscences: "Since its occupation, there has been but one opinion as to the beautiful locality, with a sunny slope, ravines made by water courses, and a natural adaptation for ornamentation." (The fact that J.B. himself donated the first 13 acres may have changed a few minds.) The cemetery was enlarged in 1880 with a donation from the Independent Order of Odd Fellows. The photograph above was taken in 1921 by Cornelia Clarke, a scientific photographer whose work was known throughout the United States as well as in England and Australia. The majority of her photographs were taken in her backyard or around Grinnell. Born in 1854, the year Grinnell was founded, she was a 1909 graduate of Iowa (Grinnell) College. (DCL.)

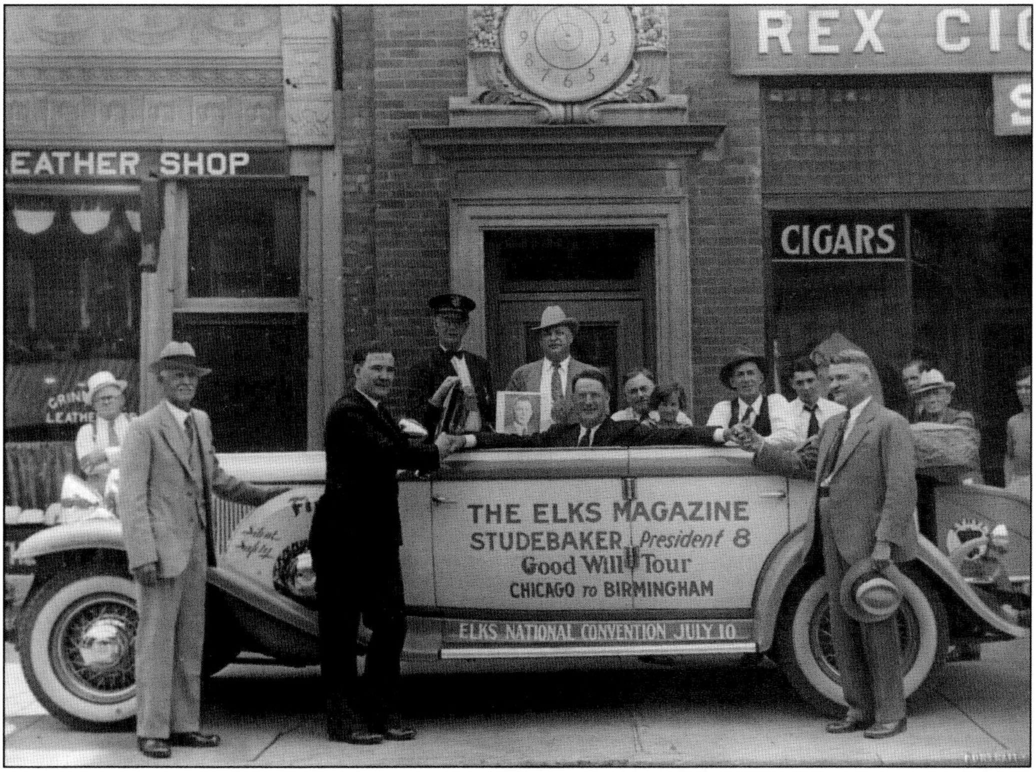

A group from Grinnell's Elks Lodge No. 1266 gathered for a photograph in 1932 before heading off to the national convention. The local lodge was organized in 1912 with 30 charter members. The meeting place for many years was the second and third floors of the commercial building at the southeast corner of Fourth Avenue and Main Street. (Joan Postels Heimsoth.)

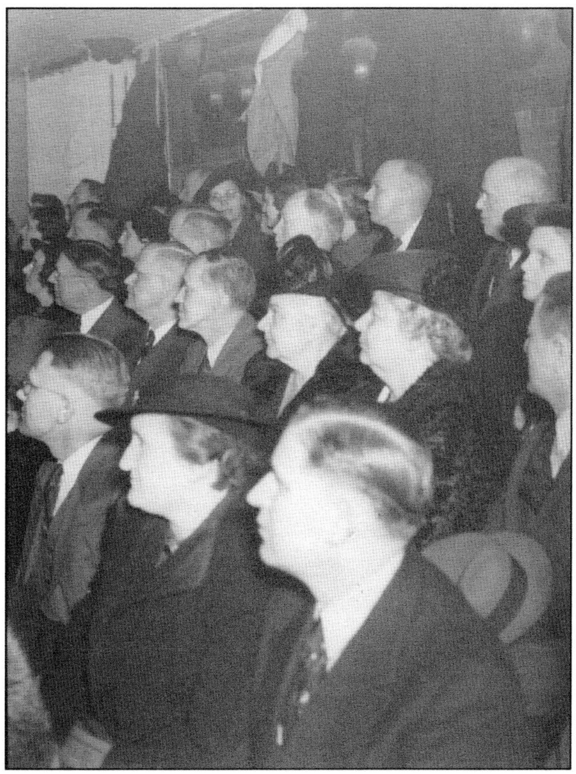

Harry Hopkins, one of Pres. Franklin D. Roosevelt's closest advisors during the Depression and World War II, was a graduate of both Grinnell High School and Grinnell College. Despite the demands of his job, he returned to Grinnell regularly to visit family and reconnect with the college. He is shown here, fourth from left in the second row, with other townspeople at a college basketball game about 1940. (Joan Postels Heimsoth.)

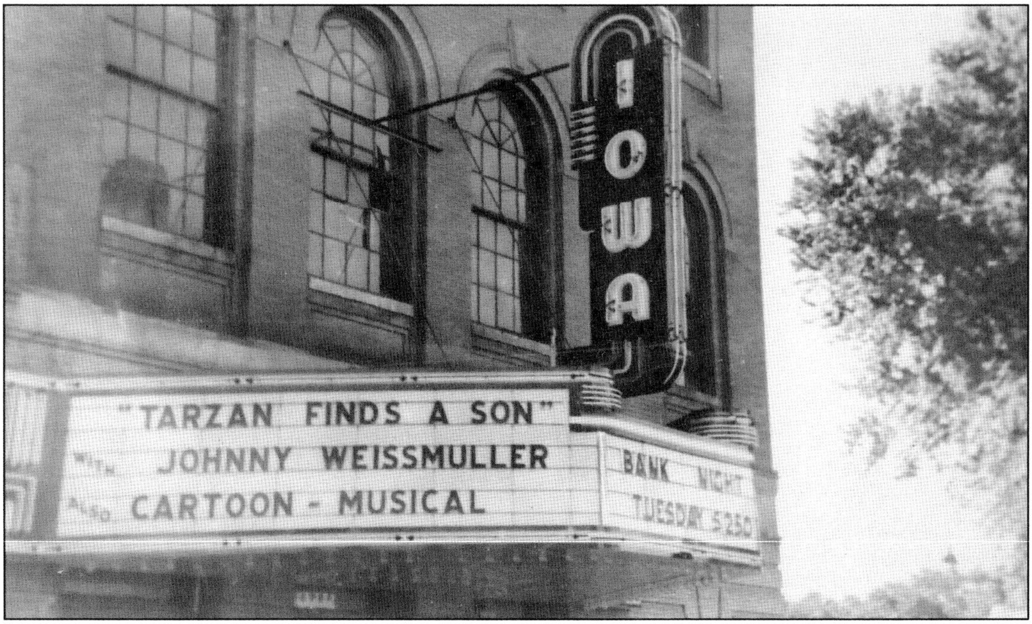

The Iowa Theater at 933 Main Street started out in 1902 as the Colonial Theater, site of touring stage plays, community events, and college productions. Films were added in the 1930s, and the theater was renamed the Iowa Theater in 1935. The marquee in the photograph advertises the 1939 film, *Tarzan Finds a Son*, and Bank Night, a lottery-type fad that was popular during the Depression. (GHM.)

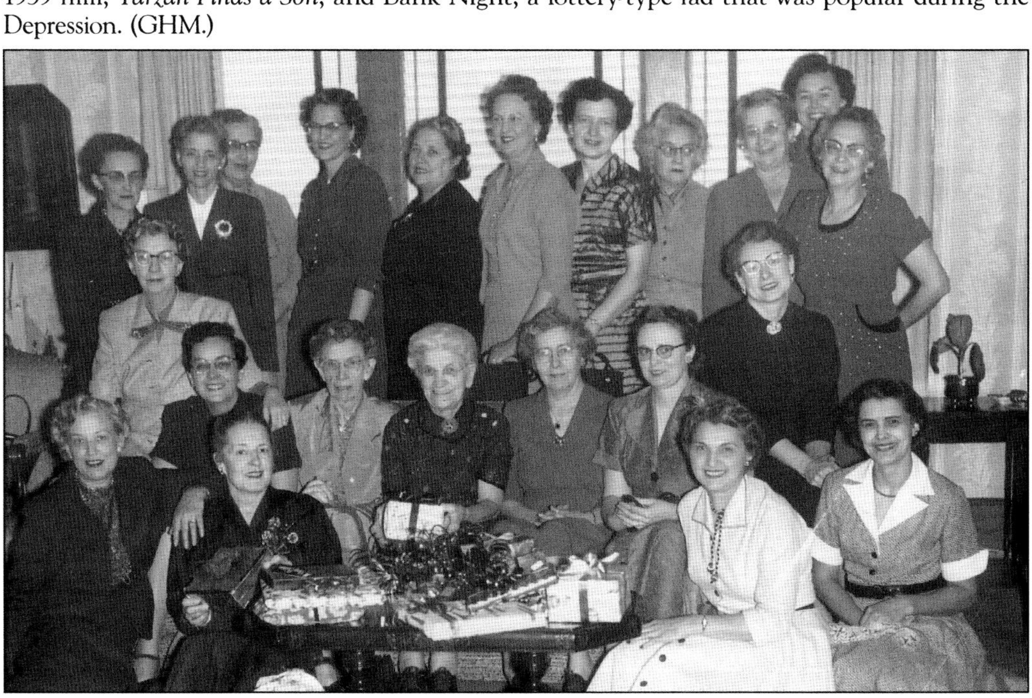

The Drummond Club gathered for a picture at its Christmas party in 1954 at the home of Orpha Mathews. Members exchanged gifts and listened to a reading of *Let's Keep Christmas*, written by Peter Marshall. The club was founded by six women in 1886 for the purpose of literary study and discussion. It was named for Henry Drummond, author of the first book read by the group. (DCL.)

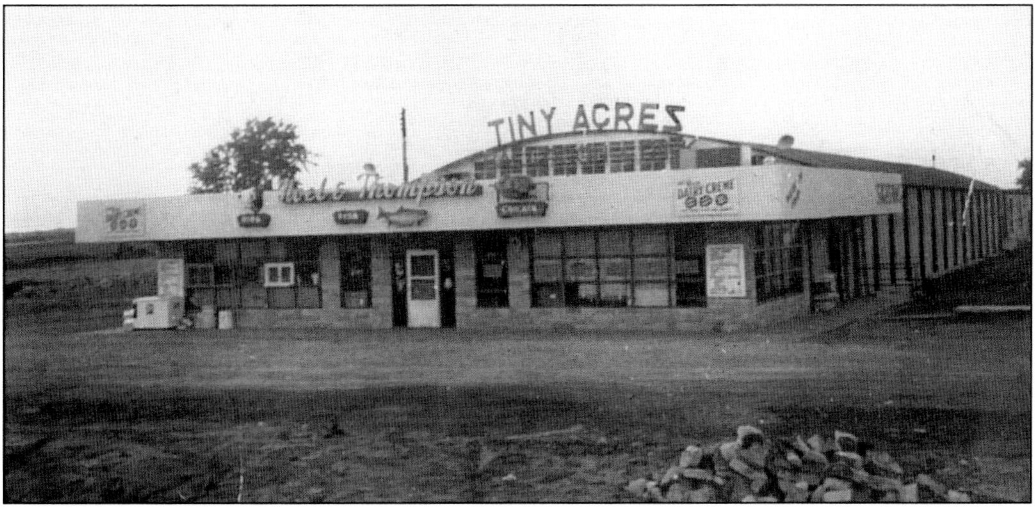

Tiny Acres, a roller-skating rink, opened on Highway 6 west of Grinnell in 1956. Farold "Dude" Murphy and his wife, Edith, along with Eddie Andersen, operated it. The Murphys started in business in the early 1950s with a skating rink under a tent in Central Park. They eventually moved the tent to the Highway 6 location and then moved into a metal building on the site. Other buildings there included the Tiny Acres apartments and a restaurant called Noels Café. The rink's star attraction (below) was a chimpanzee, Tony, who could skate on one foot, jump over obstacles, and help children get back on their feet when they fell. Adults who skated at Tiny Acres as children say they still remember the feel of Tony's leathery fingers when he grabbed their hands for a whirl around the wooden floor. Eddie Andersen was the floor manager of the rink and also operated a small manufacturing company in the building. (Both, Eddie Andersen family.)

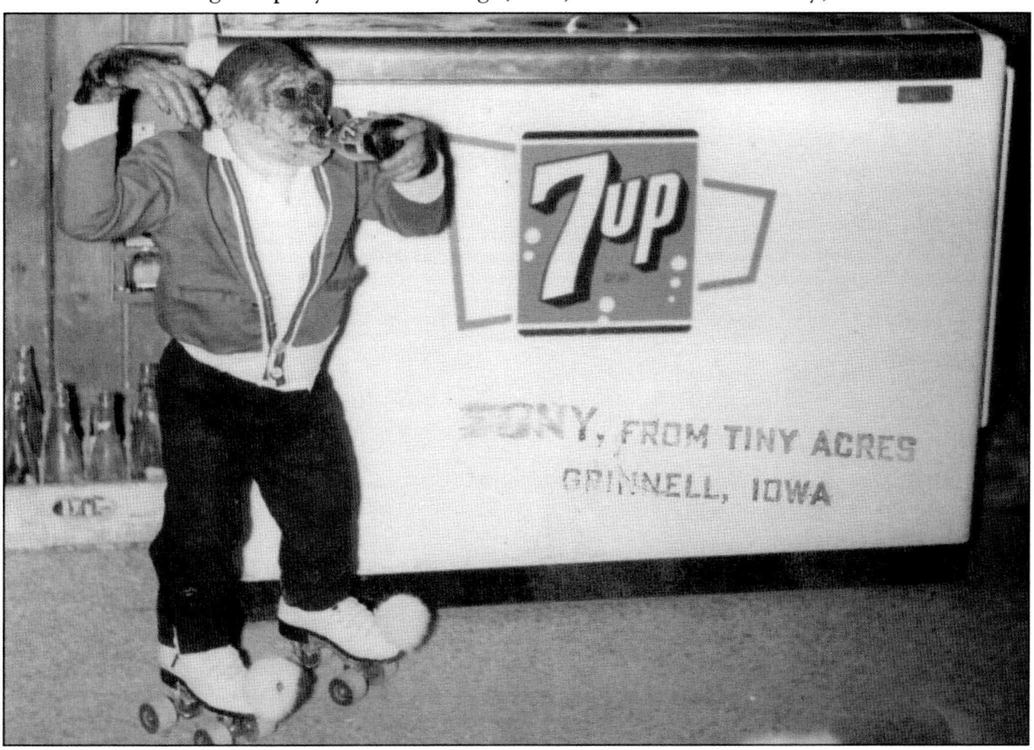

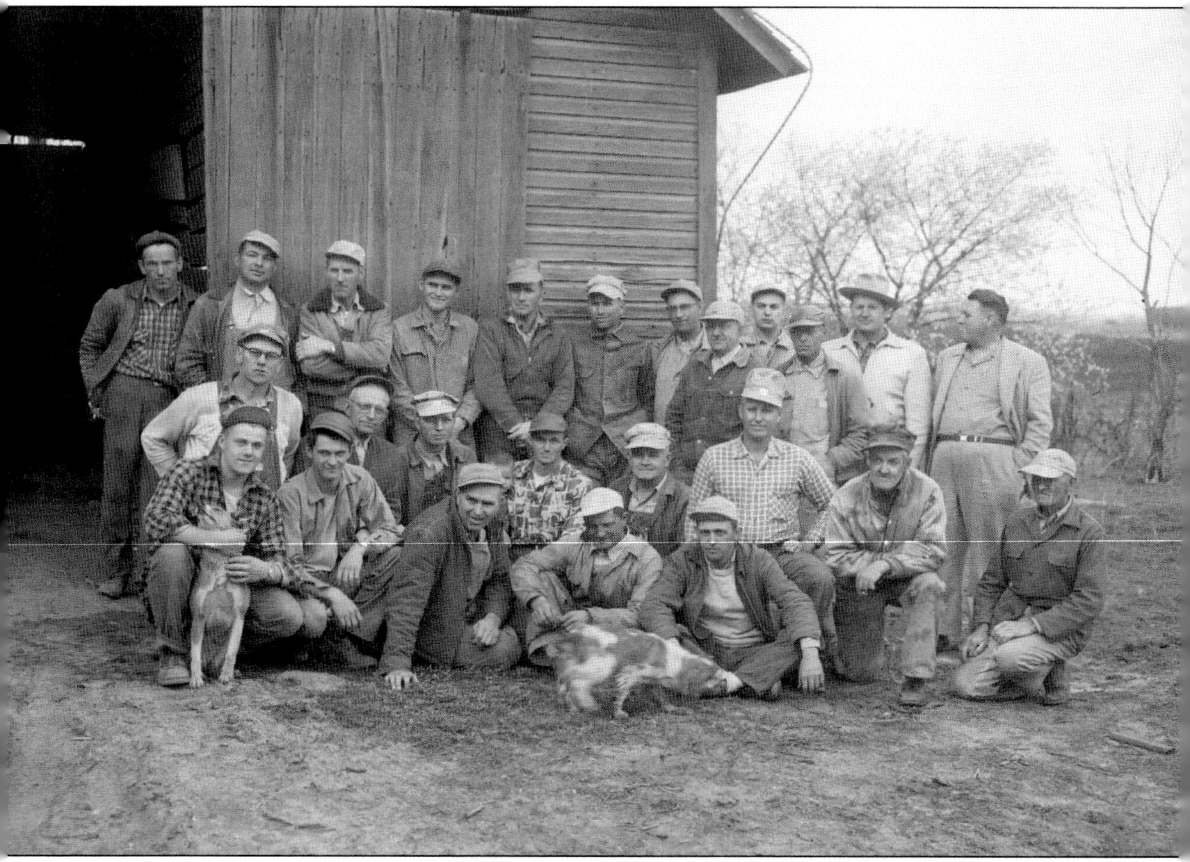

Neighbors and friends stepped in to help with spring planting in May 1954 at the farm of Dave Krumm in Chester Township north of Grinnell. Krumm had sustained a serious leg injury and could not work at the critical time in the growing season. From left to right are (first row) Richard Bailey, John Krumm, Bernard Young, Paul Krumm, Melvin Stoker, Wilbur Foster, Wilbur Elliott, and Claude Reeves; (second row) Harley McIlrath, C.B. Cross, Lawrence Wallis, Edward Breeden, and Lee Bailey; (third row) Al Cross, Don Renaud, Ross Mintle, Don Pederson, Harry Ryan, Floyd Lacina, Glen Harris, W.G. Greenwald, Harlan Shine, Paul Foster, L.W. Wright, and Sam Neff. Not pictured are Clarence Sharp and Walter Howell. The caption for the newspaper photograph noted that the men had plowed 70 acres in one hour and 10 minutes. (*Grinnell Herald-Register.*)

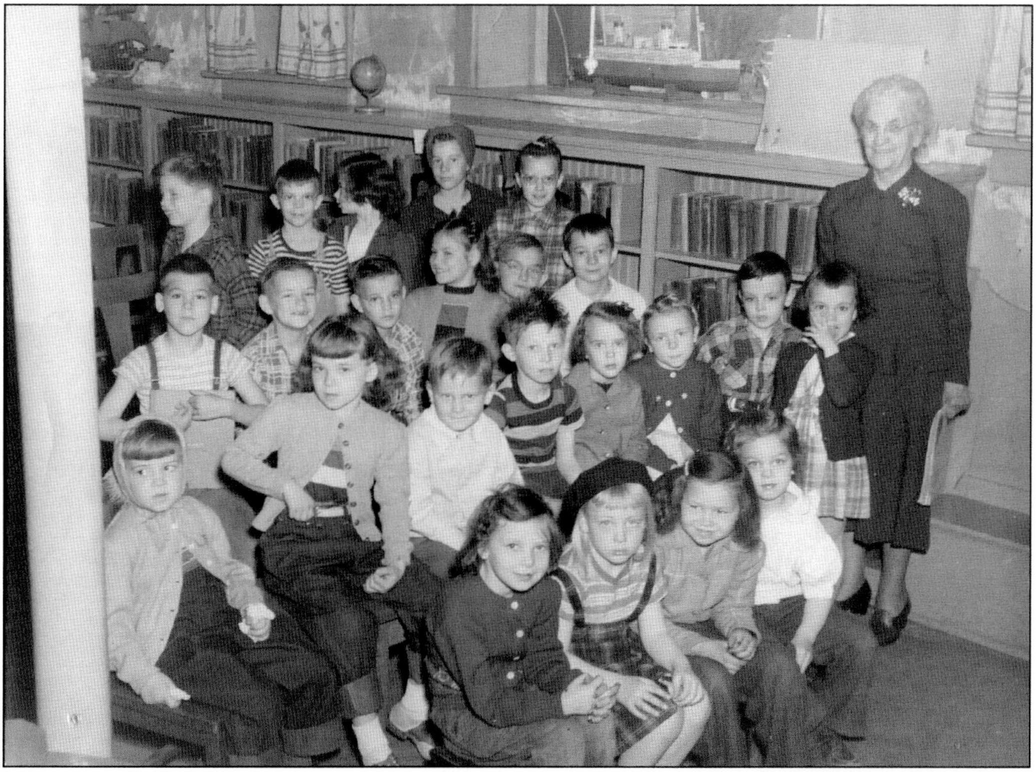

Library story hours have been popular with generations of children and parents in Grinnell. In the mid-1950s in the lower level of Stewart Library, Clara Nelson, wife of W.B. Nelson, was a popular volunteer "story lady." Records indicate that the library paid her taxi fare to and from the library, allowing a stop at the grocery store on the way home. (DCL.)

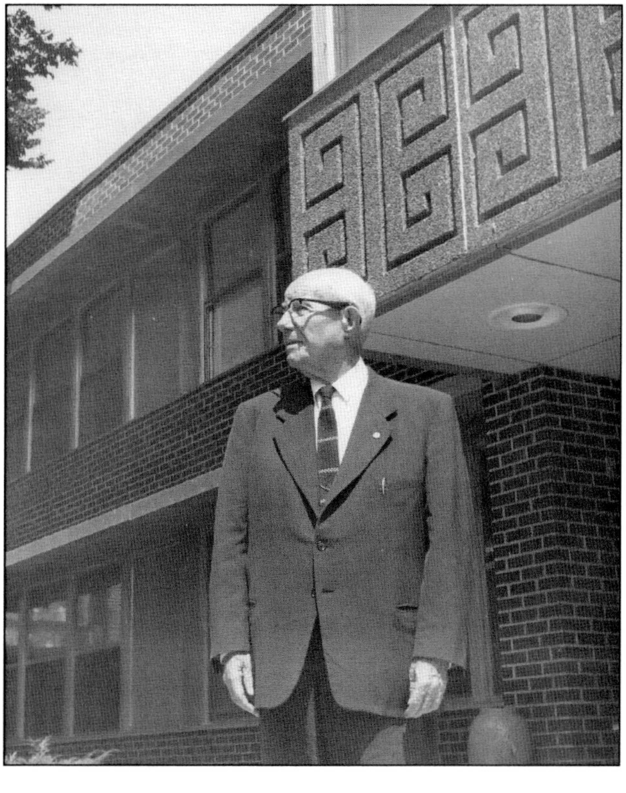

The vision of the Reverend Royal Montgomery, a retired Congregational minister, led to the founding in 1950 of the Mayflower Home. Montgomery's initial desire to provide housing for retired clergy started with a single house converted into four apartments and expanded over the years to become a large continuing-care complex called Mayflower Community that is open to all. The photograph is dated 1961. (DCL.)

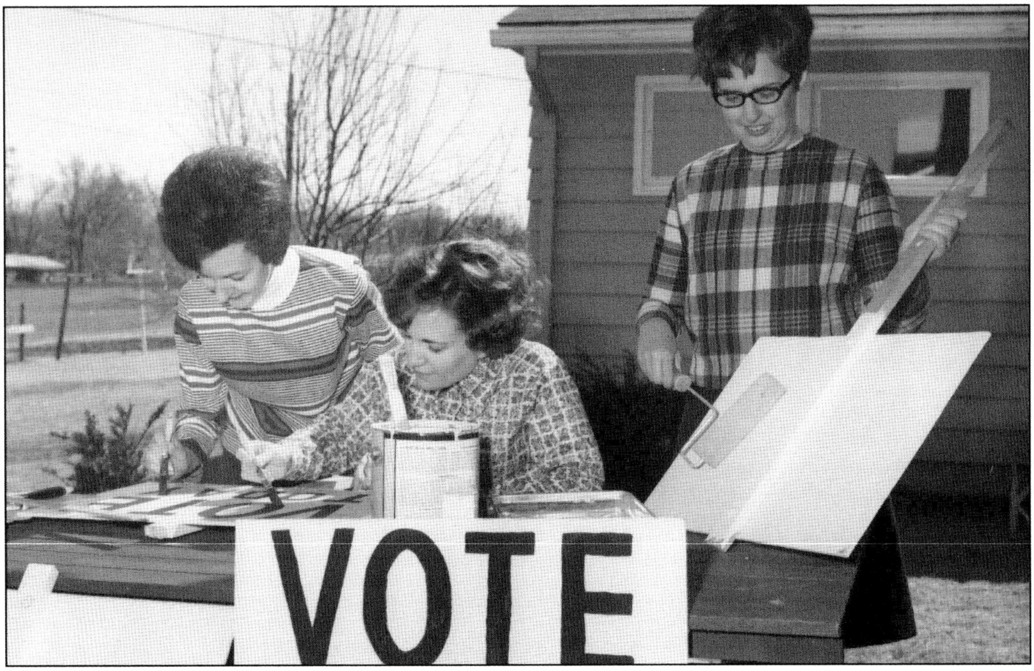

Members of the Grinnell League of Women Voters worked to create awareness of upcoming elections by making and distributing lawn signs reminding residents of Election Day. Pictured in this 1969 photograph are, from left to right, Margaret Gullett, Marilyn Strovers, and Carol Nielsen. The Grinnell League of Women Voters was organized in 1923. (DCL.)

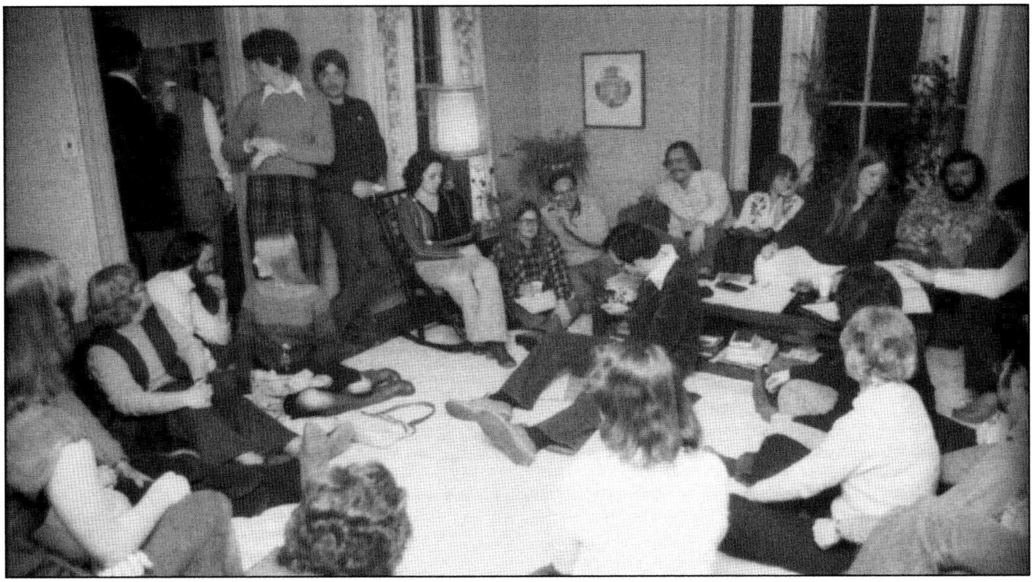

Grassroots politics took hold in Iowa starting in 1972 with party caucuses held to determine presidential preferences. In the early years, many caucuses were held in private homes, like the one pictured here in Grinnell's Fourth Ward in January 1980. Local preferences among Democrats that year were Jimmy Carter and Edward Kennedy. In a straw poll among Republicans, the preferences were, in order, George H.W. Bush, Ronald Reagan, Howard Baker, and John Anderson. (*Grinnell Herald-Register.*)

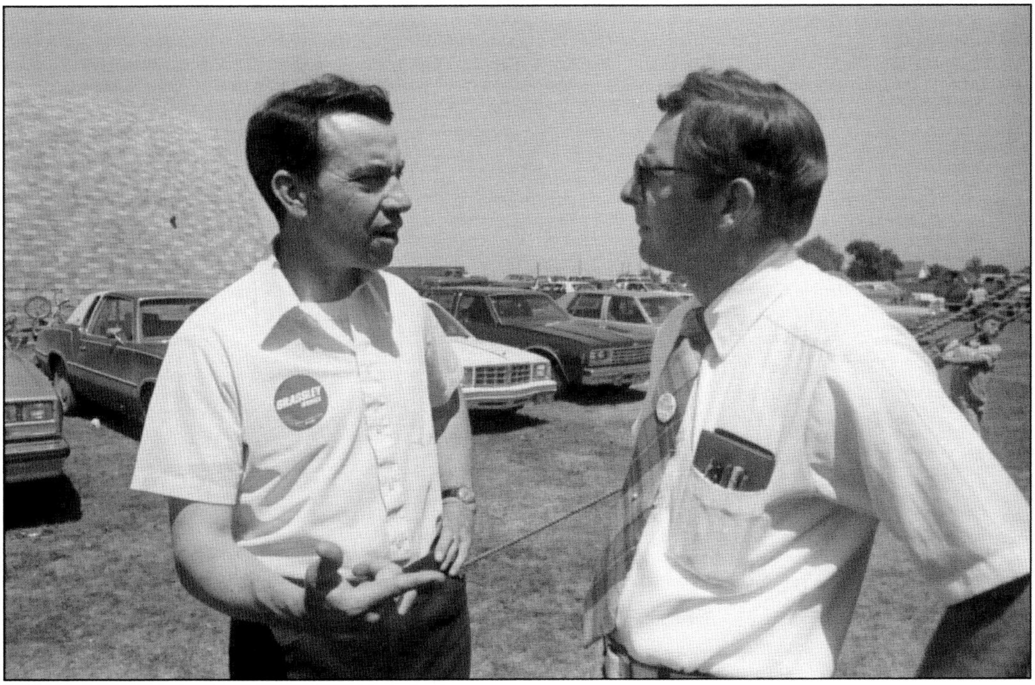

US congressman Chuck Grassley (left) chatted with Grinnell resident Montie Redenius during a campaign stop at the Poweshiek County 4H-FFA Fair in August 1980. Grassley, a Republican who had served six years in the US House of Representatives, was campaigning across the state for a seat in the US Senate. He won the November election, defeating incumbent John Culver. (*Grinnell Herald-Register.*)

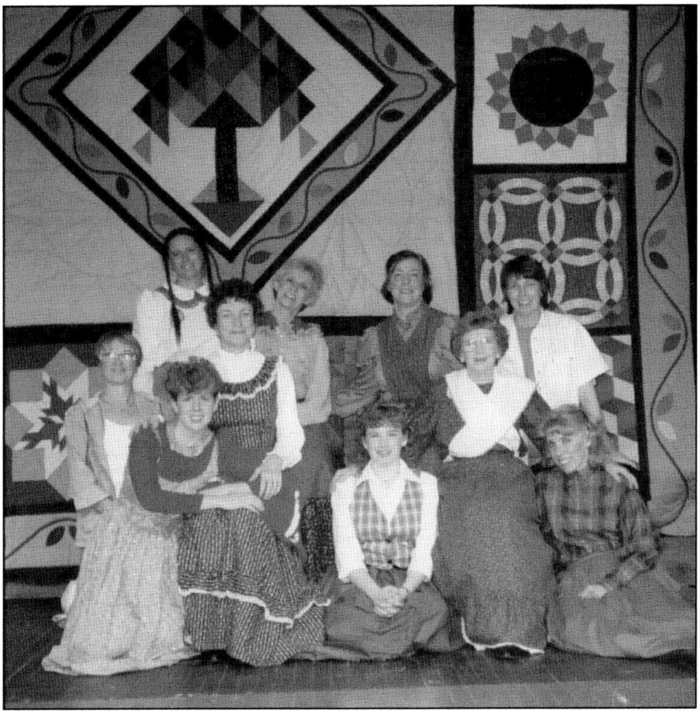

"Quilters," a musical based on the lives of American pioneer women, was produced in 1987 by the Grinnell Community Theater. Cast members included, from left to right, (first row) Christine Urfer, Beth Czechowski, and Pam Stewart; (second row) Babe Voertman, Betty Moffett, and Evelyn Lawson; (third row) Connie Gause, Berneil Mueller, Karen Phillips, and Barb Lien. The Grinnell Community Theater was organized in 1972. (DCL.)

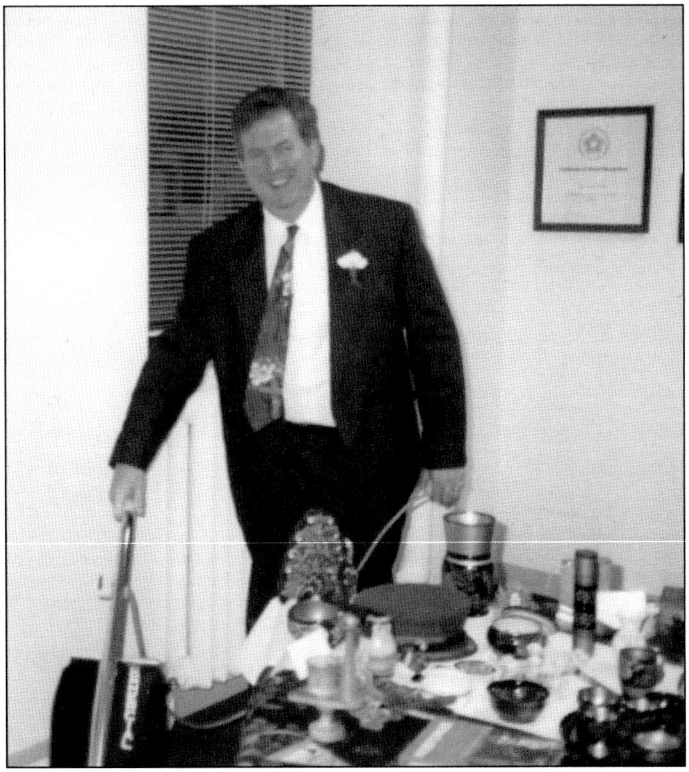

Grinnell partnered in the 1990s with Zheleznovodsk, Russia, in a Sister Cities International relationship designed to foster understanding among people around the world through citizen diplomacy. In this 1993 photograph, Jim White, a longtime member of the Grinnell City Council, prepares a room in the community center for a display of souvenirs that the Grinnell delegation brought back from a visit to Zheleznovodsk. (DCL.)

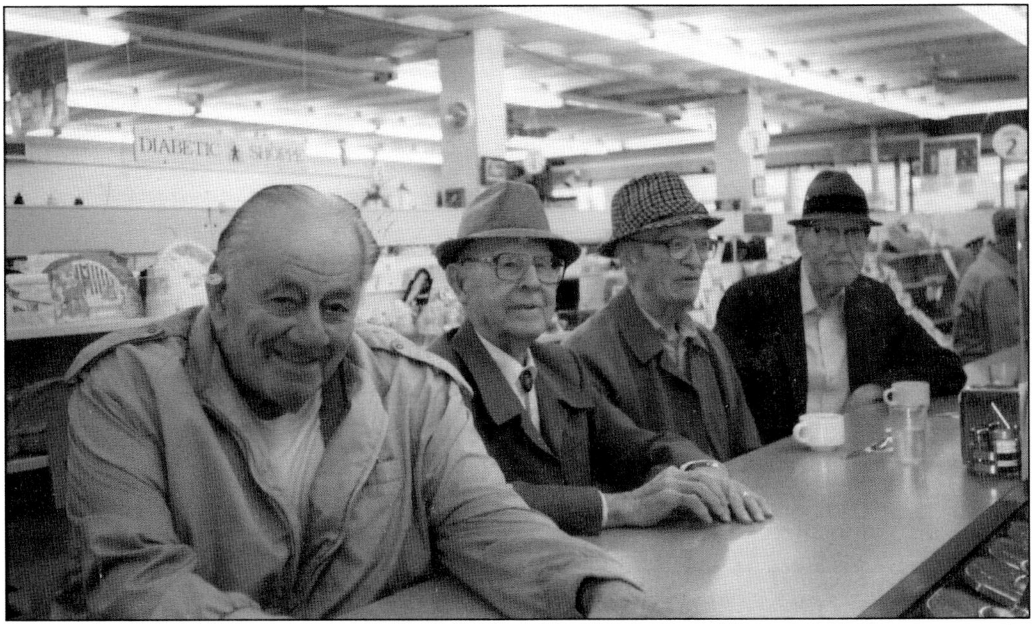

The counter at Cunningham Drug was a popular community gathering spot for many years. The regulars in 1995 included, from left to right, Fred Schmidt, Harold "Shorty" Fetzer, Stanley D. "Stub" Preston, and Art McDowell, all more than 90 years old. In addition to 5¢ cups of coffee, the attractions at Cunningham's included Candyland sundaes, a favorite treat at Candyland, a confectionery once located next door. (Jim Cunningham.)

Six

Meeting the Challenges

We never do things in a halfway fashion. When we have a cyclone, we have a good one, and when we have a bonfire, we pile up enough stuff to let the surrounding country know we are celebrating.

—*Grinnell Herald*, June 1889

Grinnell has faced its share of adversity. The town and college were just getting started in 1861 when the Civil War began, taking away most of the able-bodied males. Eleven college students died in the war.

A cyclone struck Grinnell in 1882, killing 39 and injuring hundreds. The college campus was leveled, and half the houses in town were demolished. (J.B. Grinnell personally raised money for rebuilding the college by soliciting funds from wealthy Eastern friends.) A major fire in 1889 destroyed much of the business district (including the fire department).

The Great Depression got an early start in Iowa and in Grinnell. When the government in 1920 ended price guarantees for crops and livestock that had begun during World War I, farmers experienced declining land values, surplus production, and increasing costs. The Merchants National Bank in Grinnell was among the banks in Iowa that went under in the 1920s. A more recent farm crisis occurred in the 1980s due to low crop prices, high interest rates, and a poor general economy.

Wars in faraway places took their toll on the local community. A total of 25 servicemen from Grinnell were killed in World War II. Twenty-five years later, political unrest over US involvement in Southeast Asia brought disruptions and protests at the college that spilled over into the town. The tension was so high in the spring of 1970 that the college ended classes before the end of the semester and cancelled commencement.

A tornado struck the south edge of Grinnell in 1978, killing six people.

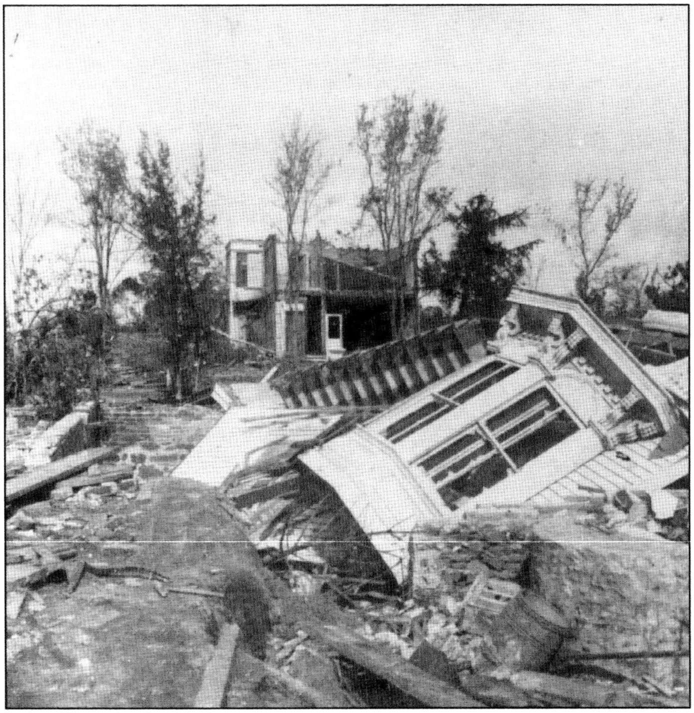

A cyclone devastated the north part of Grinnell on June 17, 1882, killing 39 people, injuring many more, and destroying most of the buildings in its path. "Houses crumbled like matchwood and people were carried for long distances," was one description. The area around Seventh Avenue and Broad Street (left) was at the center of the destruction, although the house in the background, owned by Loyal Phelps, was spared and is still standing at 1205 Broad Street. (GCA.)

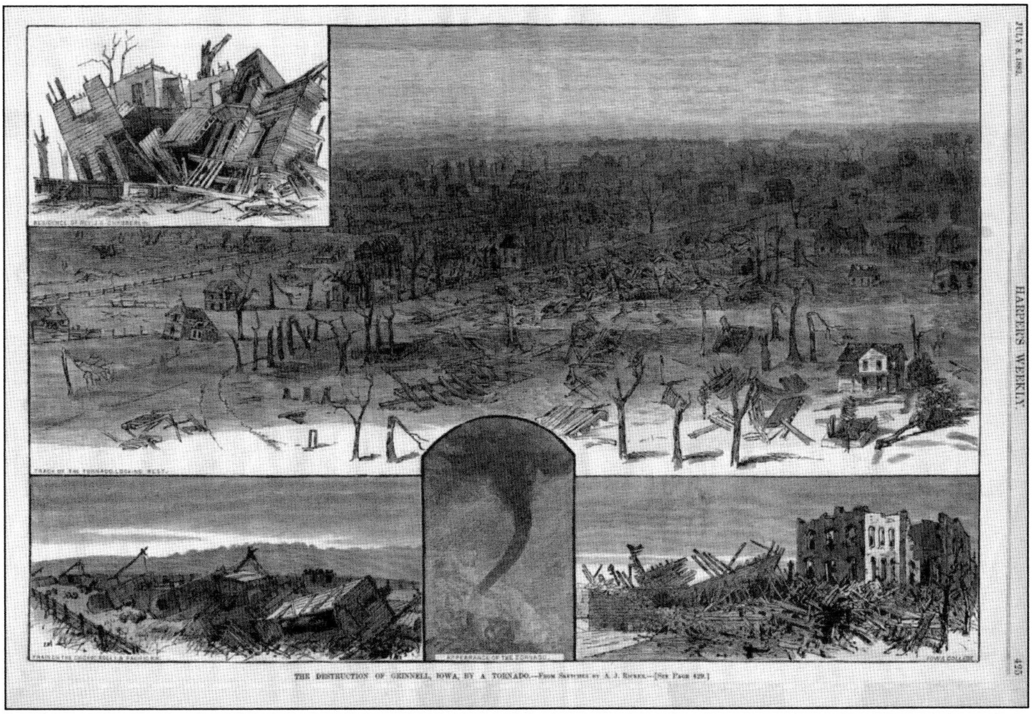

A collection of sketches of the cyclone appeared in the July 8, 1882, issue of *Harper's Weekly*—less than a month after the disaster. The national publicity spread the news in a dramatic way and helped J.B. Grinnell in his quest to raise money from his wealthy Eastern friends to rebuild the college campus. In total, J.B. personally raised $40,000 of the $150,000 that was received in aid. (GHM.)

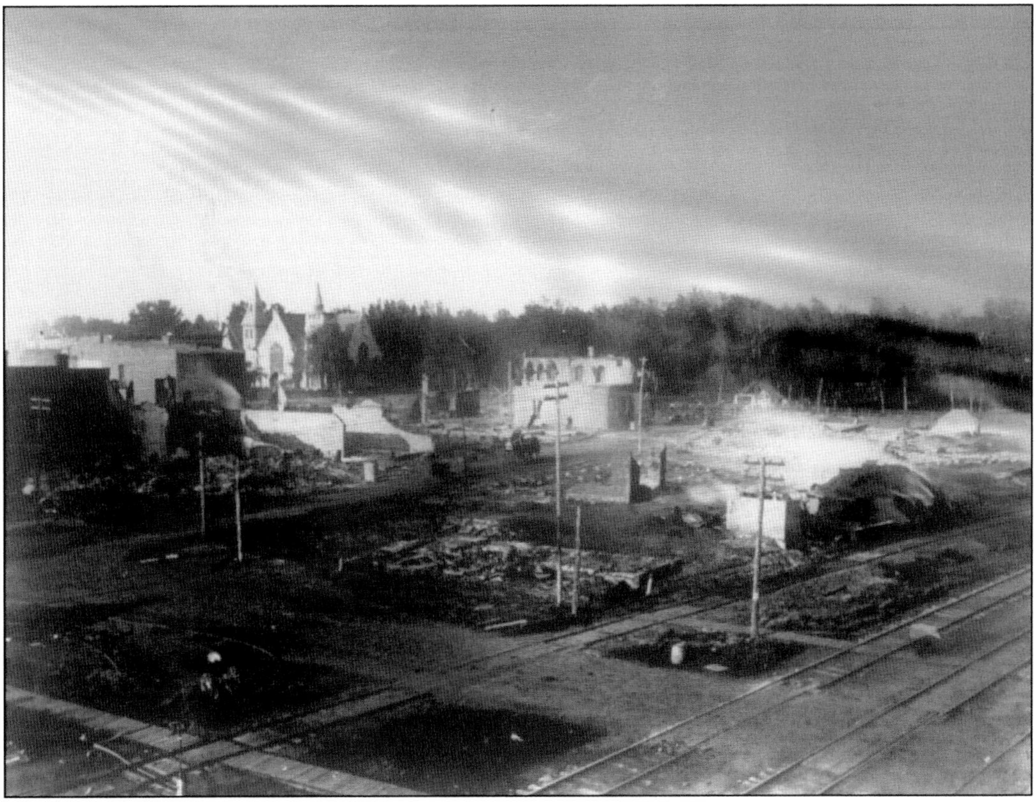

The business district south of Fourth Avenue was in ruins on June 12, 1889, after a fire that started in a grain elevator near the railroad tracks swept east and north, destroying everything in its path. The losses included businesses, the post office, and ironically the fire department. The Congregational church can be seen in the background. Central Park is at the right. (GCA.)

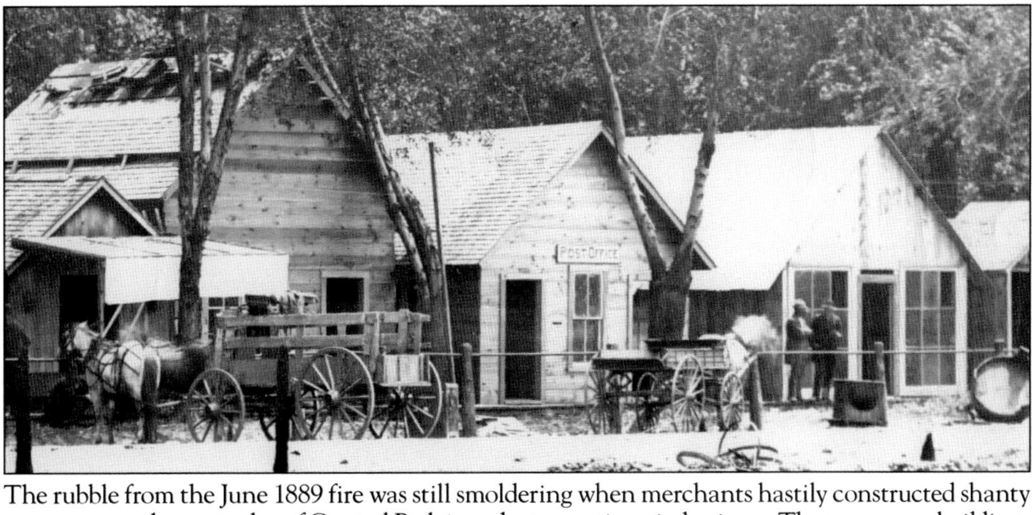

The rubble from the June 1889 fire was still smoldering when merchants hastily constructed shanty structures on the west edge of Central Park in order to continue in business. The temporary buildings included the post office and a bank. The makeshift shops were in use from June until December, when new buildings were ready. (GCA.)

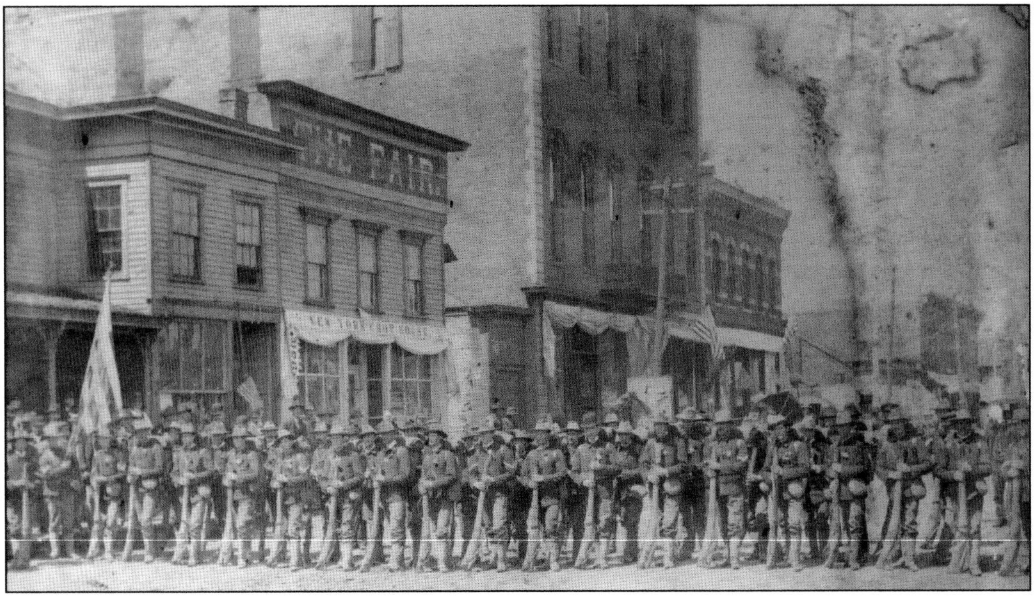

Company K of the Iowa National Guard is shown in front of the Preston Opera House, 831 Main Street, at the start of the Spanish-American War. The company was called up in May 1898, camped for a time in Des Moines, and then was sent to Florida, where it waited out the war until discharge in November. The company used the third floor of the opera house for an armory. (GCA.)

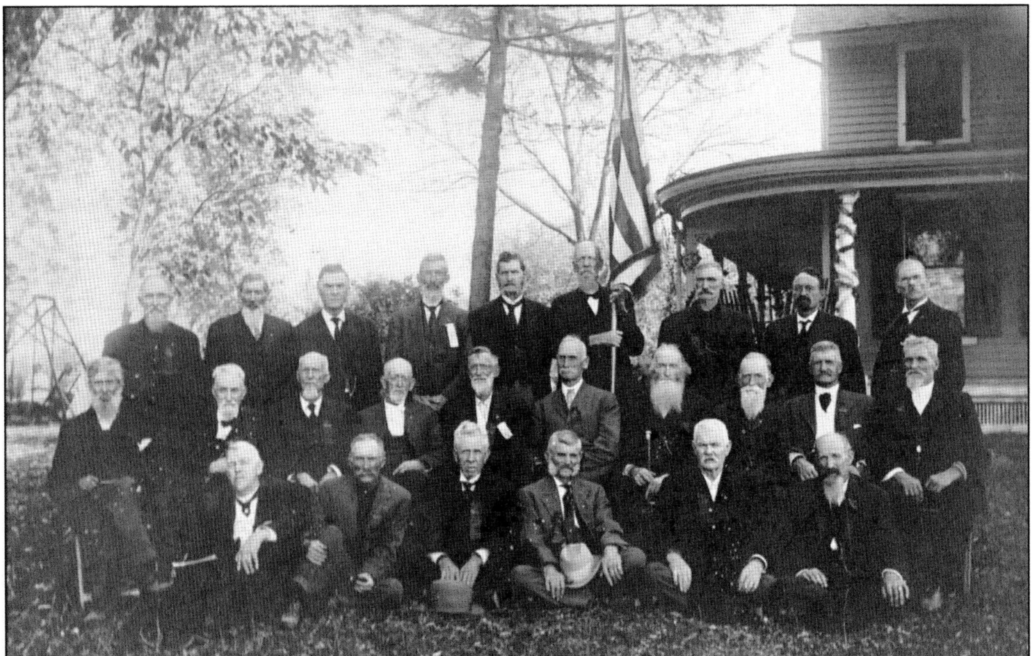

Civil War veterans assembled for a photograph in front of 1302 Broad Street. While some of the veterans were born in Poweshiek County, others came to Grinnell from other states after the war. All were members of the Gordon Granger Post No. 64 of the Grand Army of the Republic. More than 200 Civil War soldiers are buried in Hazelwood Cemetery. The photograph is undated. The house is no longer standing. (Bill McNally.)

Grinnell native Robert J. Garrigan flew a single-engine Army Air Force fighter plane low over the northeast corner of Fourth Avenue and Main Street in downtown Grinnell in the summer of 1942. His daring act apparently was not punished, for he retired as an Air Force colonel. (Bill McNally.)

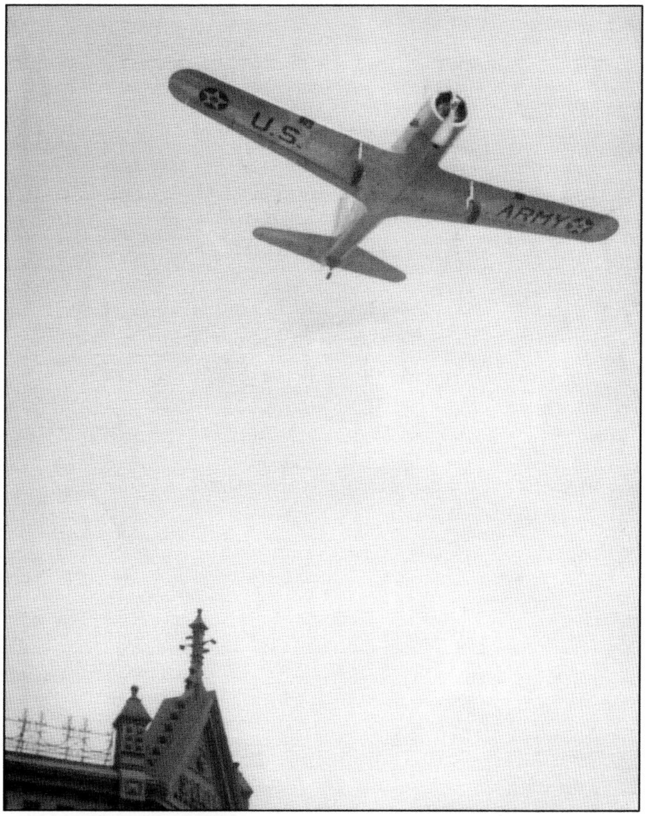

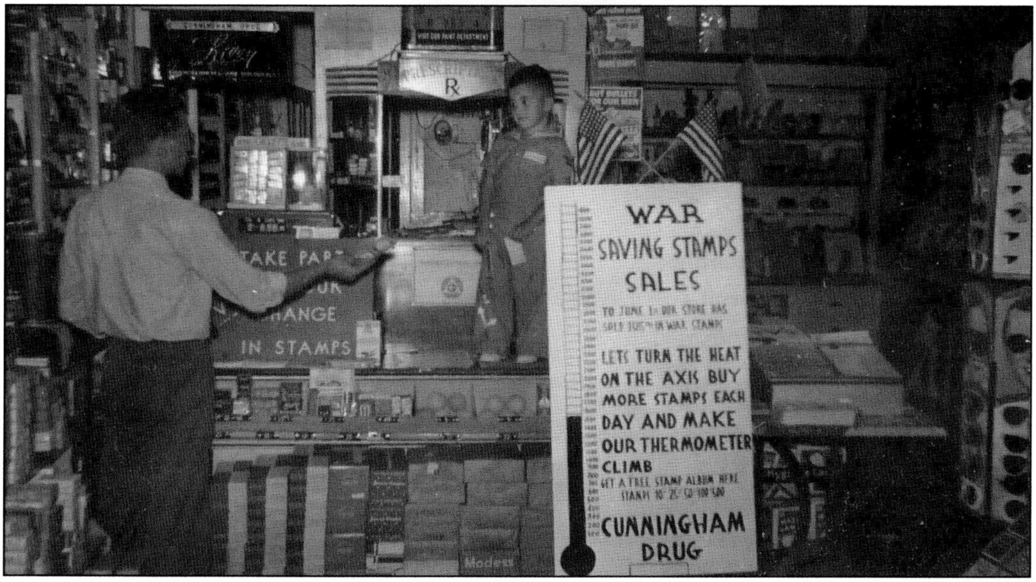

Cunningham Drug, like many local businesses during World War II, promoted the sale of war stamps issued by the US Treasury Department to fund the war effort. Stamps, sold in amounts ranging from 10¢ to $5, were collected in booklets that could be redeemed for war bonds. The photograph shows store owner Don Cunningham and his young son Jim with the many patriotic signs advertising the stamps. (Jim Cunningham.)

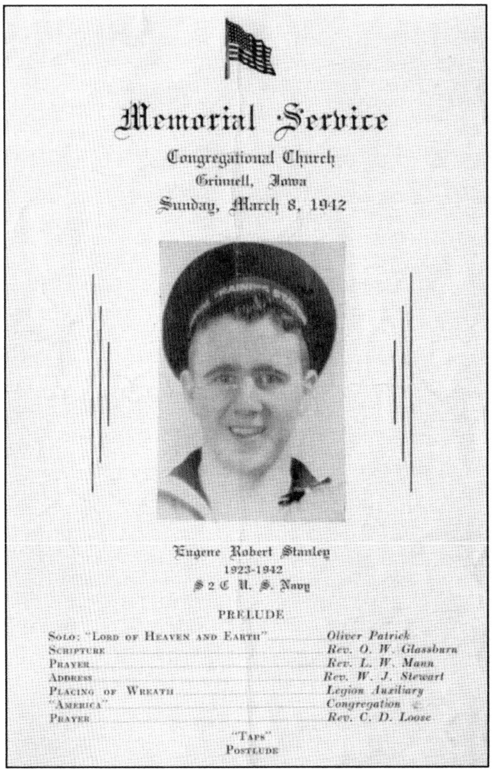

Memorial Service
Congregational Church
Grinnell, Iowa
Sunday, March 8, 1942

Eugene Robert Stanley
1923-1942
S 2 C U. S. Navy

PRELUDE

Solo: "Lord of Heaven and Earth"	*Oliver Patrick*
Scripture	*Rev. O. W. Glassburn*
Prayer	*Rev. L. W. Mann*
Address	*Rev. W. J. Stewart*
Placing of Wreath	*Legion Auxiliary*
"America"	*Congregation*
Prayer	*Rev. C. D. Loose*

"Taps"
Postlude

Grinnell's first casualty in World War II was 19-year-old Eugene Robert Stanley, a member of the US Navy who was killed in 1942 in the South Pacific. His funeral service was held in the Congregational church and conducted by the local American Legion with assistance from Legion posts in Montezuma, Kellogg, and Brooklyn. A total of 54 servicemen from Poweshiek County were killed in World War II, including 25 from Grinnell. (GHM.)

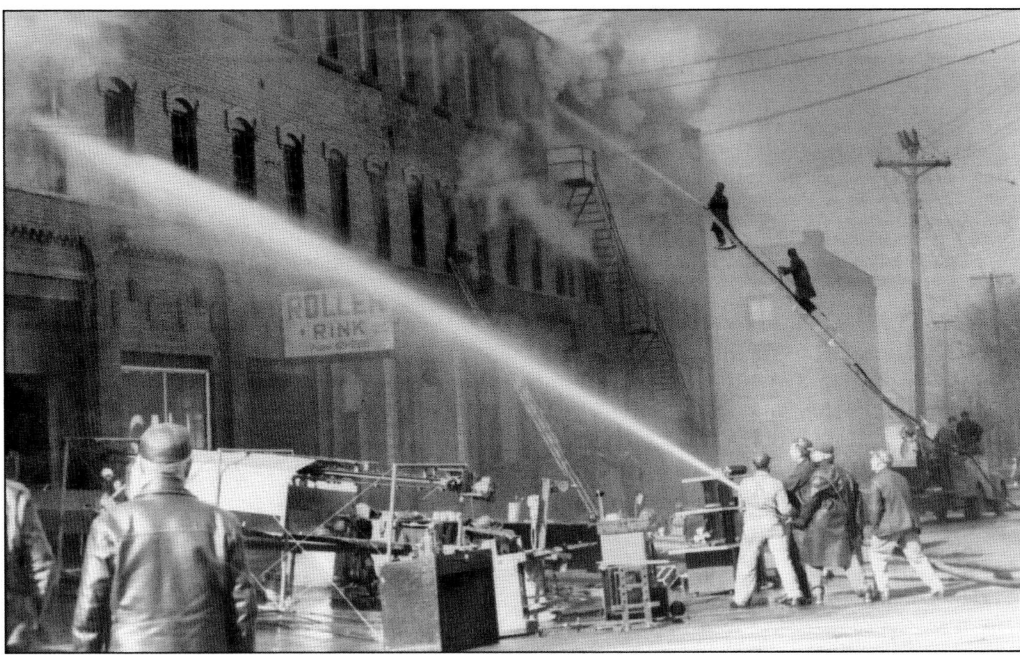

A fire on April 12, 1948, destroyed the building at Fourth Avenue and Spring Street that housed Grinnell Implement Co., Grinnell Axle and Body Co., and Vic's Garage. For the implement company, which sustained the biggest loss, the fire came at a particularly bad time because the store was stocked with new equipment for the upcoming planting season. (Grinnell Fire Department.)

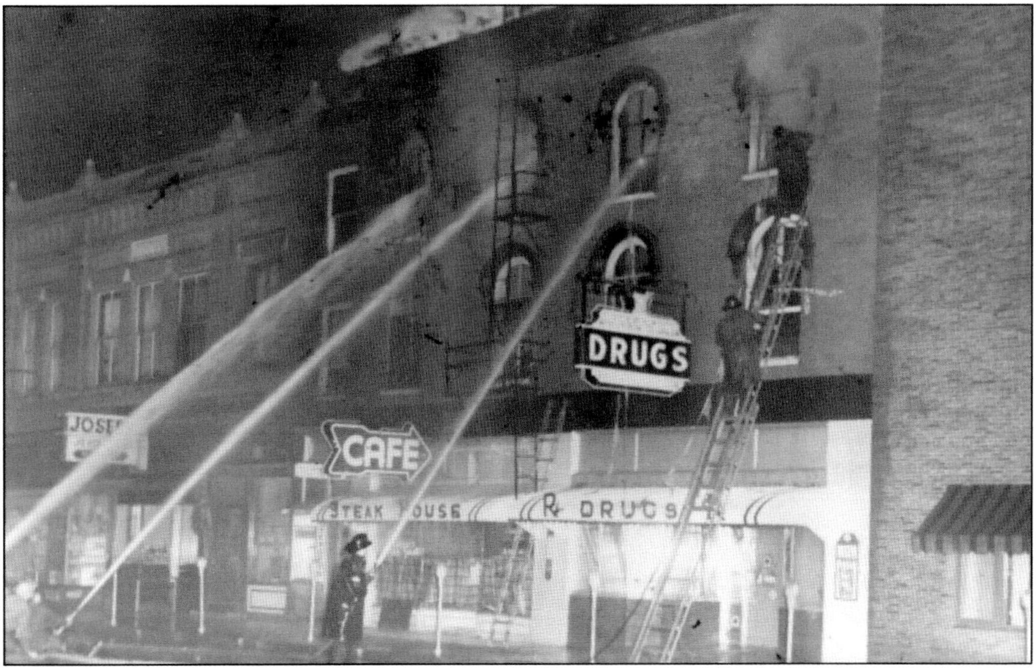

The second and third floors above Cunningham Drug on Fourth Avenue were destroyed in an early-morning fire in October 1954 (above). The street-level drugstore and the neighboring restaurant sustained smoke and water damage. The blaze ended plans by the Grinnell Historical Society to open a museum on the upper floors. Despite the proximity to the fire, the architectural treasure next door, the Merchants National Bank (at right in image below), was spared. Cunningham's relocated to temporary quarters on Broad Street and was back filling prescriptions within three working days. A new one-story building was constructed on the original site and the drugstore reopened in August 1955. It continued in business until closing in 2003. (Above, Grinnell Fire Department; below, Jim Cunningham.)

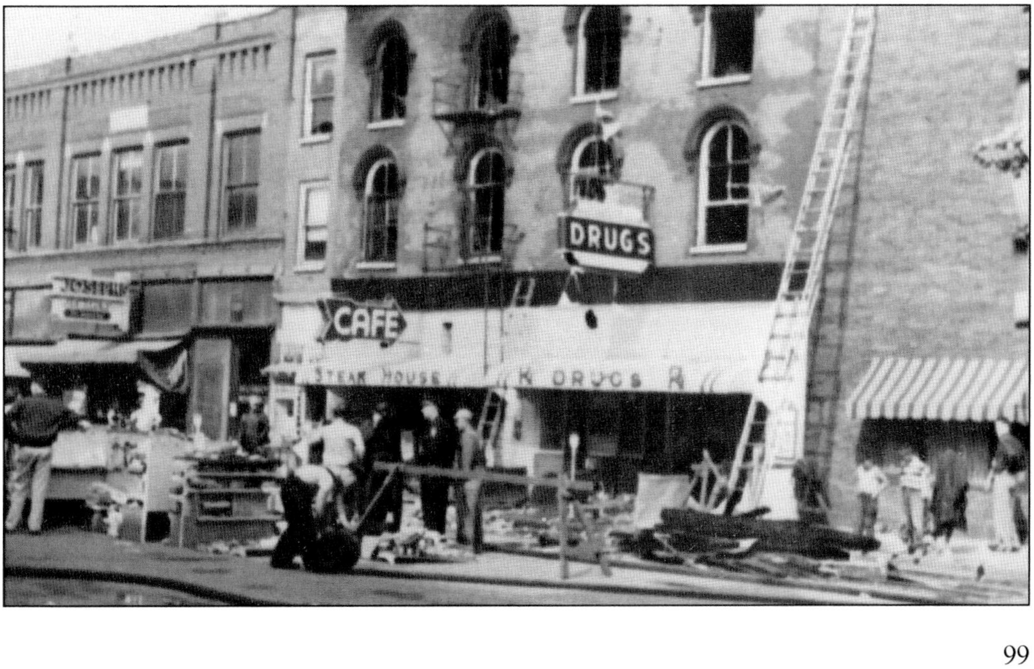

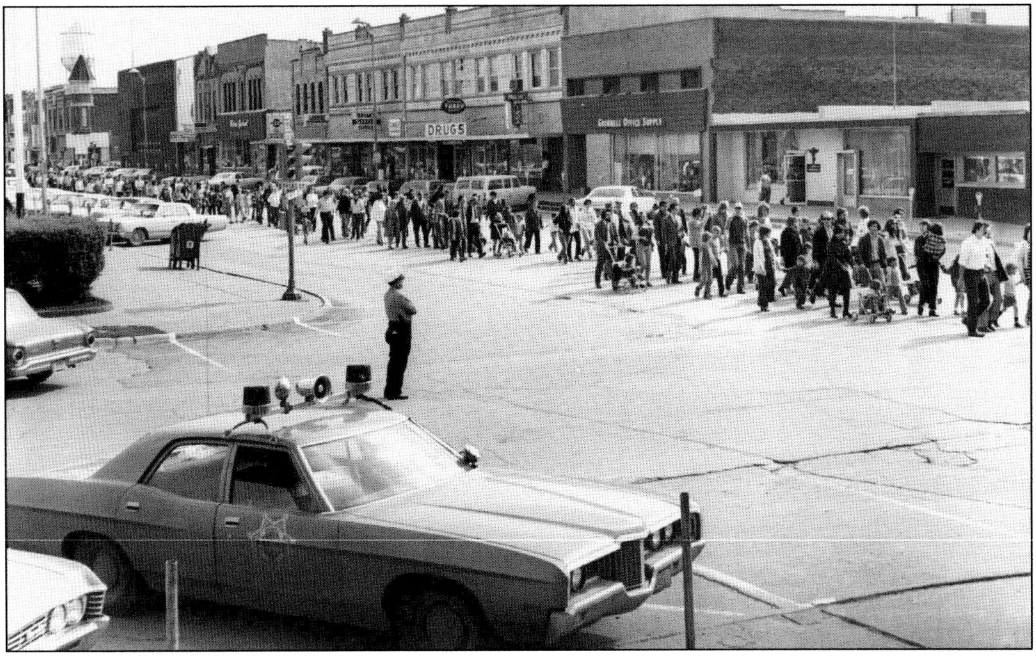

Campus protests against the Vietnam War that started in the late 1960s spilled over into the community as the fighting dragged on. In May 1972, students, faculty, and townspeople of all ages marched for seven days in solemn processions through the streets in opposition to Pres. Richard Nixon's announcement of further escalation of the war. (GCA.)

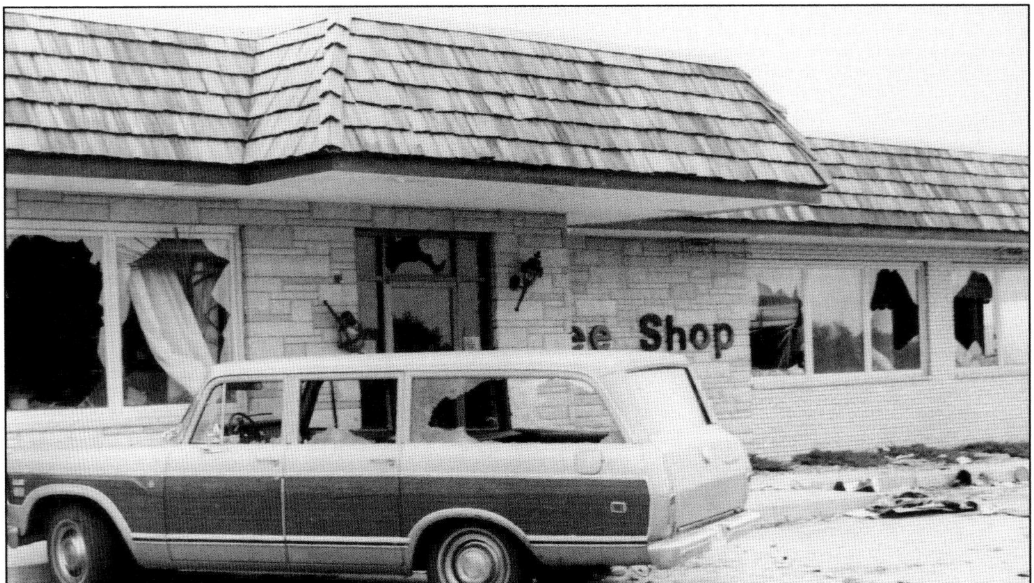

A tornado struck south of Grinnell near Interstate 80 on September 16, 1978, killing six people, overturning semitrailer trucks, and damaging a motel-restaurant-service station complex. A large crowd in the Silhouette Restaurant escaped with only minor injuries when a waitress, noticing bulging windows and sensing a tornado, rushed into the dining room shouting "tornado—hit the floor!" Only minor wind and hail damage occurred in the city of Grinnell. (DCL.)

Seven

Walking around Town

And above all, we like to think of Grinnell as a city of homes. When the founders came, the site was bare prairie without trees of any kind. Now the trees overshadow our streets with their canopy of gracious shade, and the streets are lined with pleasant homes.

—*Grinnell: A Century of Progress*, 1954

Homes are indeed among the gems of Grinnell—the Jewel of the Prairie. In addition, the downtown business district is considered among the best preserved in Iowa.

The homes in Grinnell represent a wide variety of architectural styles. A few are nearly pure examples of popular modes of the late 1800s and early 1900s. Many combine various architectural elements and defy exact stylistic definition. The mix is largely because most homes in early Grinnell were designed not by trained architects but by skilled local craftsmen.

The first substantial homes were built in the southeast part of town on High and East Streets, between Third and Fifth Avenues. Later, the area of Broad and Main Streets north of Sixth Avenue attracted families with means.

Notable individual buildings include the Merchants National Bank, designed by Louis Sullivan and built in 1914, and two Prairie-style residences—the B.J. Ricker House on Broad Street designed by Walter Burley Griffin, an associate of Sullivan and Frank Lloyd Wright, and the E.H. Spaulding House on Main Street and Sixth Avenue, designed by the Des Moines architectural firm of Hallett and Rawson.

Architecture of note on the college campus includes Goodnow Hall, built in 1895 in the Romanesque Revival style; Mears Cottage, the first dormitory, built in 1888 in the Queen Anne style; and the Bucksbaum Center for the Arts, designed by Cesar Pelli and built in 1999.

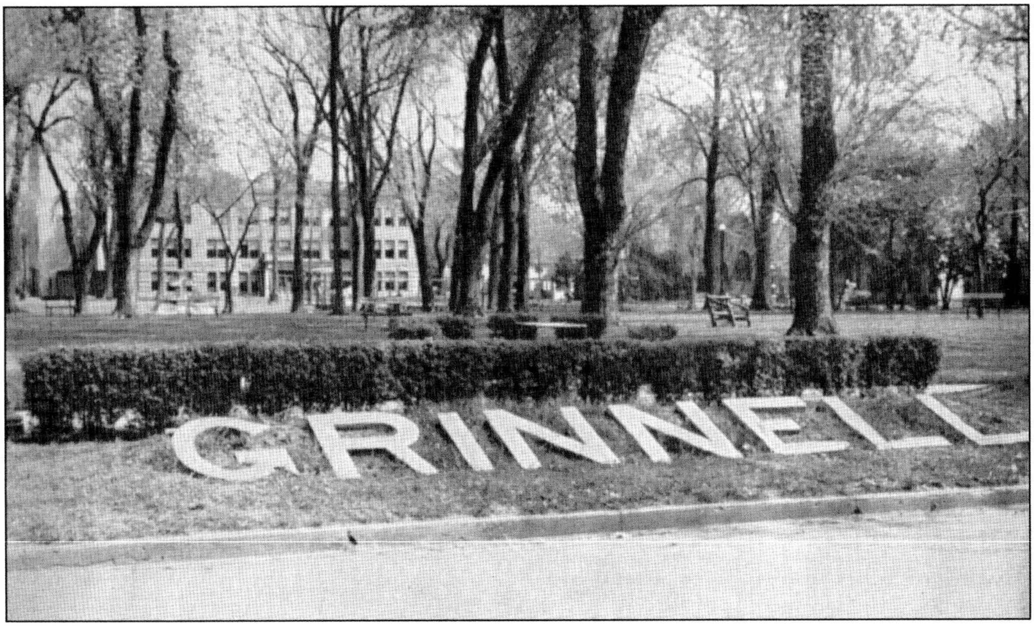

In the early 1900s, rail passengers were reminded of their location when they passed the large GRINNELL letters on the south side of Central Park. Although J.B. Grinnell chose the site for his new town because of a promised rail line, the first train did not arrive until 1863, nine years later. A diary entry by Josephus Eastman on June 27, 1863, exclaimed the following: "It looks like the eastern style of living. Hurrah! Hurrah!" (DCL.)

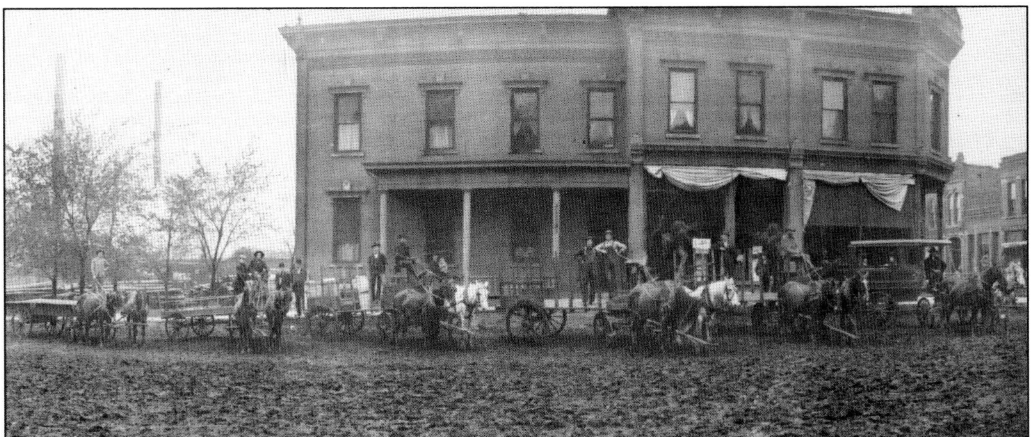

The Mack Building at Commercial and Broad Streets was constructed in 1889 in the months after the disastrous fire in the area. An addition to the south of the building in 1895 created the Mack Hotel, known by many other names over the years, including the Monroe Hotel Annex and the Park Hotel. The buggy at the right was used to transport travelers to and from the depot. The Park Hotel, Grinnell's last downtown hotel, closed in 1983. (GCA.)

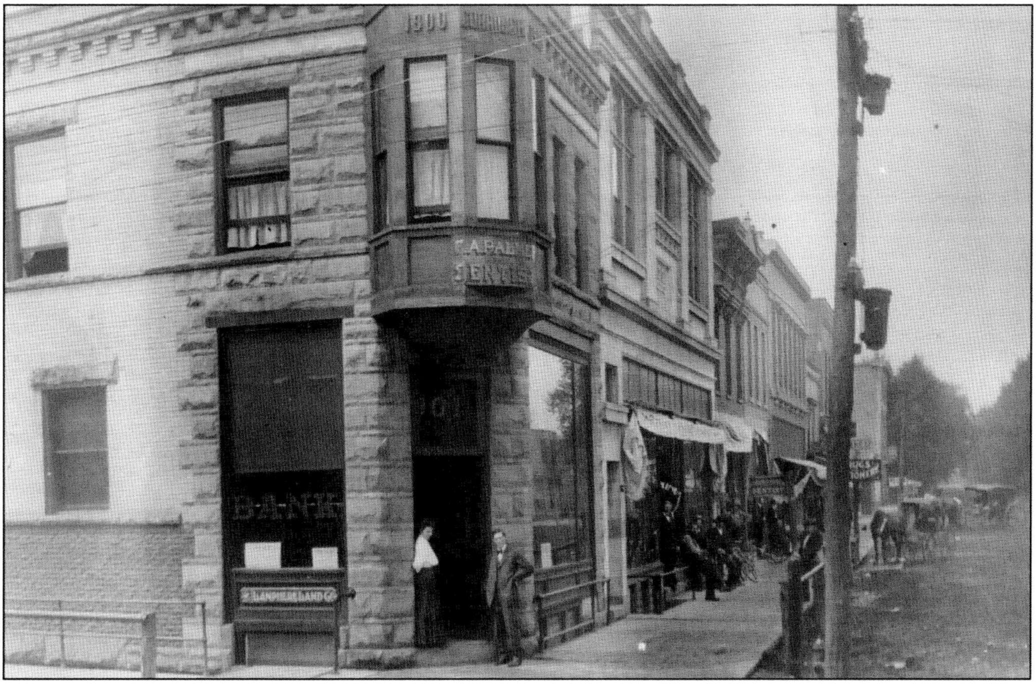

The Romanesque-style building known as the Corrough Block was constructed in 1900 at the northwest corner of Fourth Avenue and Main Street. (In early Grinnell, individual buildings in the business district were often known as blocks.) Early businesses in the building were a bank, drugstore, and land office on the first floor and dentist on the second floor. The oriel (bay) window on the second floor was for the dental chair, in order to take advantage of natural light. (DCL.)

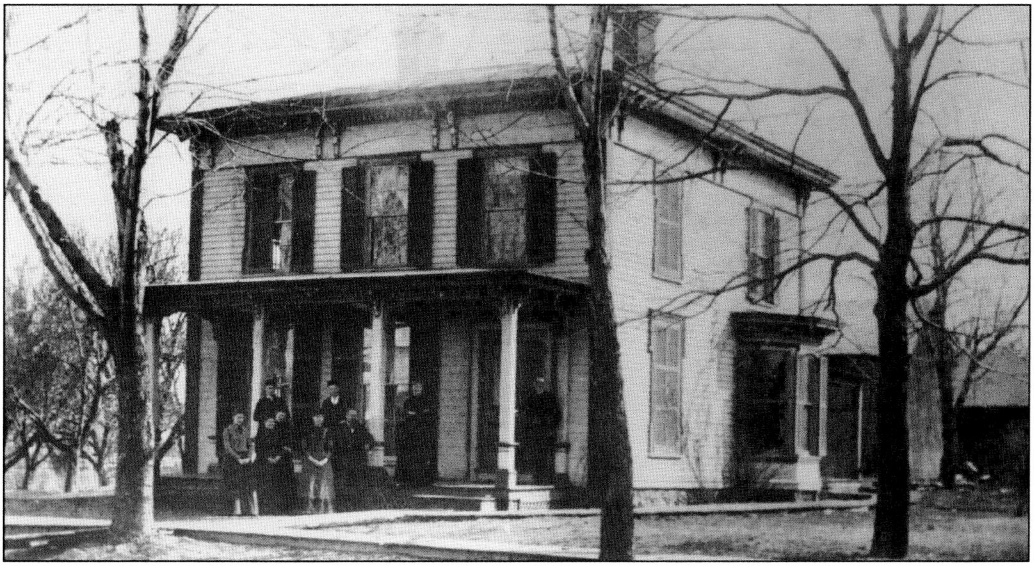

Abby Williams Hill, a noted artist who specialized in landscapes of the American West, grew up in the home at 1008 High Street (shown here in 1889). Hill studied at the Art Institute of Chicago and taught at Iowa (Grinnell) College and then began a career as a painter. Many of her works were commissioned by the railroads. The home today is used for rental housing by college students. (GHM.)

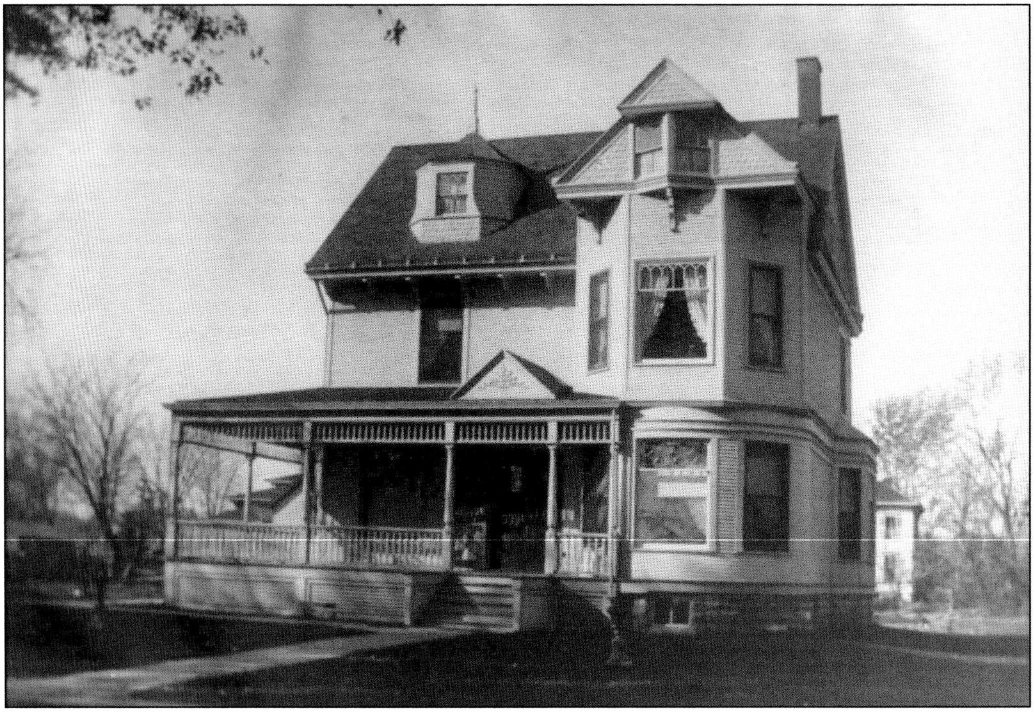

The Queen Anne home at 817 East Street, built in 1894, was one of the first on the block. It was built for E.B. Brande, a prominent businessman and local benefactor. A newspaper account from 1895 described the house as "one of the most attractive of our many beautiful dwellings." (GCA.)

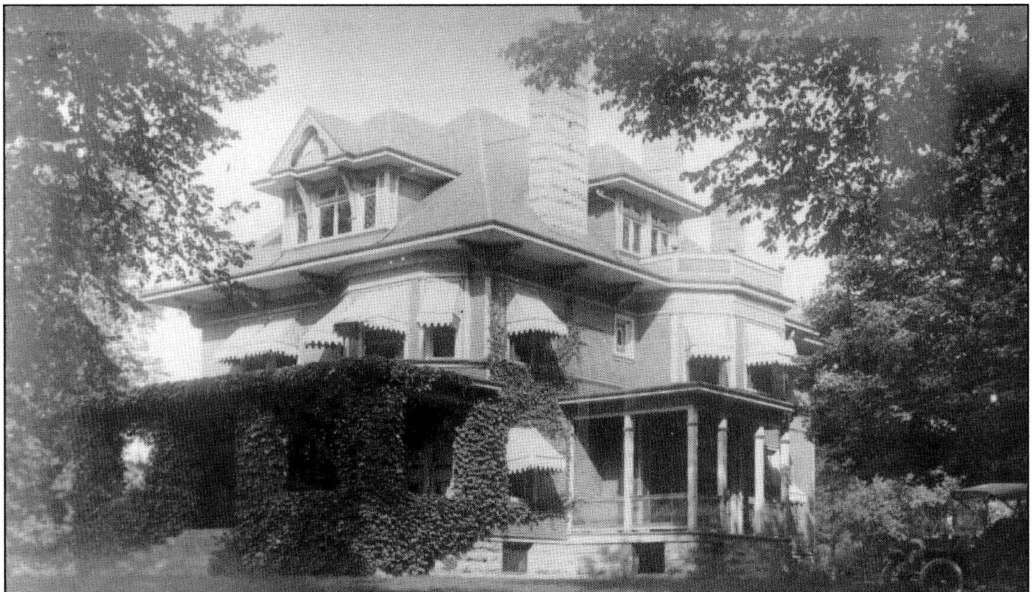

The home at 904 High Street was designed by noted Chicago architect George Maher and built in 1894. It features several Victorian elements along with a hint of the emerging Prairie style. The home was built for Charles R. Morse, a prominent businessman involved in grain and banking. Morse also served as a councilman and mayor and was on the school board. (GCA.)

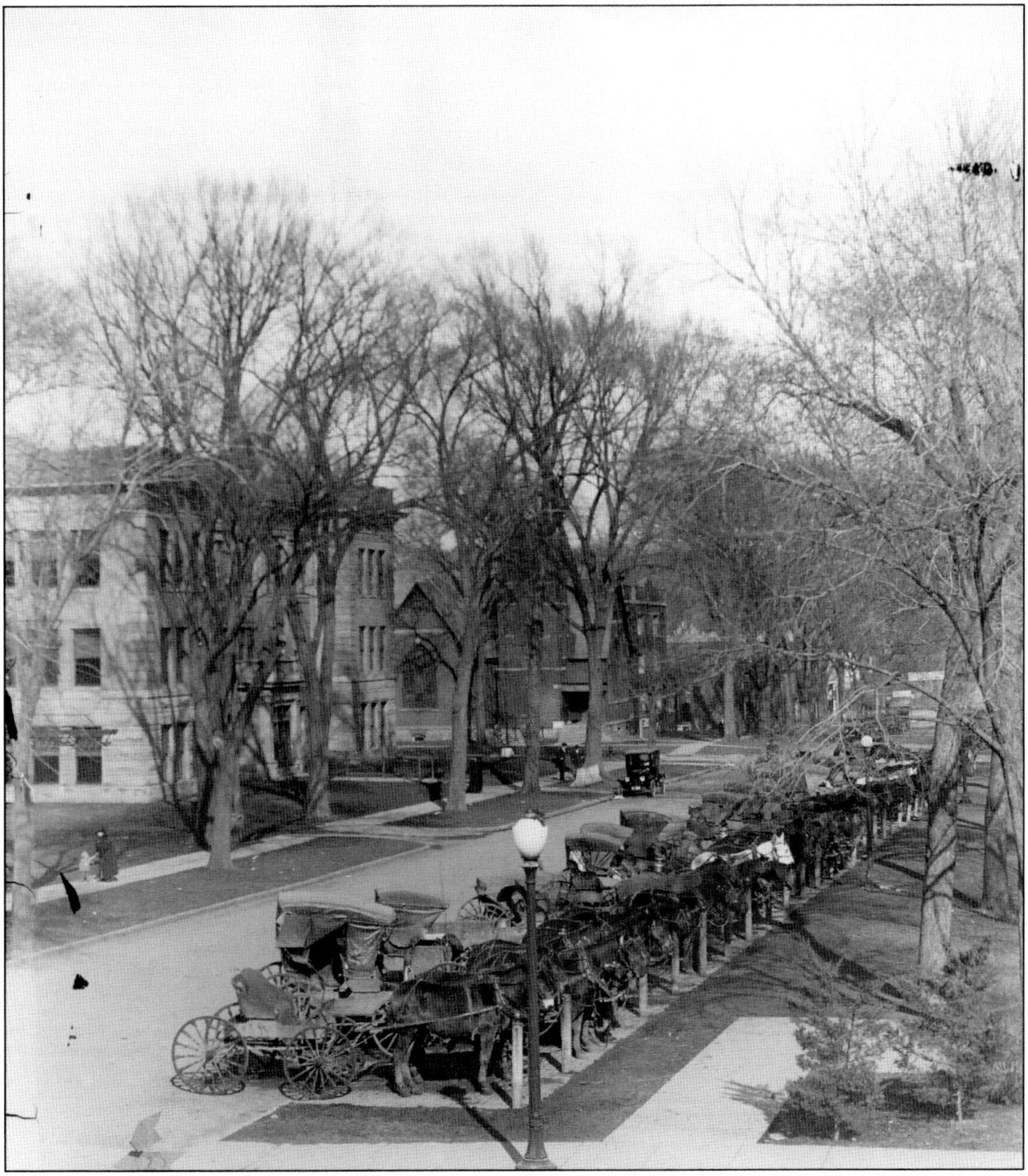

Horse-drawn and horseless carriages shared Fourth Avenue in the early 1900s. The row of parked carriages with horses likely belonged to worshipers attending services at the Baptist church (top right) or at the Congregational church (not visible at left). The high school, built in 1904, is also in the background. At right is Central Park. For a time, Grinnell's Spaulding Manufacturing Company produced both buggies and automobiles. At the height of its buggy production, the company announced its intention to produce an automobile. Between 1909 and 1916, approximately 5,000 Spaulding automobiles were manufactured in Grinnell. In 1913, one model broke the world record for a trip over a dirt road—337 miles from Davenport to Council Bluffs in 9 hours and 14 minutes. (GHM.)

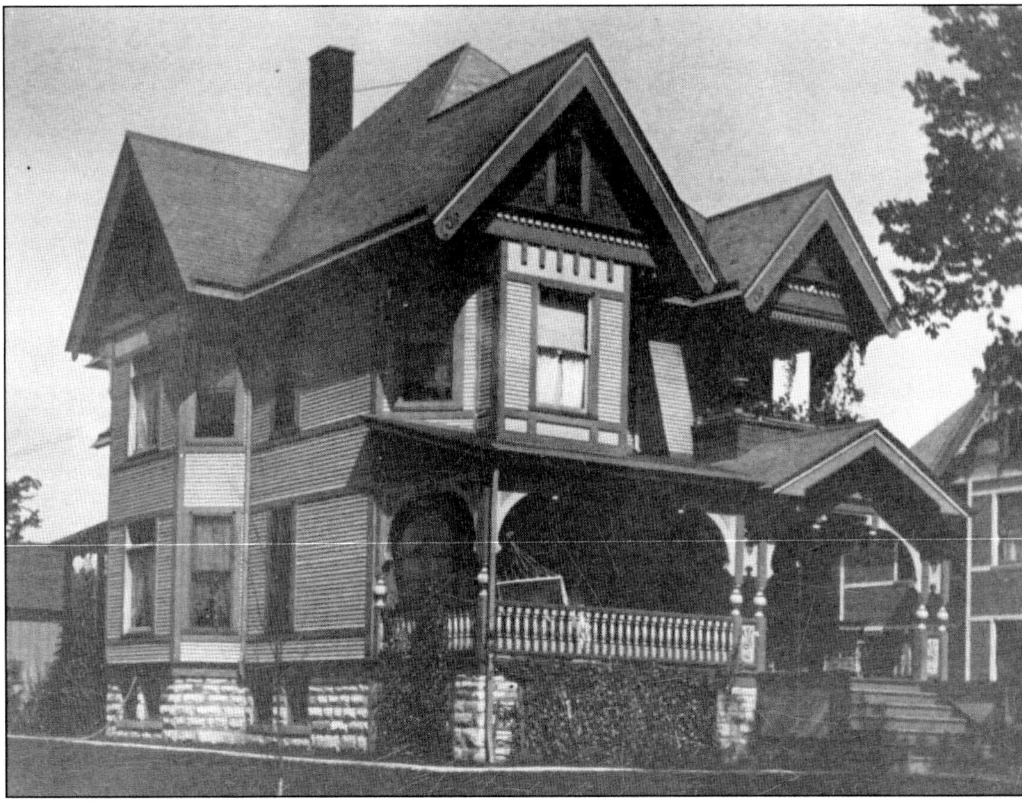

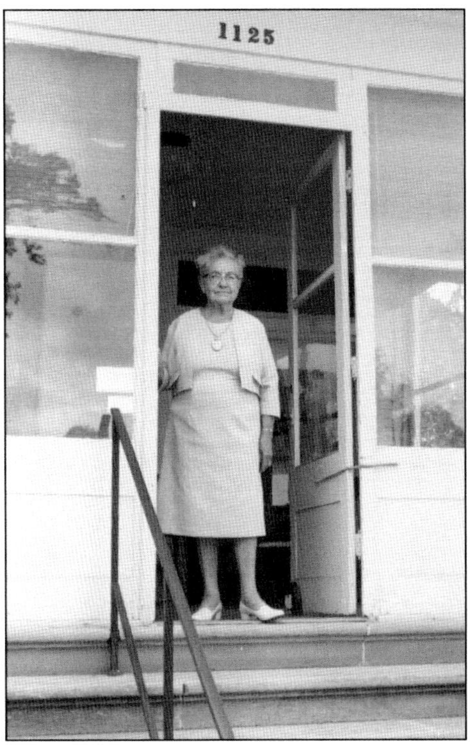

The Victorian residence at 1125 Broad Street has been home to the Grinnell Historical Museum since 1965. The home was built in 1894 for mercantile merchant J.H. McMurray. The McMurrays bequeathed the house at their deaths to their longtime housekeeper, Kate Siehl. At her death, her heirs sold the house to the museum trustees. The photograph was taken prior to 1912, when the front porch was enclosed. (GHM.)

Rose Stoops played a major role in creating and sustaining the Grinnell Historical Museum. A longtime curator at the museum as well as president of the museum's auxiliary, she is shown here in 1978 on the museum steps. She died in 2001 at the age of 105. The museum annually awards a college scholarship in Rose Stoops's name to a Grinnell High School student. (GCA.)

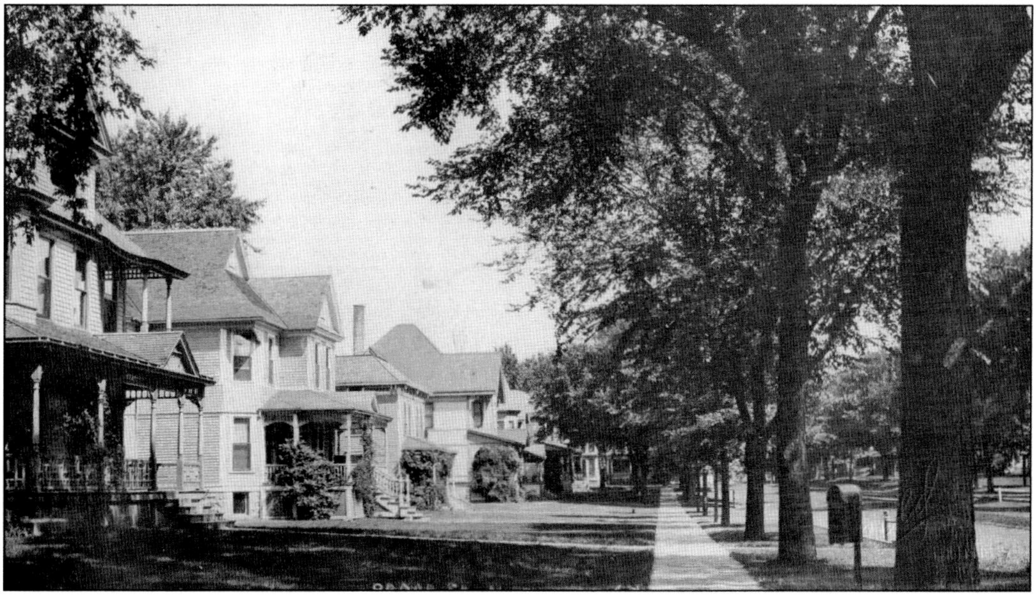

Broad Street north of Sixth Avenue was rebuilt after the 1882 cyclone into a fashionable neighborhood that was home to some of the city's leading families. The house at left was converted into the present Smith Funeral Home. The house at the end of the block is now the Carriage House Bed and Breakfast. (GHM.)

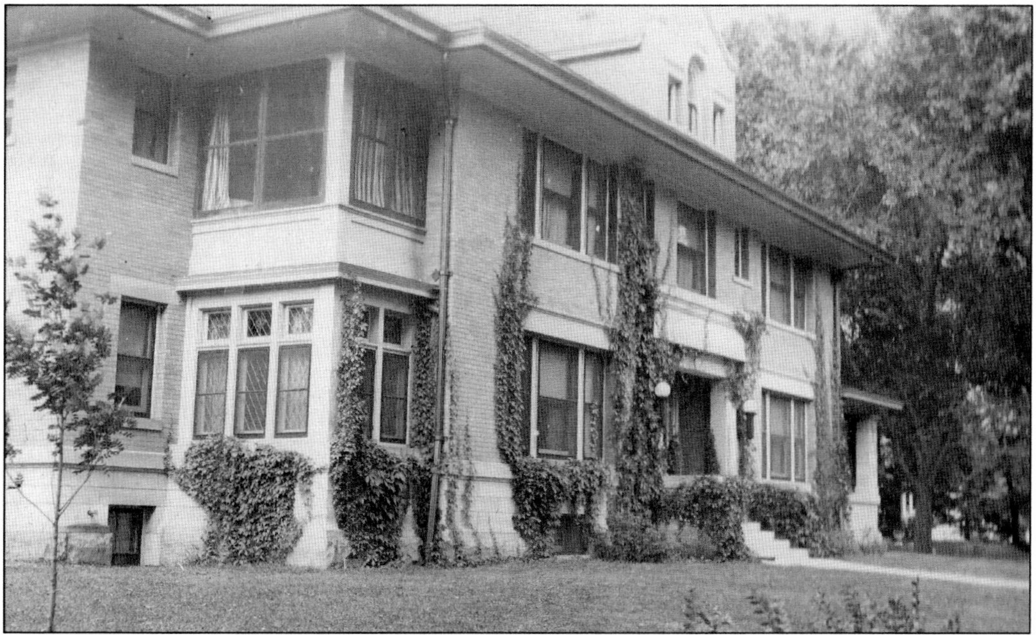

Ernest H. Spaulding, son of the founder of Spaulding Manufacturing Company, maker of buggies and automobiles, built a Prairie-style house at 1103 Main Street between 1905 and 1907. The home, now a bed and breakfast named the Spaulding Inn, originally had a porte cochere on the north and a semicircular veranda on the east. Three other homes on the block were also built by Spaulding family members. (GHM.)

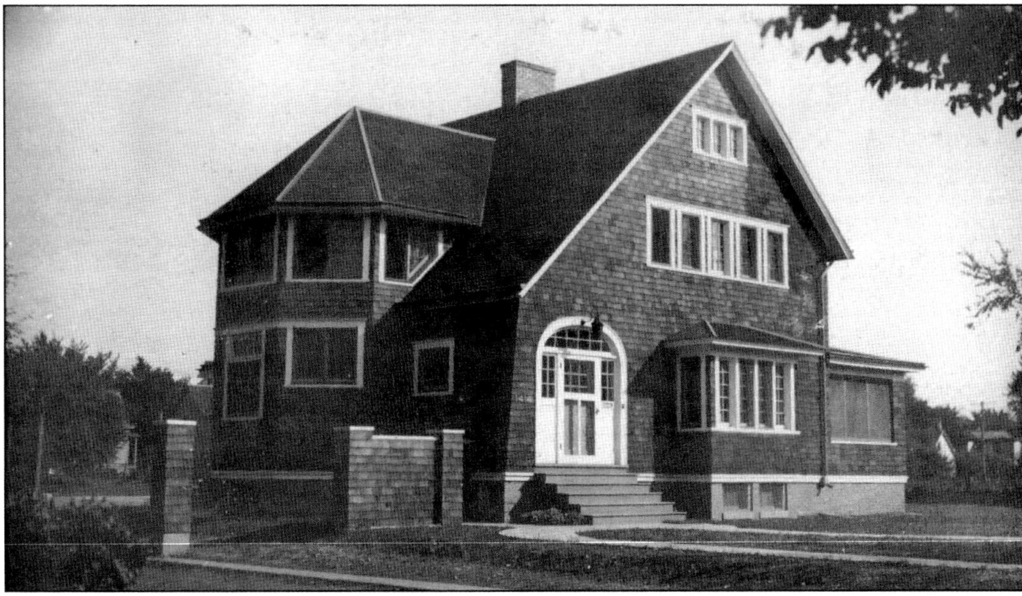

The picturesque shingle-style home at 1414 Broad Street is tucked among Victorian residences more common in the neighborhood. Designed by the Des Moines architectural firm of Hallett and Rawson, it was built in 1910 for attorney H.L. Beyer. A similar home is located across the alley at 1415 Park Street. (GHM.)

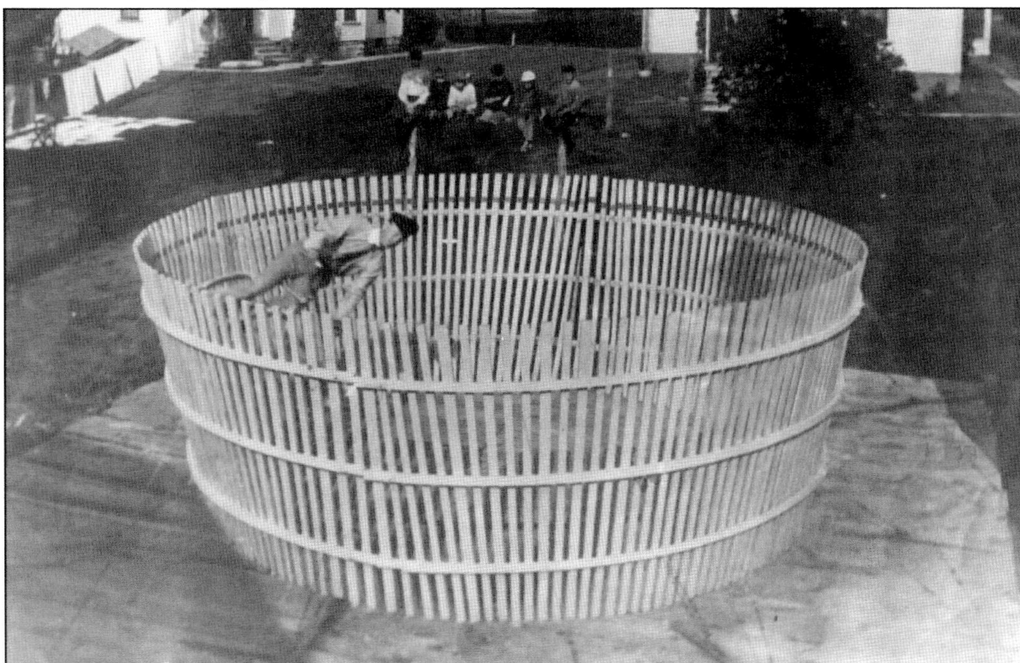

Here, a cyclist got his exercise and provided entertainment in the early 1900s in the backyard of 817 Seventh Avenue, the home of Richard C. Ross. The velodrome was made of a concrete slab with wooden slats held together by guy wires. The home was constructed of red-tinted block manufactured by the Ross family's Grinnell Stone Company. Other homes made of the same block are located at 1114 Broad Street and 1310 Main Street. (GHM.)

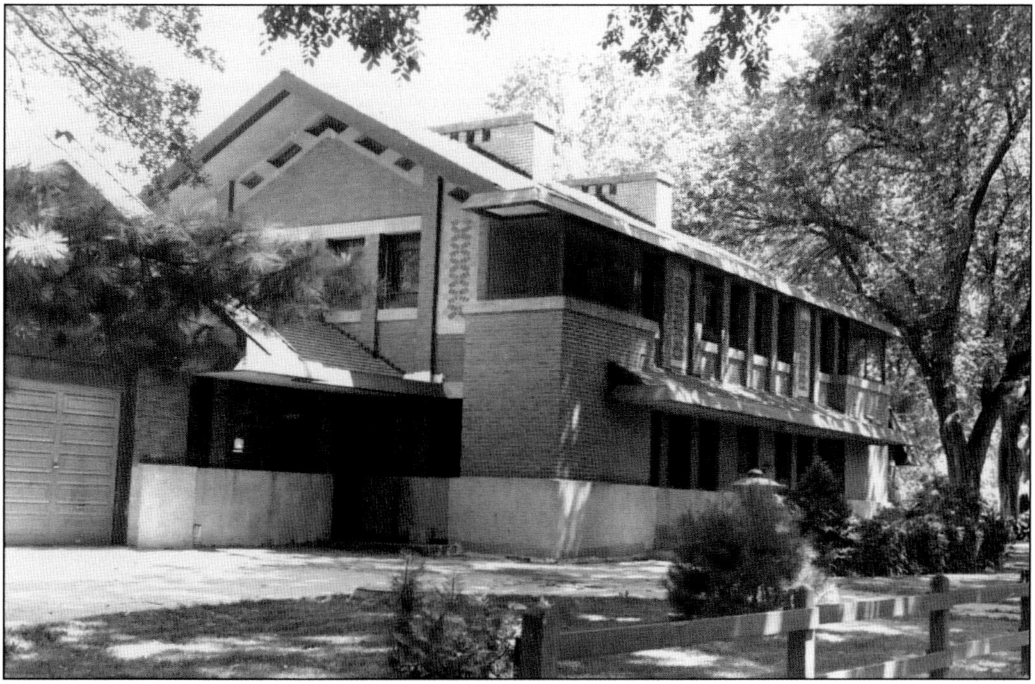

Grinnell's most notable home is the Prairie-style residence at 1510 Broad Street, designed by Walter Burley Griffin, who worked with both Louis Sullivan and Frank Lloyd Wright. The home was built in 1911 for Benjamin J. Ricker, a partner in the prosperous Morrison-Ricker Manufacturing Company, maker of leather gloves. The house is owned today by Grinnell College, which uses it as a guesthouse. (GCA.)

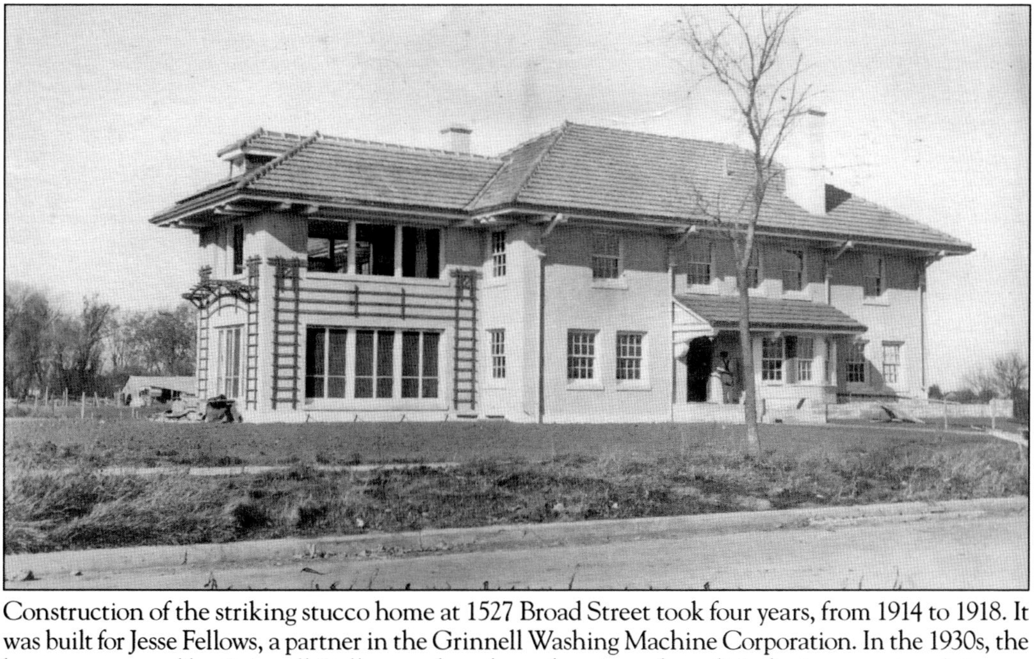

Construction of the striking stucco home at 1527 Broad Street took four years, from 1914 to 1918. It was built for Jesse Fellows, a partner in the Grinnell Washing Machine Corporation. In the 1930s, the house was owned by Grinnell College and used as a dormitory for political science majors. It is now a private residence. The house was nearing completion in this photograph. (Mickey Munley.)

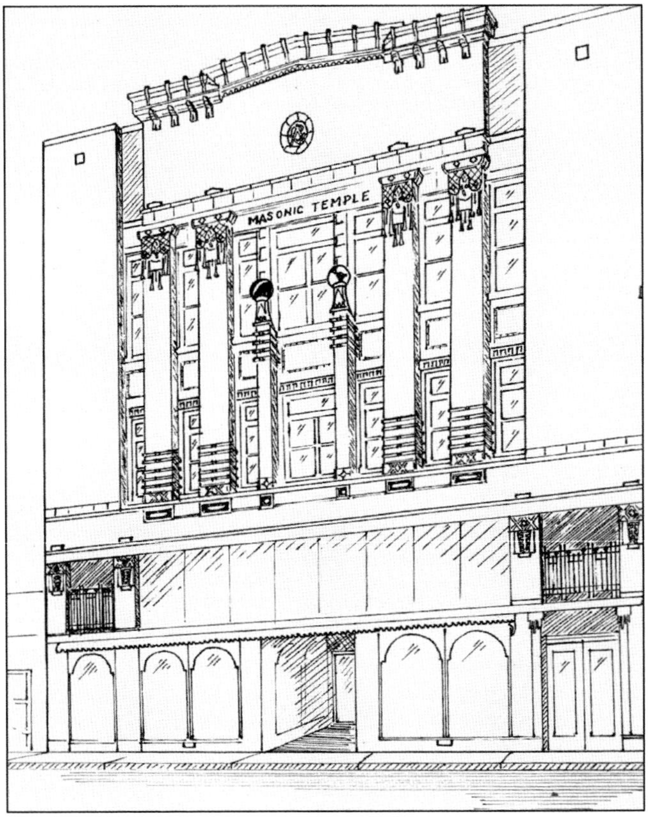

The Hermon Lodge of the Masons was chartered in 1869, just 15 years after the town was founded. After years of renting space, the lodge constructed its own building (left) in 1918 at 928 Main Street. The building's distinctive exterior carries out the temple motif, with pilasters adorned at the top with lilies, pomegranates, and spheres. The sketch was done by Earl Blair, a Grinnell resident who used pen and paper to record many of the city's historic buildings. (DCL.)

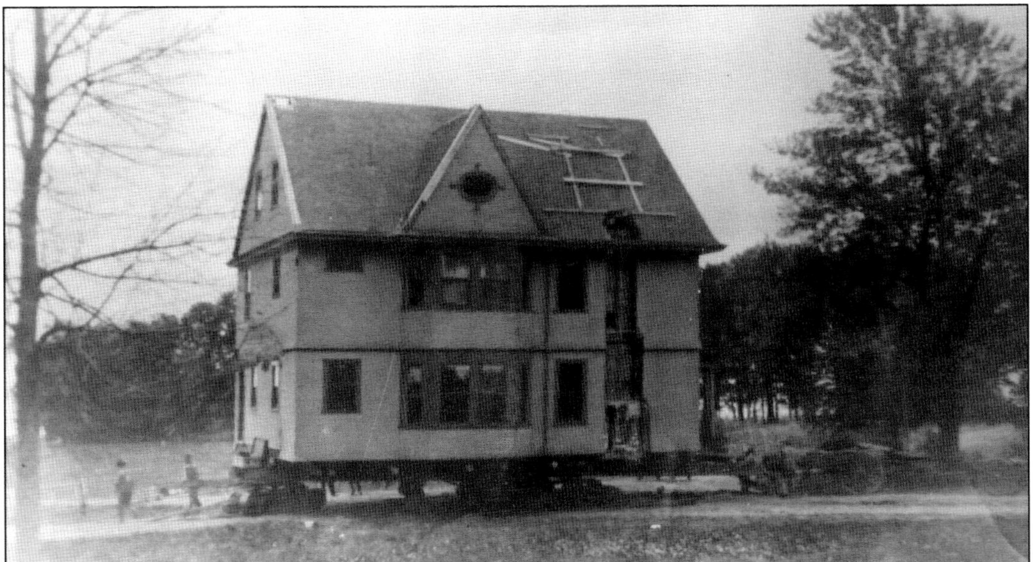

Houses were often on the move in the early 20th century, including this one that was relocated about 1921 from the northwest corner of Fifth Avenue and Broad Street to its present location at 1533 Sixteenth Avenue. The house was transported by a horse-drawn apparatus along Sixth Avenue to Penrose Street and then north to Sixteenth Avenue. (GCA.)

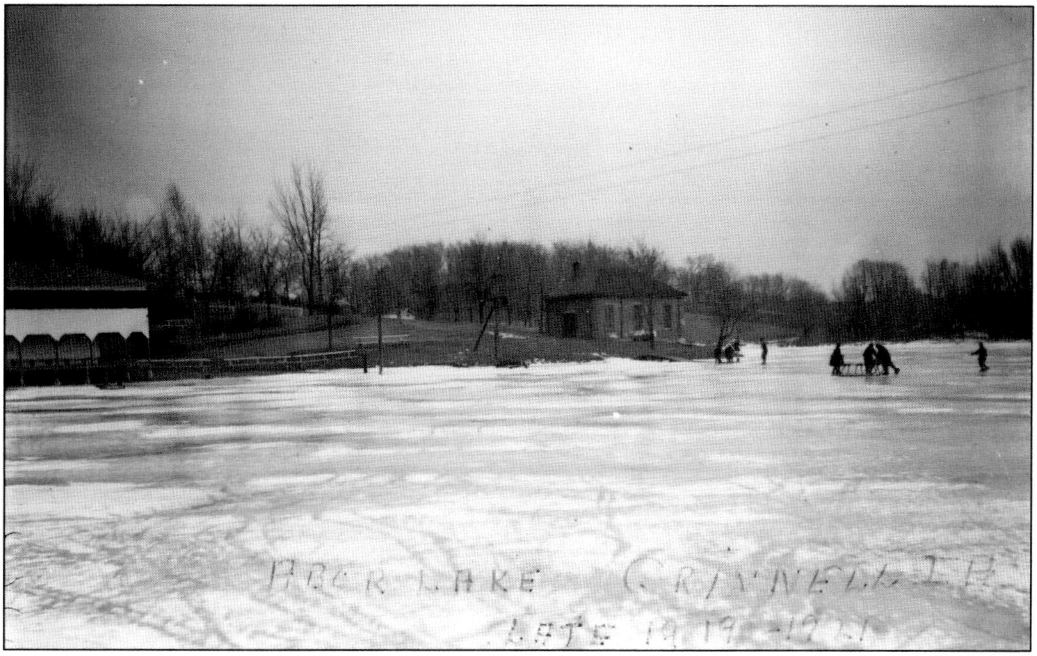

While Arbor Lake was used for swimming and boating in summer, it was also a popular spot for ice-skating in winter. Cornelia Clarke, a noted local photographer who roamed the town capturing scenes of beauty and activity, particularly in winter, took the photograph, dated sometime between 1919 and 1921. (DCL.)

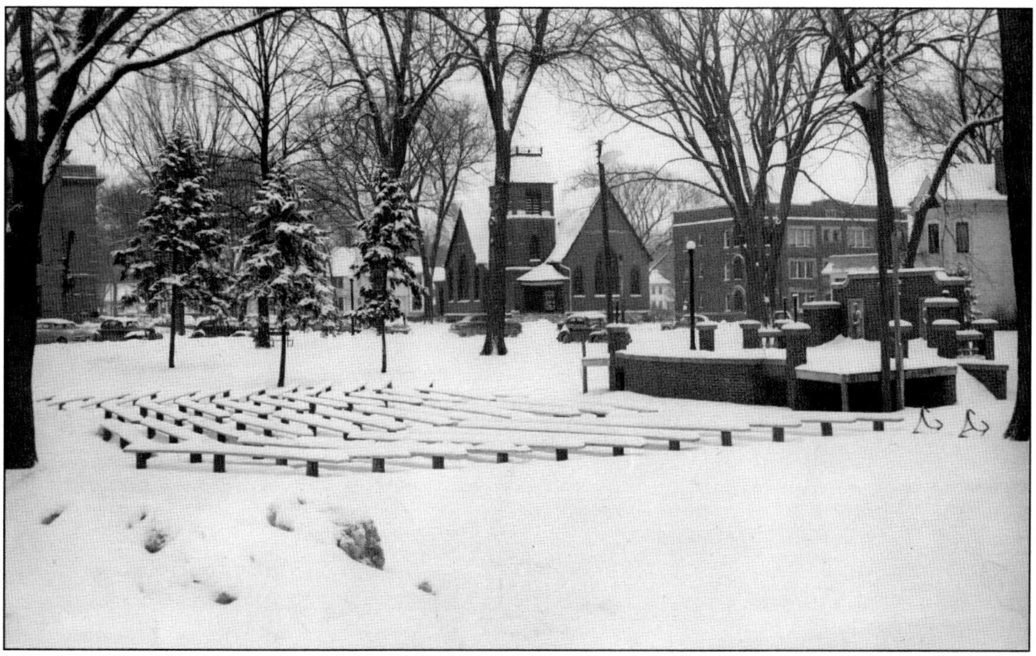

A brick bandstand on the east side of Central Park was built in 1924 to honor World War I veterans. The benches were added in the 1940s. The structure was removed in the 1960s. A music venue returned to Central Park in 1990, when a gazebo was constructed in the center of the park and dedicated on the Fourth of July of that year. (DCL.)

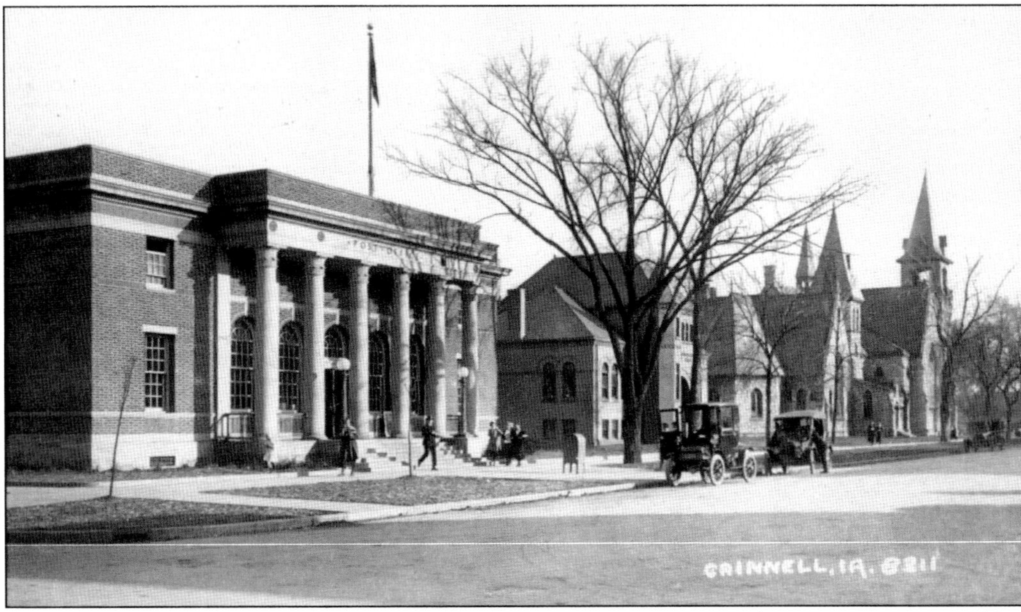

Three distinguished buildings lined the east side of the 900 block of Broad Street between 1917 (date of construction of the post office, shown at left) and 1951 (date of demolition of the Congregational church, shown at right). In between is Stewart Library, built in 1902 and now home to the Grinnell Arts Center. (GCA.)

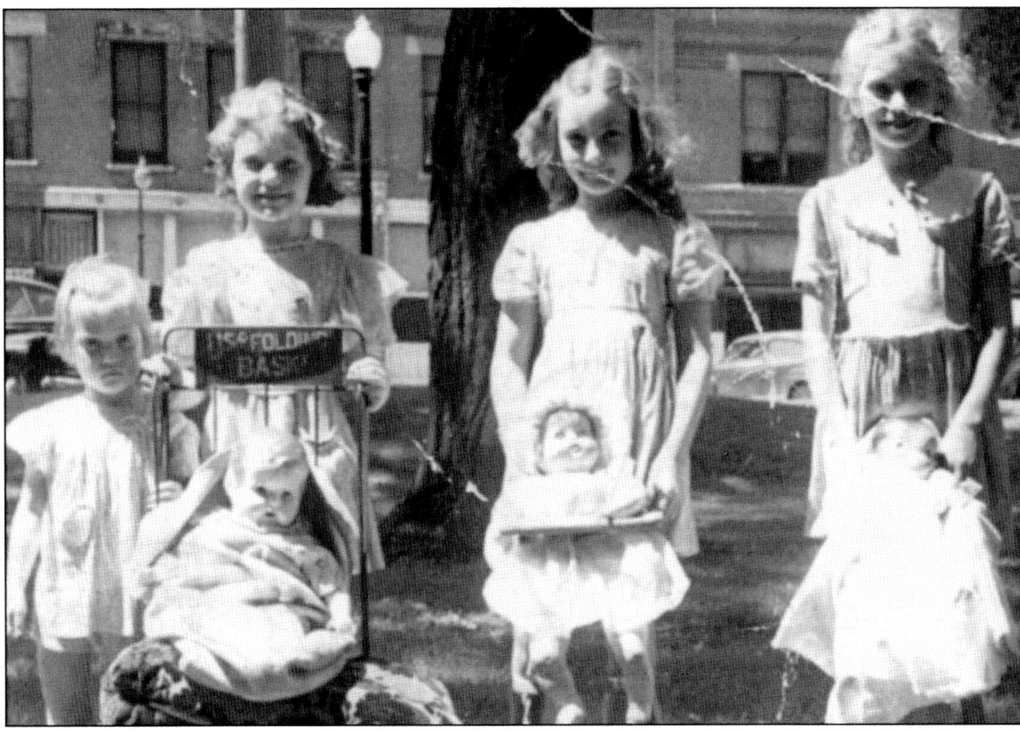

Four little girls and three baby dolls celebrated a summer day in 1945 with an outing in Central Park. The girls are, from left to right, Charlotte Ditzler, Sandra Kelly, Judy Bunch, and Marjorie Ditzler. Names of the dolls are likely forgotten. (Marjorie Ditzler Hellman.)

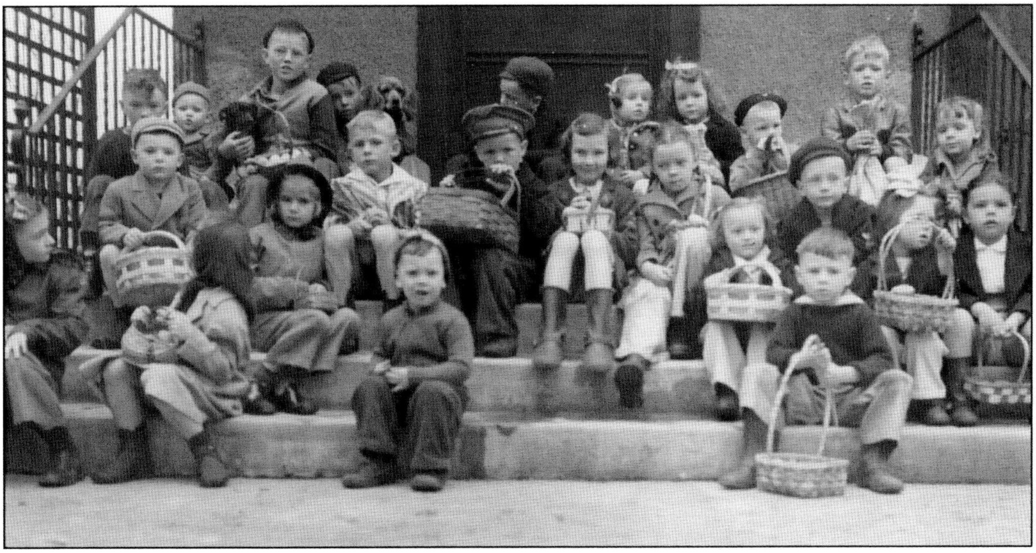

Neighborhood children and two dogs gathered in 1943 for an Easter egg hunt at the home of Richard and Jane Seeland, 803 Tenth Avenue. Richard Seeland, a Grinnell College graduate, was a vice president of Lannom Manufacturing Company. Seeland Park, a Grinnell retirement community, is named in his honor. (DCL.)

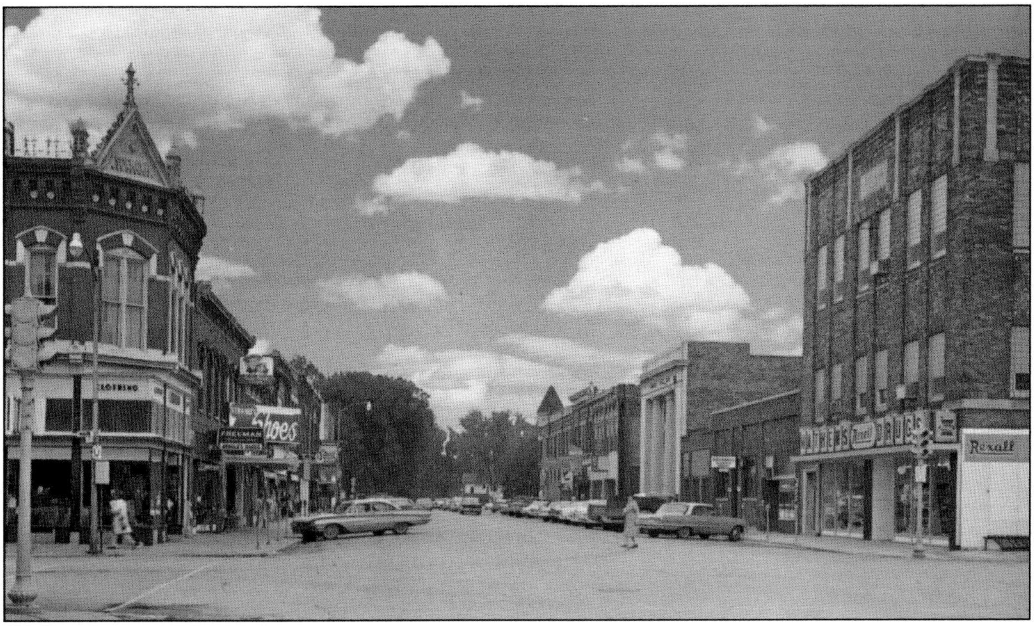

Fourth Avenue between Main and Broad Streets was lined with longtime retail businesses in the early 1960s. At right is the Rexall Drugstore, which anchored the southeast corner of Fourth Avenue and Main Street from 1916 to 1970. At left are Preston's Clothing Store, which operated at that location from 1898 to 1965, and Arnold's Shoes, which was in business for 53 years. Note the traffic lights at the corners. (Bill McNally.)

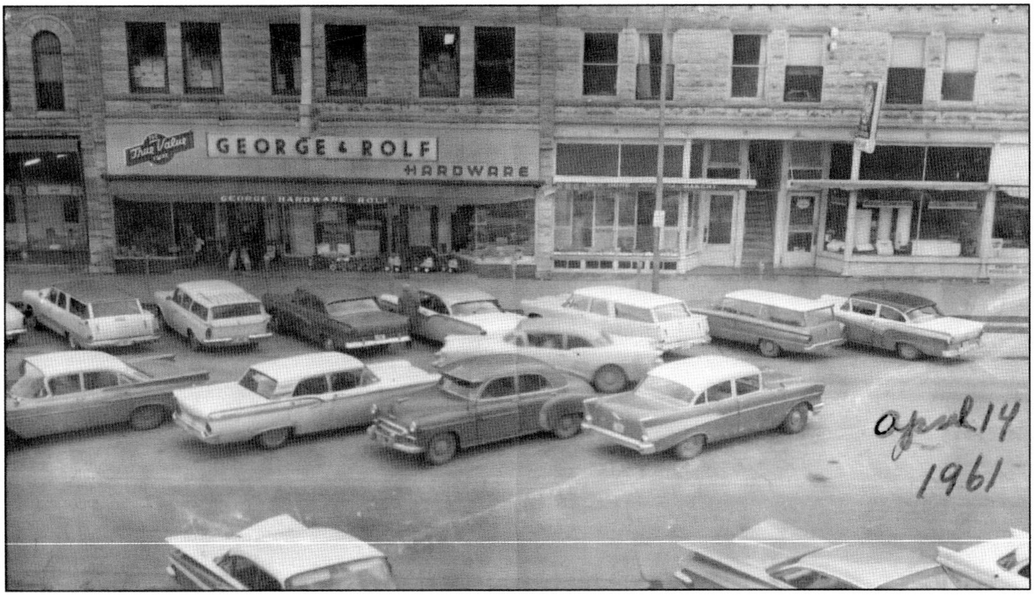

Among the many parking and traffic configurations in downtown Grinnell over the years was a period between 1949 and 1961 when parking was allowed in the center of Broad Street between Fifth Avenue and Commercial Street. One-way streets were in place downtown between 1974 and 2005. Stop-and-go lights were introduced in the early 1950s and removed in 1974. (Bill McNally.)

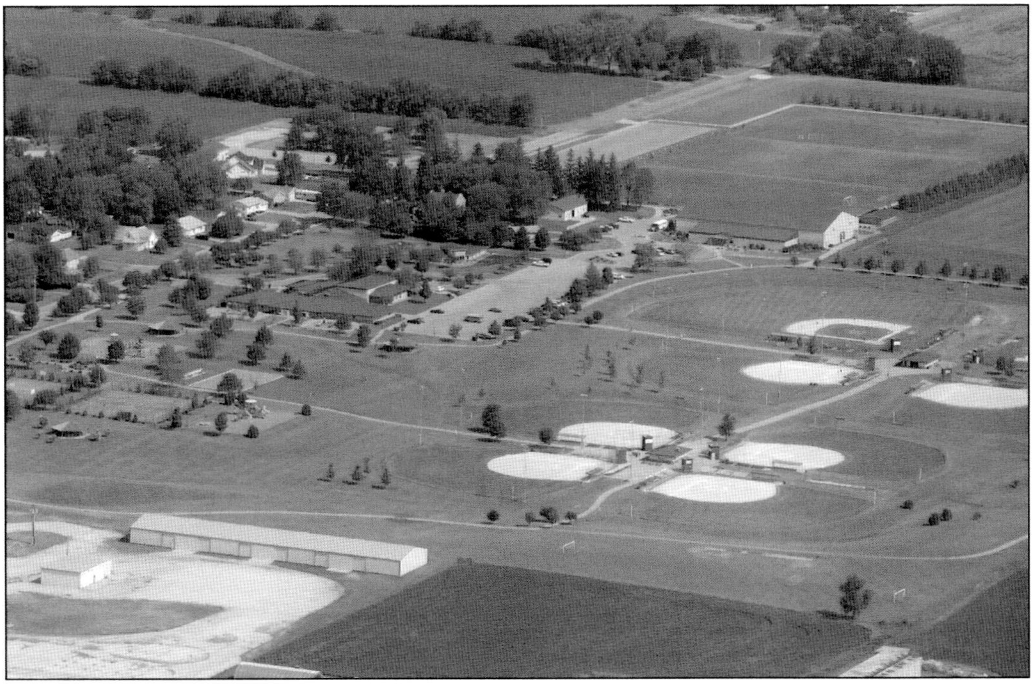

Thanks to the generosity of local entrepreneur Claude Ahrens and his wife, Dolly, a 100-acre recreation complex was carved out of farmland at the east edge of Grinnell in the 1990s. Called Ahrens/Paschall Memorial Park, it includes sports fields and courts, a golf driving range, and a walking path as well as the Ahrens Family Center (with a day care center and indoor pool) and the Grinnell Athletic and Recreation Center. (Claude W. and Dolly Ahrens Foundation.)

Eight

Celebrating the Good Times

The children were not forgotten [on the first Fourth of July in 1854], for Mr. Grinnell himself went to Chicago to buy nuts, candy, and firecrackers to distribute among them. The bell was rung, speeches were made, and a roll call ordered, which showed representatives from 20 different states besides England, Canada, and Scotland.

—Julia Chapin Grinnell, wife of J.B. Grinnell

Just a few months after the first settlers arrived in Grinnell, more than 150 people showed up to celebrate the first Fourth of July in the new town. They came from miles around by ox team, horseback, and on foot.

Twenty-five years later, in 1879, when the population had grown to 2,415, the Fourth of July holiday was celebrated with a program that lasted 16 hours. The event included "gas balloon ascensions, a magnificent parade, exciting races, and historical and literary exercises by prominent men. Music was provided by four cornet bands."

In 1954, Grinnell marked 100 years with a celebration that went on for a full six months. Activities began in March, with church services that incorporated the centennial theme. Schoolchildren wrote about Grinnell's history as part of a citywide essay contest. Volunteers constructed a replica of the Long Home, the town's first building, on the lawn of Stewart Library. A grand pageant with a cast of 700 was performed in May at Ward Field on the college campus.

Throughout the town's history, parades around the business district have been a part of school and community festivities. Many culminate with special activities in Central Park. Family and class reunions and high school and college graduations are milestones that have been shared in celebrations.

J.B. Grinnell did a lot for the town he founded. Establishing the tradition of celebrating the good times appears to be one of his best contributions.

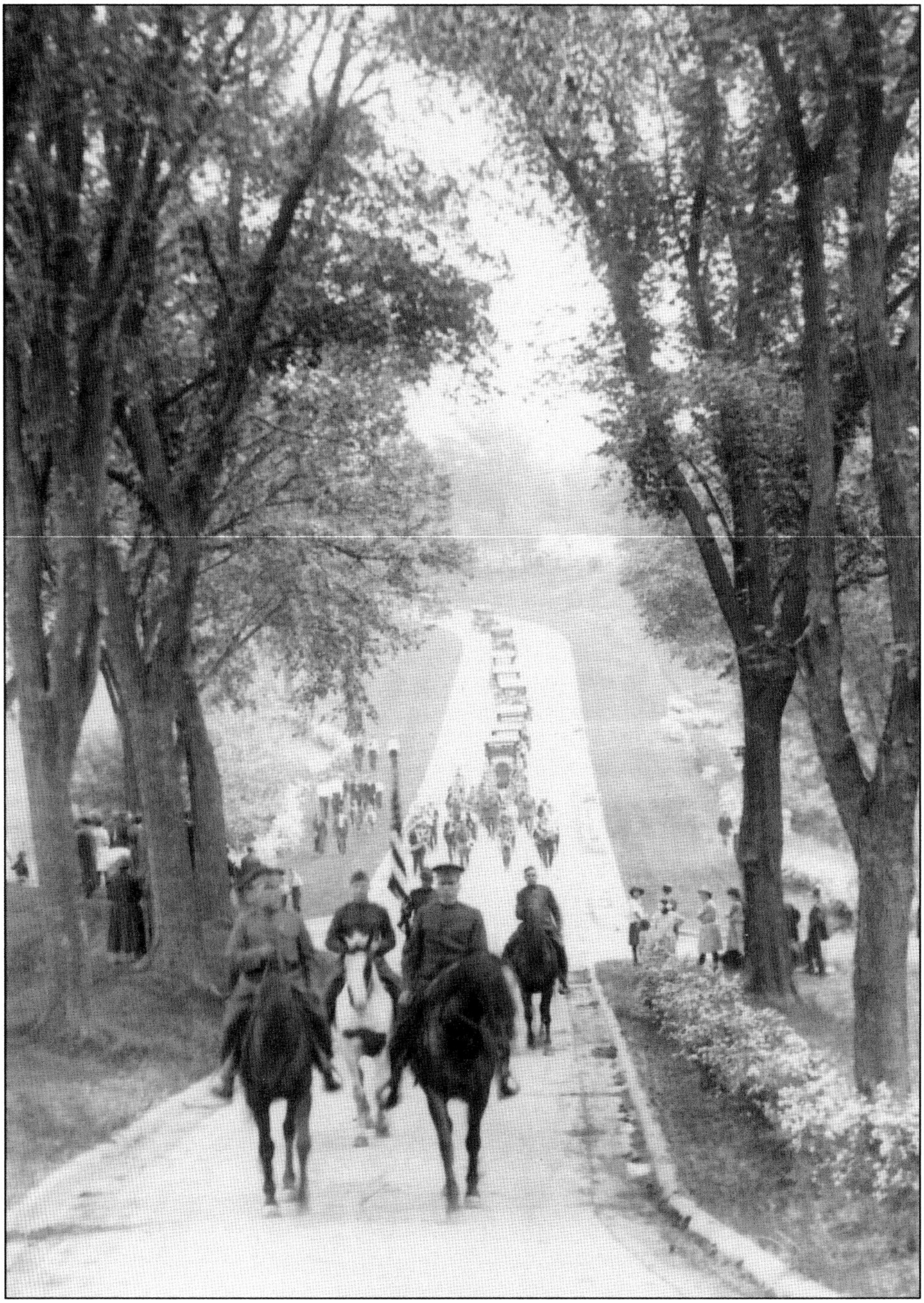

Hazelwood Cemetery, named for its hazel-brush thicket, has long been the site of Memorial Day observances. In the early 1900s, a typical Memorial Day event included a parade to the cemetery from downtown composed of bands, schoolchildren, members of the local Grand Army of the Republic and Women's Relief Corps, and representatives of civic organizations. The ceremony concluded with the traditional laying on of wreaths. The first burial at Hazelwood was that of Jane Patterson, who died in 1857. J.B. Grinnell noted in his 1890 autobiographical reminisces that he had attended hundreds of burials but that "none was so solemn as the first, in the opening of the virgin breast of earth, and the vision of a home none of us seek, but most all ere long inhabit." (DCL.)

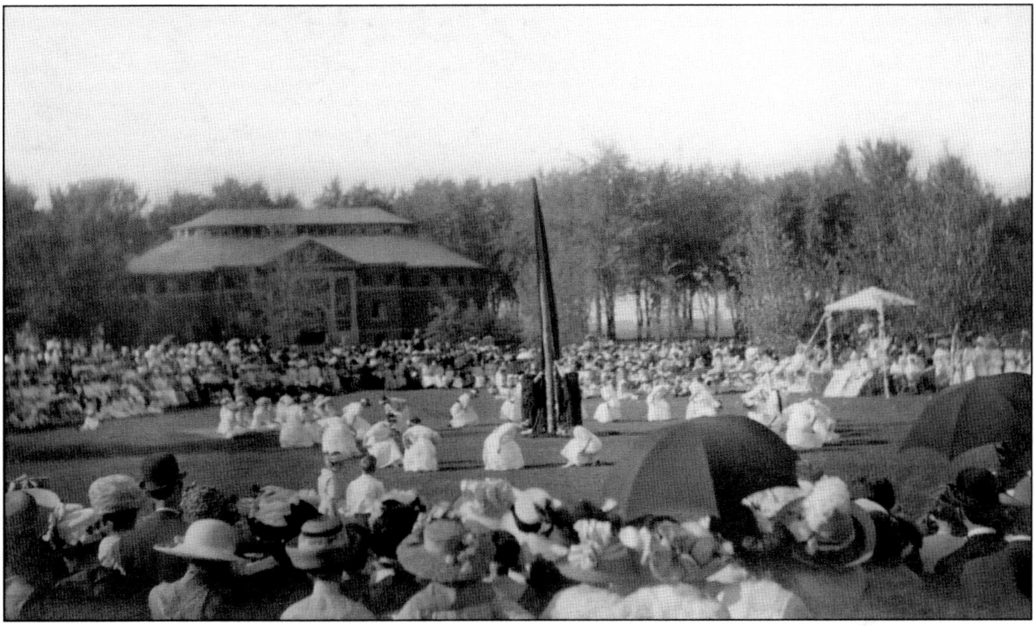

Spring was welcomed in Grinnell during the early 1900s with a May Day pageant put on by Grinnell College students. Held on central campus south of Rand Gymnasium, the event attracted both students and townspeople. The college band played as groups of college women, in gowns of white with wreaths of flowers in their hair, moved in graceful dances around a maypole and crowned a May queen. (GCA.)

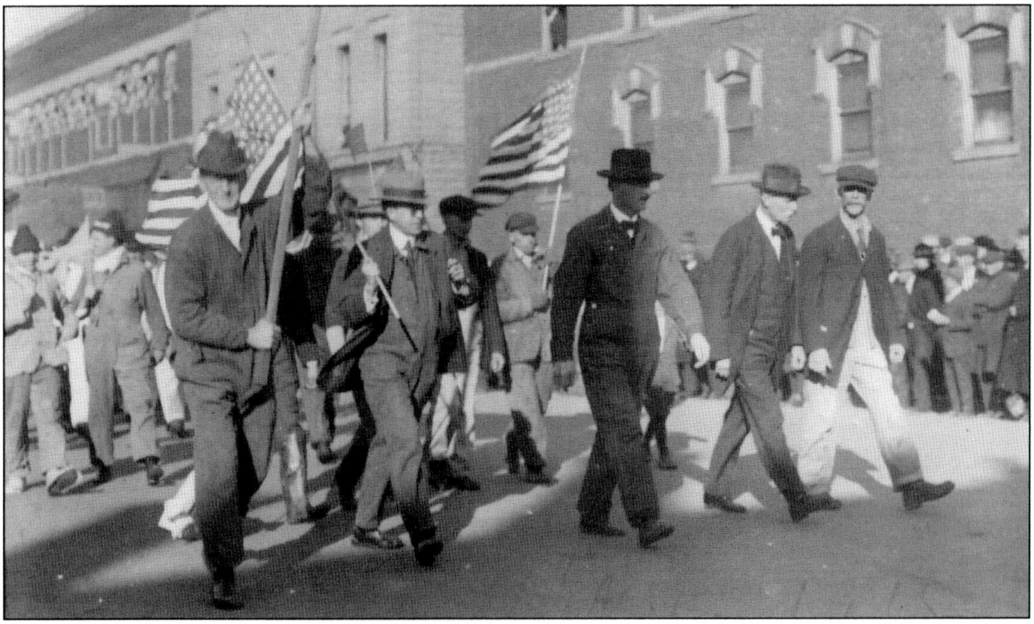

A group of jubilant businessmen led by Harry T. Barber (second from left) celebrated the end of World War I on November 11, 1918, by marching through the downtown within hours of the signing of the armistice in France. The impromptu parade extended the length of several blocks and included people in automobiles, trucks, carts, and on foot "all flying flags, great and small," according to the *Grinnell Herald*. Note the crowd lining the sidewalk. (GHM.)

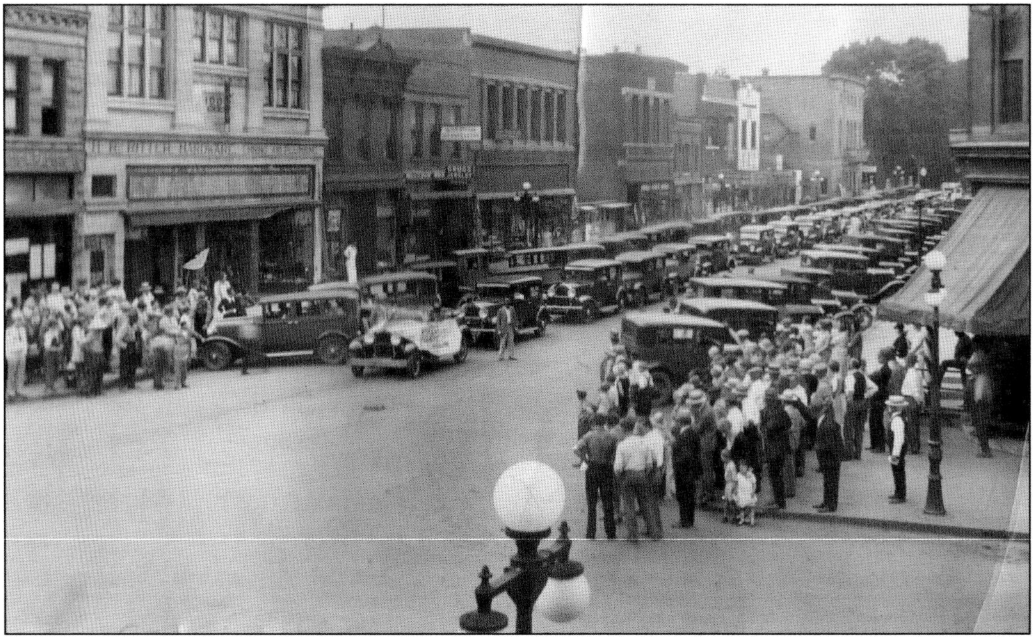

Curious onlookers lined Main Street in 1929 to see Whippet automobiles as they rolled through Grinnell. Whippets were built by the Willys-Overland Company of Toledo, Ohio, between 1926 and 1931. Named after the Whippet dog, the automobiles were small and swift and meant to appeal to budget-conscious buyers. Their innovative design featured "finger-tip control," which was a button in the center of the steering wheel that activated the horn and switched on the lights. (GHM.)

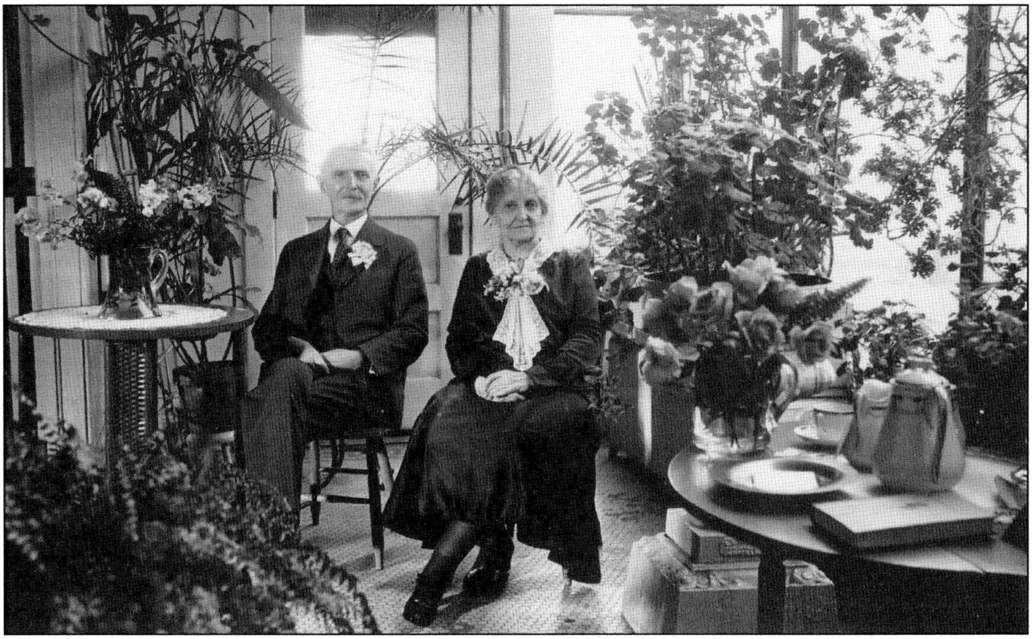

George H. and Elizabeth Hamlin celebrated their 50th wedding anniversary in 1931 with a portrait in the conservatory of their home at 619 Sixth Avenue. Hamlin was the son of the Reverend Homer Hamlin, one of the four founders of the town. George Hamlin and his twin sister Emma were the first children born in Grinnell. (GHM.)

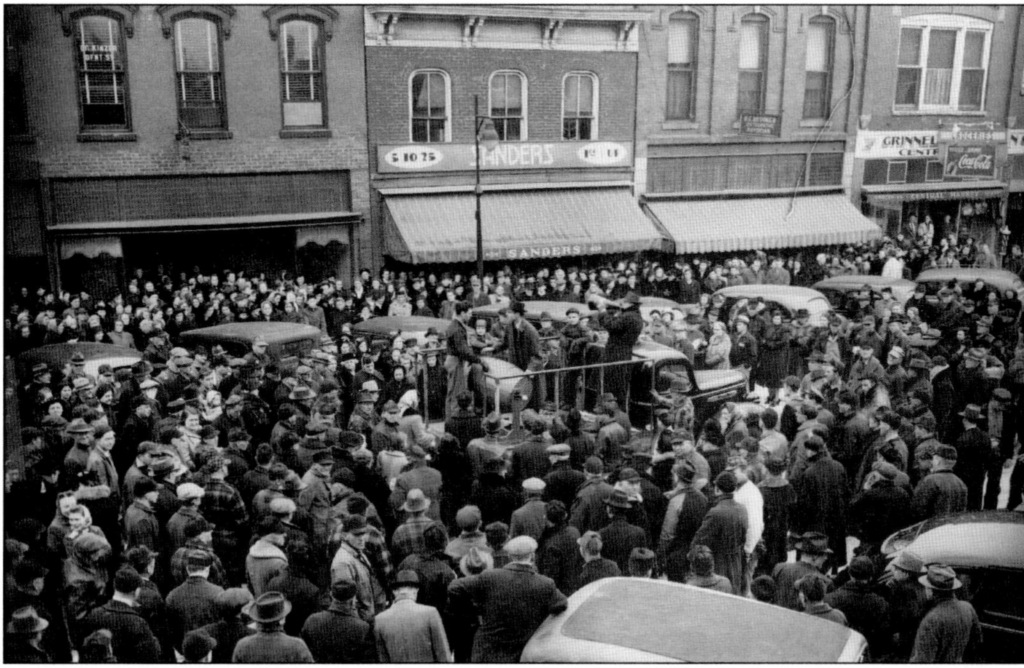

A customer appreciation day in November 1940 drew a huge crowd to Fourth Avenue between Main and Broad Streets. To boost business in the last years of the Depression, merchants gave away coupons with purchases that were good for prizes awarded in drawings, such as the one pictured. Sanders Variety Store—one of three variety stores located within a half-block at the time—can be seen in the background. (DCL.)

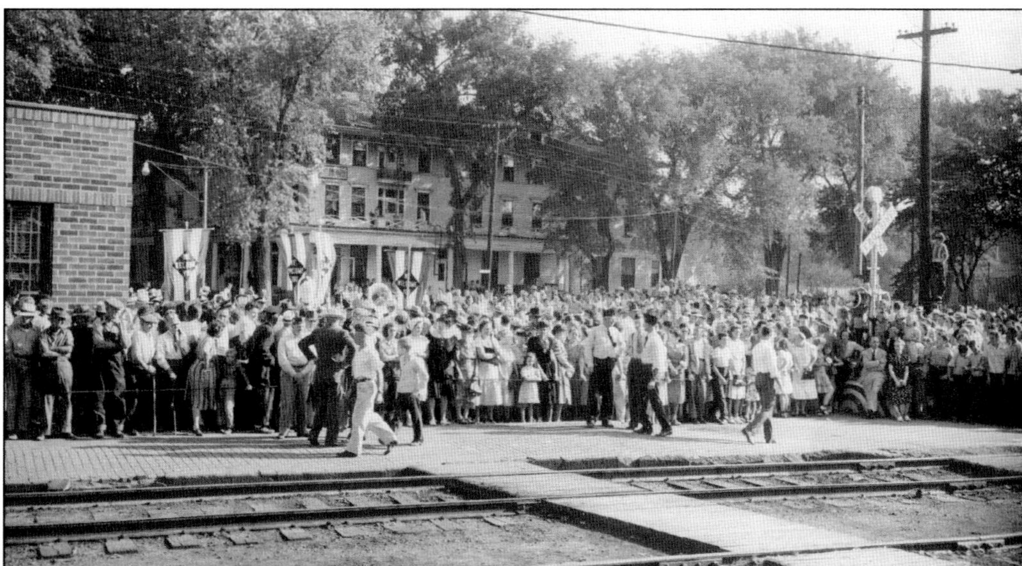

More than 5,000 people turned out to greet Pres. Harry Truman on September 18, 1948, when his 17-car train stopped briefly in Grinnell en route to Dexter, Iowa, where he was the principal speaker at a plowing match. Speaking from the train's observation platform, Truman praised the crops he had seen in Iowa and urged everyone to vote in the November election. He recalled that in 1944, as a senator, he had received an honorary degree from Grinnell College. (DCL.)

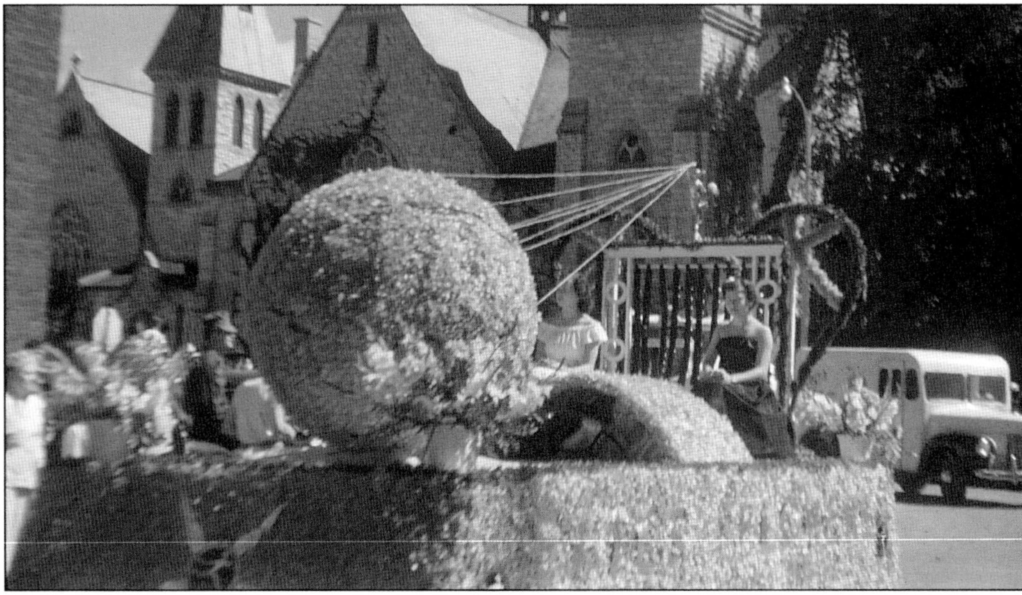

Grinnell has always loved parades. This one on September 5, 1949, part of Grinnell Days sponsored by the chamber of commerce, drew an enthusiastic crowd as it wound its way through the downtown streets, passing by the Congregational church. Bates Flowers sported a float (above) decorated with lilac-colored tissue paper and real flowers. Gladys Ann Smith (left) and Barbara Bailey (right) are pictured on the float. Note the driver crouched in front of the women. The image below shows farm machinery, which has always been prominent in Grinnell parades. Cylinders on the tractor are detasseling mechanisms meant to remove corn tassels. Many tassels were missed or not completely removed. The follow-up machine, carrying the girls, was meant to enable them to pull the remaining tassels. In later years, detasselers walked the fields to pull the tassels. (Both, DCL.)

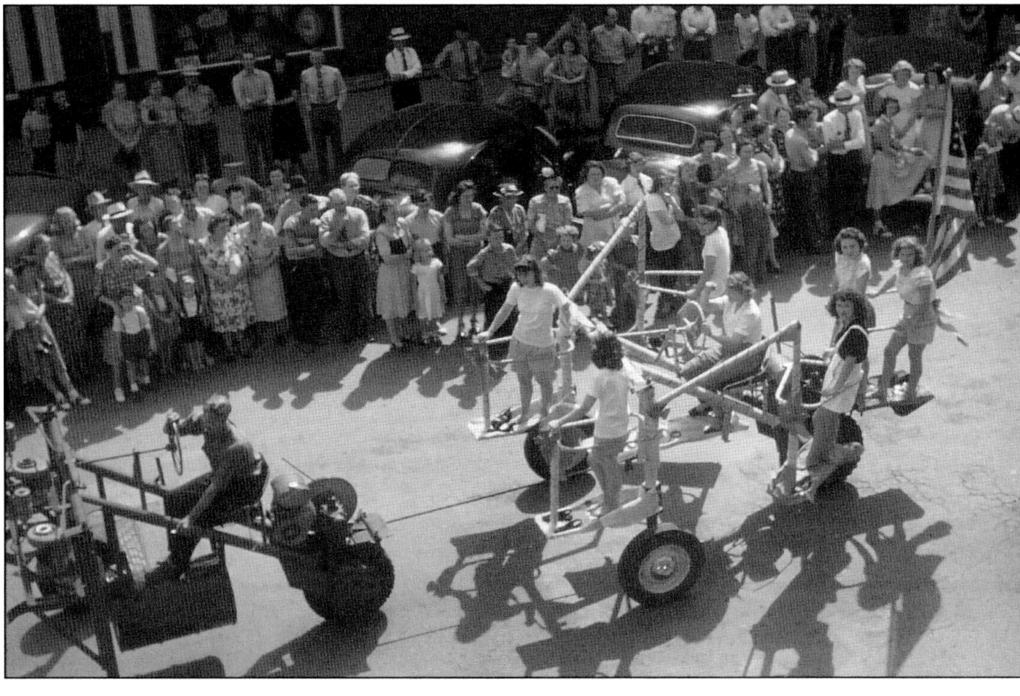

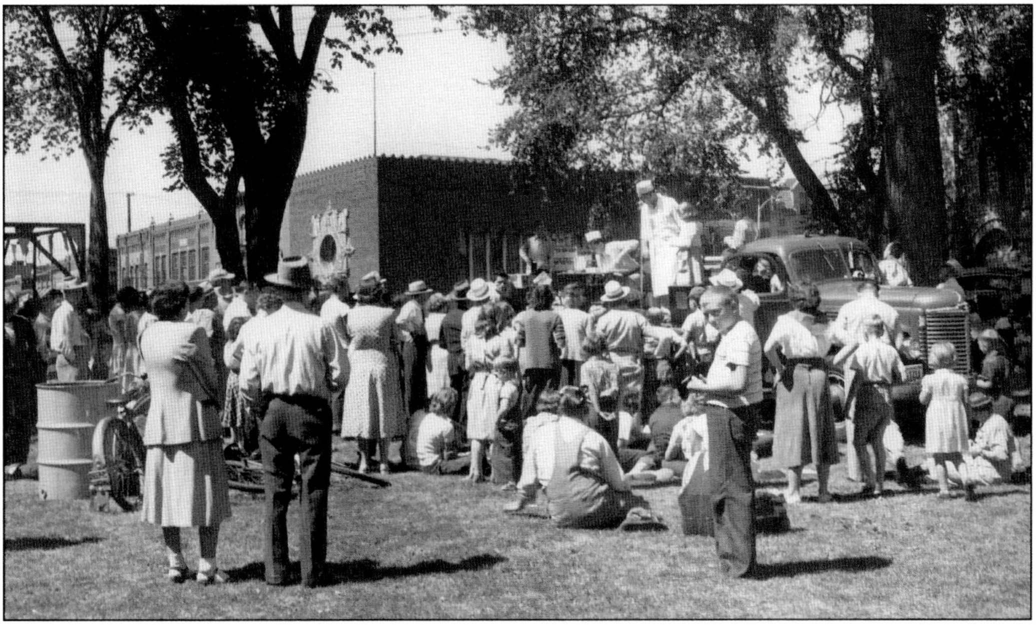

Pancakes were served in September 1950 at a Pancake Dollar Day event in Central Park sponsored by the chamber of commerce. More than 100 business people worked short shifts at eight griddles doling out "all the free pancakes with syrup, honey, and coffee one can eat and drink." Grinnell Dairy and Lang's Dairy furnished the milk and cream. The event was designed to promote downtown business with incentives such as bargain shopping and drawings for free gifts. (Bill McNally.)

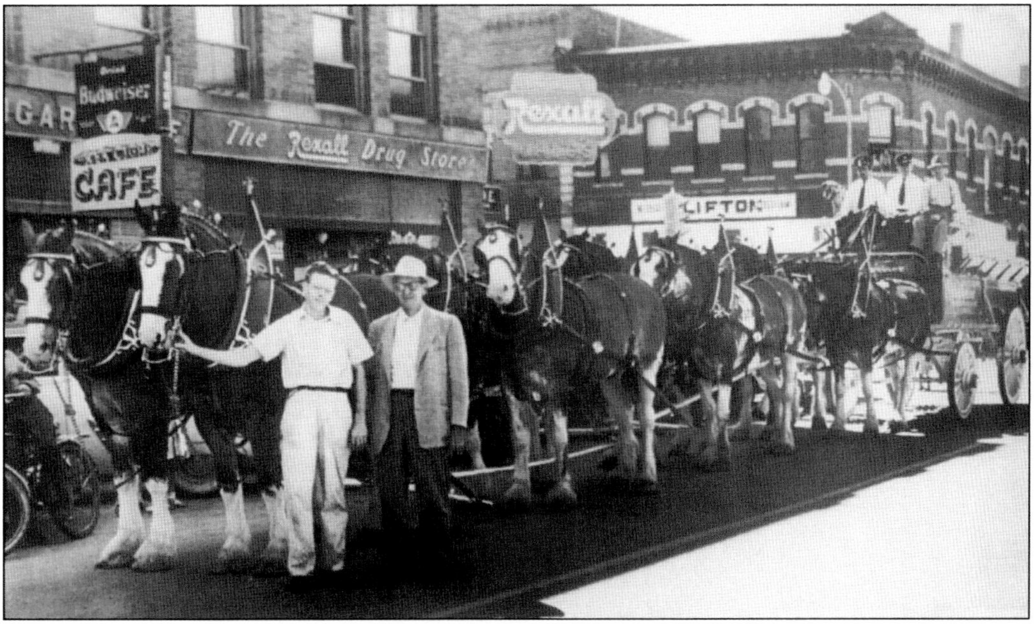

The famous Budweiser Clydesdales attracted a huge crowd when they visited Grinnell in September 1952. Sponsored by the Grinnell Beverage Company, the beer wagon showed off its obedience-trained Dalmatian, seated next to the drivers. In the photograph, Sid Gustafson (left), owner of the Rex Cigar Store, and Harry Crowder (second from left), owner of the Grinnell Beverage Company, pose with the hitch on the corner of Fourth Avenue and Main Street. (Joan Postels Heimsoth.)

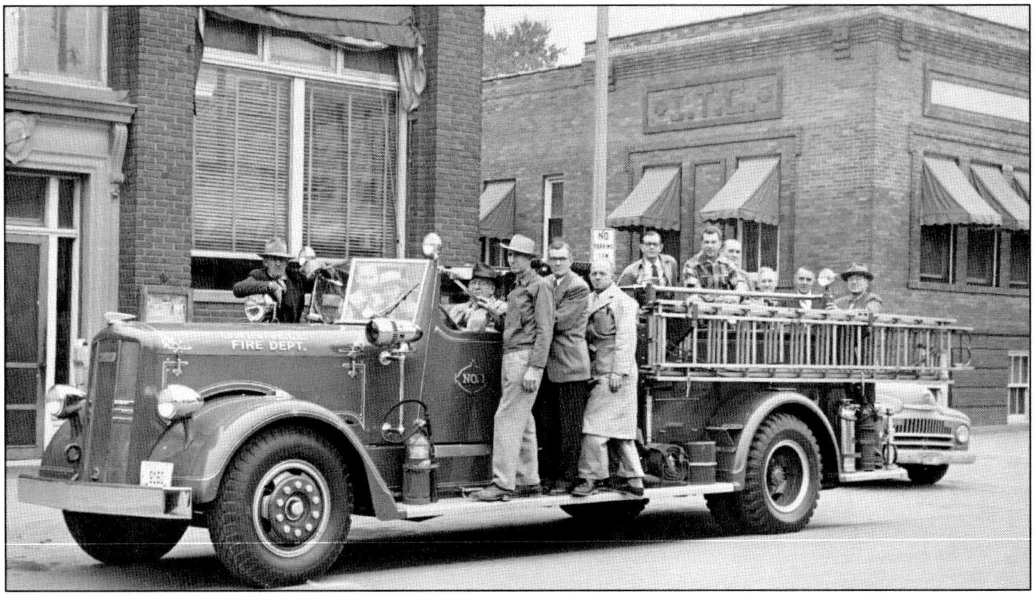

As part of a National Fire Safety Week in the 1950s, local businessmen took a spin past the Grinnell Herald-Register Building on Fifth Avenue. On board Engine No. 1, a 1913 American LaFrance model, were, from left to right, L.S. Sieberth, secretary-treasurer of the local firemen's association; Keith Gregory; Jim McNally; Chris McNally; Herb Waltersdorf; John Queen; Francis Walling; M.F. Zimmerman; Bill Ritter; the Reverend William Overhulser; Herb Greve; G. Lester Duke; and Frank Lynch. (Bill McNally.)

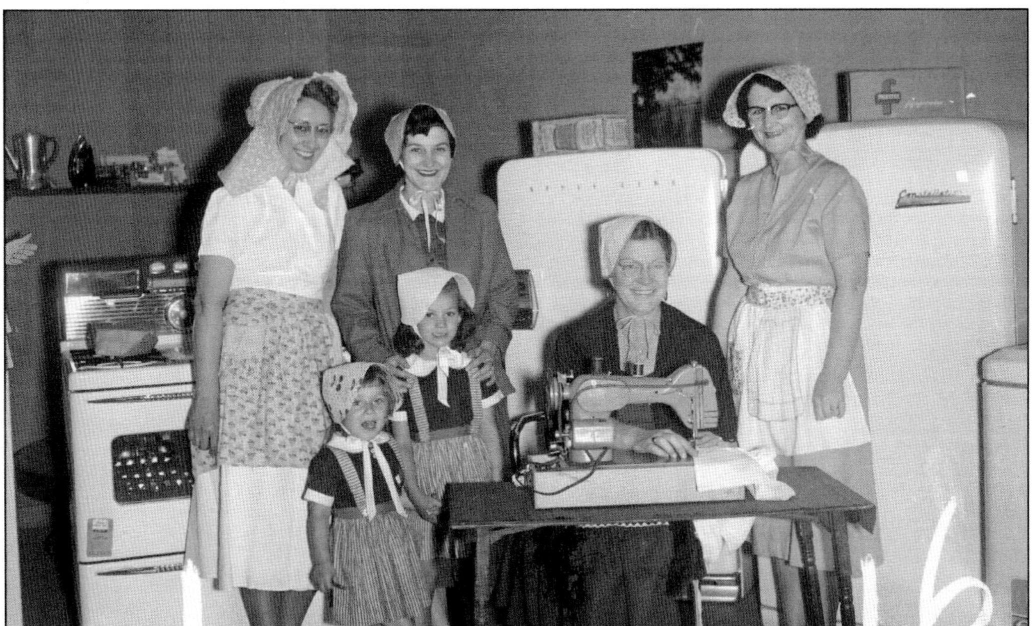

Members of the Altar and Rosary Society of St. Mary's Catholic Church made and sold aprons and bonnets for Grinnell's centennial celebration in 1954. Modeling the products are, from left to right, Mrs. George Hansen, Mrs. Robert Henderson, Mrs. Ed. Hughes, and Mrs. John Hotchkin. The girls were Margaret and Suzanne Henderson. (*Grinnell Herald-Register.*)

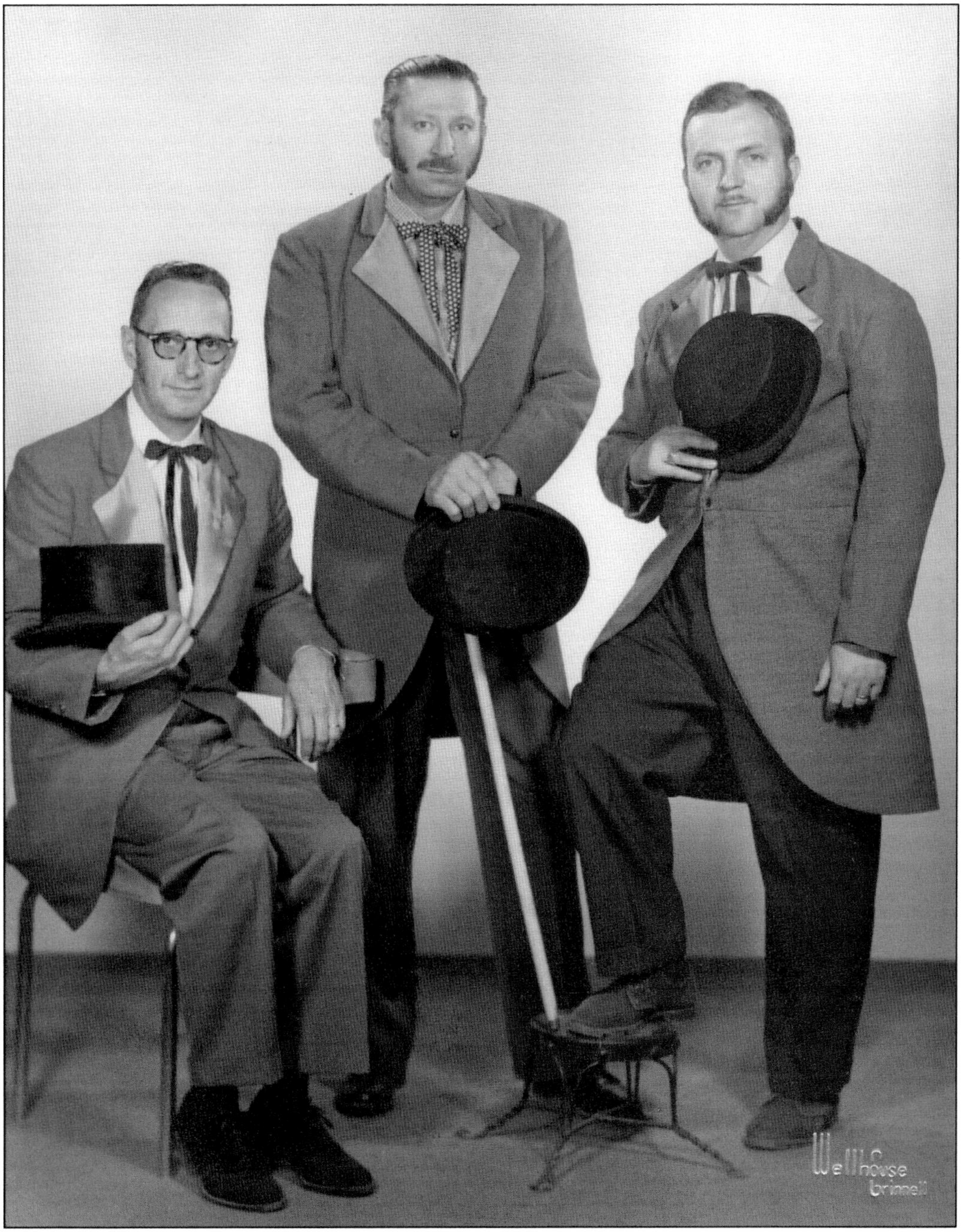

Heading the 1954 centennial celebration in Grinnell were local businessmen, from left to right, Don Cunningham, Jim McNally, and A.J. (Al) Pinder. The three men drummed up participation and enthusiasm for the many and varied centennial activities that extended over a six-month period. The highlight was a pageant titled "A Town Grows," presented in late May at Ward Field on the college campus. It is reported to have featured a cast of 700. A *Grinnell Herald-Register* advertisement in the centennial publication read, "Grinnell prospered because men believed in Grinnell . . . and they worked to make their dreams of a better Grinnell come true." Note the muttonchop sideburns on Jim and Al. (GHM.)

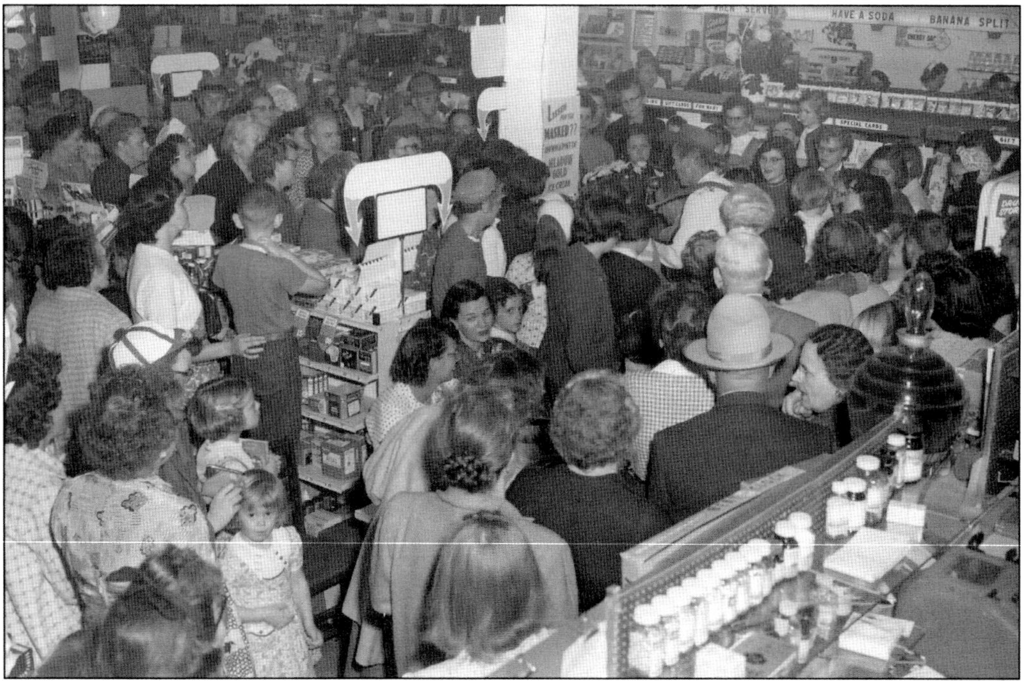

Loyal customers flocked to the reopening of Cunningham Drug in August 1955 on its first day back in business after a disastrous fire 10 months earlier in the building on Fourth Avenue. Even a musician was on hand to provide entertainment. (Jim Cunningham.)

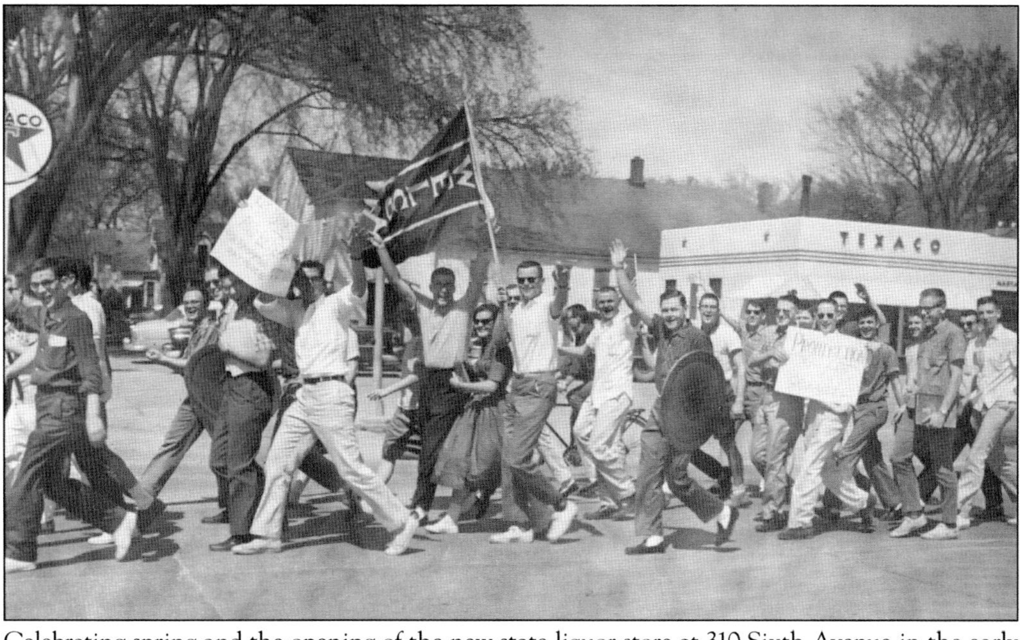

Celebrating spring and the opening of the new state liquor store at 310 Sixth Avenue in the early 1960s, a group of about 100 Grinnell College students marched from campus "with signs and flags waving, car horns honking, and drums beating a steady rhythm," according to a newspaper account. The signs read, "Eat, Drink and Be Merry for Tomorrow It May Close" and "Prohibition Repealed in Grinnell." (Bill McNally.)

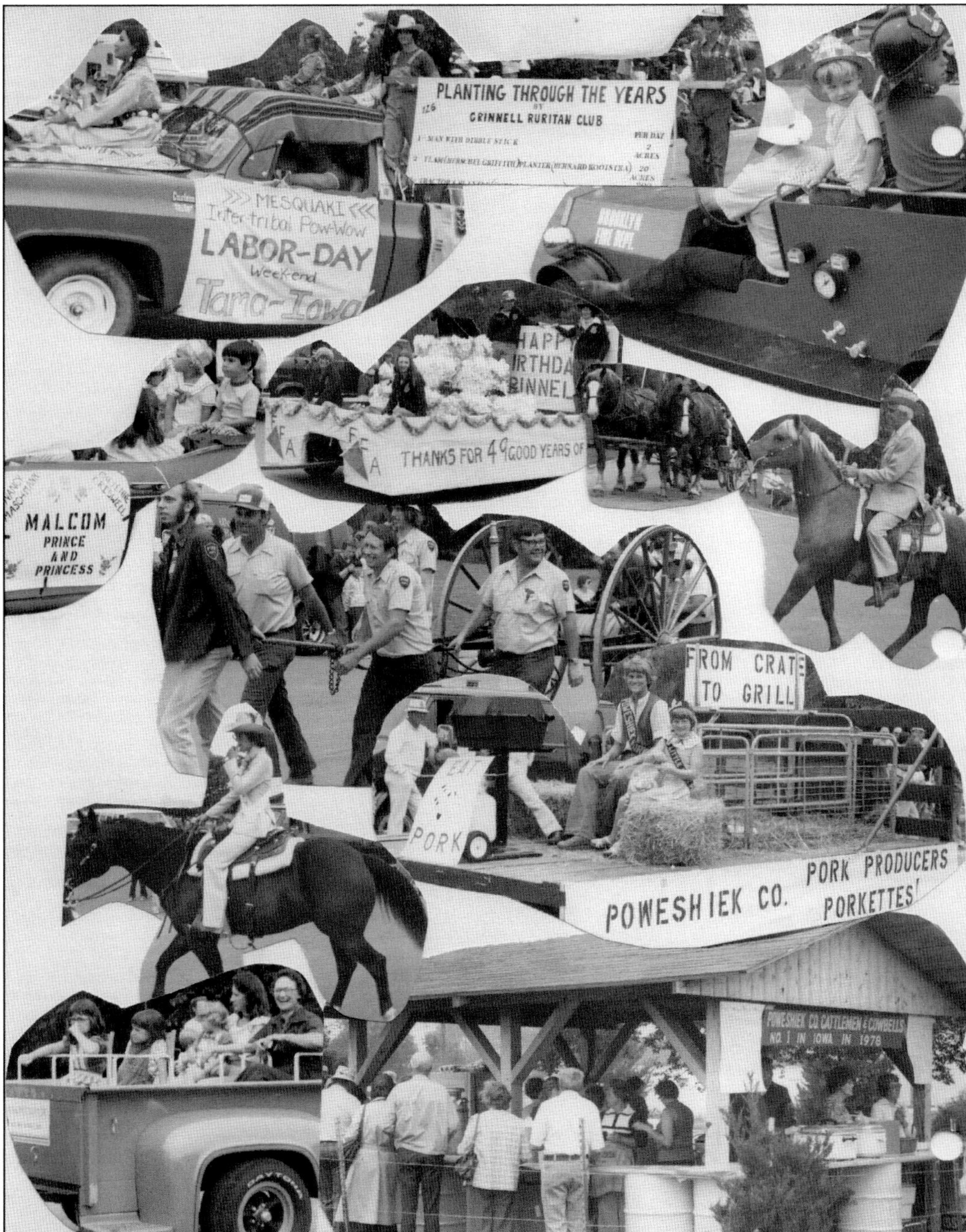

Grinnell mayor Floyd Beaver, a local veterinarian and mayor from 1964 to 1984, rode a horse in the 1979 Fourth of July parade that marked Grinnell's 125th anniversary. Other highlights of the parade included a decorated pickup truck advertising the Mesquaki Inter-tribal Pow-Wow in August, farmers from the Grinnell Ruritan Club, the Malcolm prince and princess, the high school Future Farmers of America float celebrating its 49th year in Grinnell, and the Poweshiek County Pork Producers float carrying the Poweshiek pork queen and the little princess. The line was steady at the Poweshiek County Cattlemen and Cowbells refreshment stand. (DCL.)

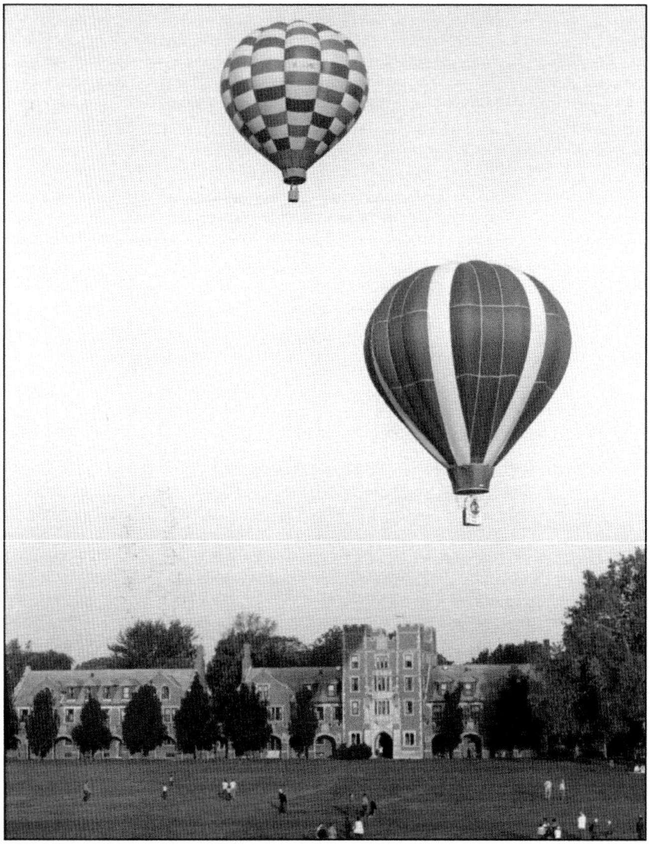

For several years in the 1980s, hot-air balloons ascended over Grinnell in mid-July. Sponsored by the chamber of commerce as part of its Ridiculous Days retailing events, the mass ascensions occurred from Mac Field and Ward Field on the college campus on a Saturday evening or a Sunday morning. Sponsors were allowed to ride if the weather permitted, and spectators were encouraged to assist with the event. (GCA.)

The 1950s came alive in Grinnell decades later in the annual Happy Days celebration held in and around Central Park. Highlight of the weekend was a classic car show featuring vintage automobiles with engine compartments as gleaming as the exteriors. This 1992 photograph shows a 1957 Chevrolet Bel Air hardtop coupe. Note the owner's pride expressed in the license plate–57 4EVR. (DCL.)

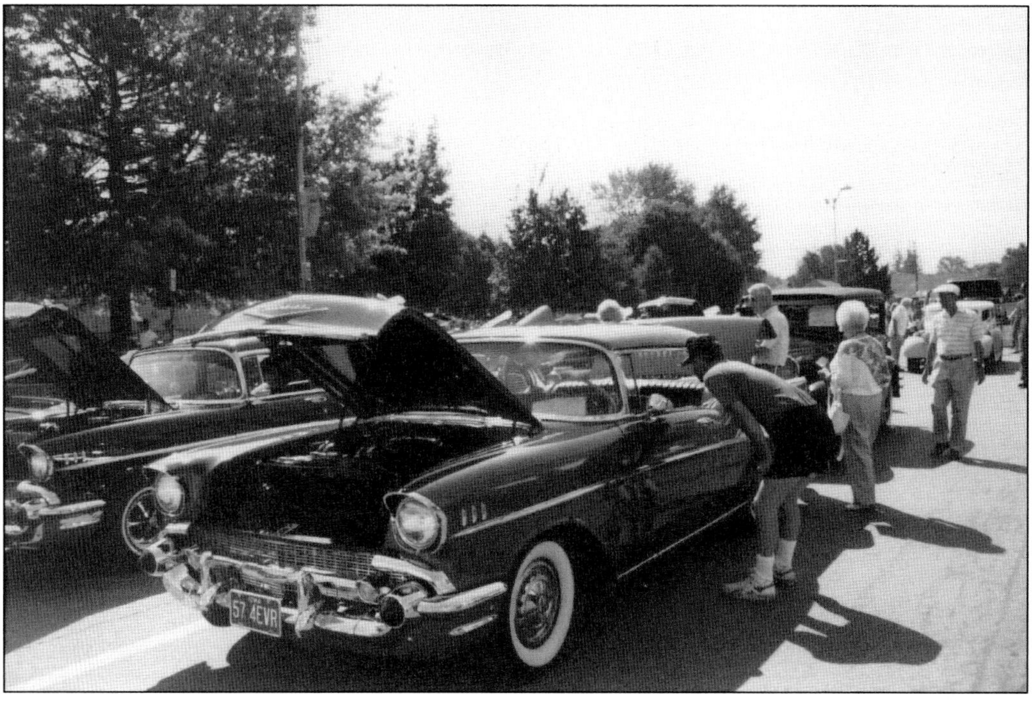

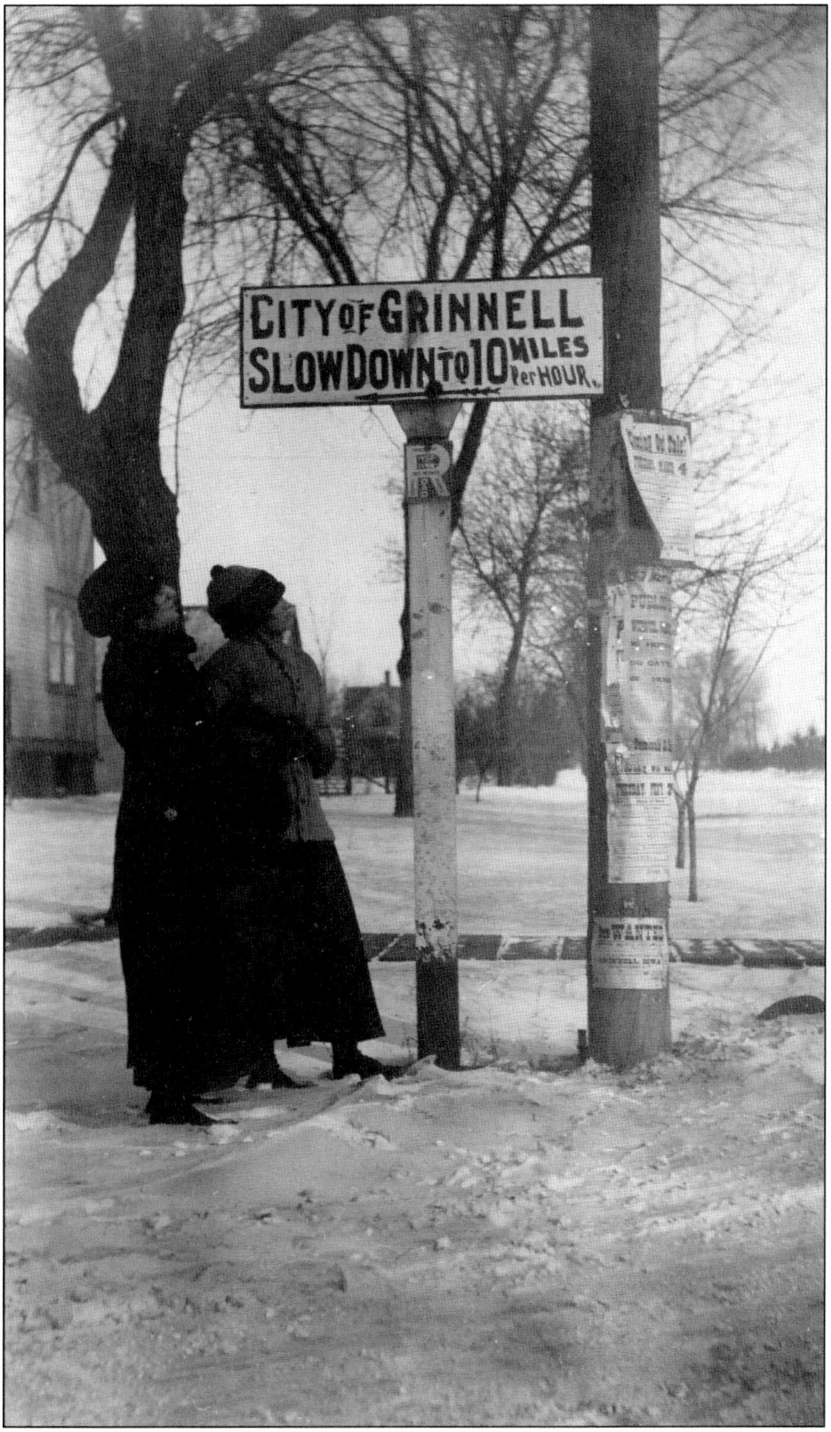

Two women stopped to reflect on a sign showing a 10-mile-per-hour speed limit posted along the River to River Road at the city limits of Grinnell. The two-lane east-west road, completed July 2, 1910, linked Davenport on the Mississippi River to Council Bluffs on the Missouri River. The road went through Grinnell, jogging south along Fourth Avenue through the downtown. (GCA.)